Open Agile Architecture™ Standard, Version 2.0

The Open Group Publications available from Van Haren Publishing

The TOGAF® Standard, 10th Edition:
Introduction and Core Concepts
Architecture Development Method
Content, Capability, and Governance
Leader's Guide
ADM Practitioners' Guide
Business Architecture
Enterprise Agility and Digital Transformation
A Pocket Guide
TOGAF® Business Architecture Foundation Study Guide
TOGAF® Enterprise Architecture Foundation Study Guide
TOGAF® Enterprise Architecture Practitioner Study Guide

The TOGAF Series (Version 9.2):
The TOGAF® Standard, Version 9.2
The TOGAF® Standard, Version 9.2 – A Pocket Guide
TOGAF® 9 Foundation Study Guide, 4th Edition
TOGAF® 9 Certified Study Guide, 4th Edition

The Open Group Series:
The IT4IT™ Standard, Version 3.0
IT4IT™ for Managing the Business of IT – A Management Guide
IT4IT™ Foundation Study Guide, 2nd Edition
The IT4IT™ Reference Architecture, Version 2.1 – A Pocket Guide
Cloud Computing for Business – The Open Group Guide
ArchiMate® 3.1 Specification – A Pocket Guide
ArchiMate® 3.2 Specification
ArchiMate® 4 Specification
ArchiMate® 4 Specification – A Pocket Guide
The Digital Practitioner Pocket Guide
The Digital Practitioner Foundation Study Guide
Open Agile Architecture™ – A Standard of The Open Group
Open Agile Architecture™ Standard, Version 2.0
Open Agile Architecture™ Standard, Version 2.0 – A Pocket Guide
Hospital Reference Architecture Guide: The Complete and Expanded English Translation of the Dutch ZiRA

The Open Group Press:
The Turning Point: A Novel about Agile Architects Building a Digital Foundation
Managing Digital
Ecosystems Architecture
For Your Information – About Information, the Universe, and the Modern Age

The Open Group Security Series:
O-TTPS™ – A Management Guide
Open Information Security Management Maturity Model (O-ISM3)
Open Enterprise Security Architecture (O-ESA)
Risk Management – The Open Group Guide
The Open FAIR™ Body of Knowledge – A Pocket Guide

All titles are available to purchase from:
www.opengroup.org
www.vanharen.net
and also many international and online distributors.

Open Agile Architecture™ Standard, Version 2.0

THE Open GROUP

Van Haren PUBLISHING

Title:	Open Agile Architecture™ Standard, Version 2.0
Series:	The Open Group Series
A Publication of:	The Open Group
Publisher:	Van Haren Publishing, 's-Hertogenbosch, www.vanharen.net
ISBN Hard copy:	978 94 018 1477 5
ISBN eBook (pdf):	978 94 018 1478 2
ISBN ePub:	978 94 018 1479 9
Edition:	Second edition, first impression, April 2026
Layout:	The Open Group

Document Number: C262
Published by The Open Group, April 2026

Comments relating to the material contained in this document may be submitted to:
The Open Group
Apex Plaza
Reading
Berkshire, RG1 1AX
United Kingdom
or by electronic mail to: ogspecs@opengroup.org

Table of Contents

Preface

The Open Group

The Open Group is a global consortium that enables the achievement of business objectives through technology standards and open source initiatives by fostering a culture of collaboration, inclusivity, and mutual respect among our diverse group of 900+ memberships. Our membership includes customers, systems and solutions suppliers, tool vendors, integrators, academics, and consultants across multiple industries.

The mission of The Open Group is to drive the creation of Boundaryless Information Flow™ achieved by:

- Working with customers to capture, understand, and address current and emerging requirements, establish policies, and share best practices
- Working with suppliers, consortia, and standards bodies to develop consensus and facilitate interoperability, to evolve and integrate specifications and open source technologies
- Offering a comprehensive set of services to enhance the operational efficiency of consortia
- Developing and operating the industry's premier certification service and encouraging procurement of certified products

Further information on The Open Group is available at www.opengroup.org.

The Open Group publishes a wide range of technical documentation, most of which is focused on development of Standards and Guides, but which also includes white papers, technical studies, certification and testing documentation, and business titles. Full details and a catalog are available at www.opengroup.org/library.

This Document

This document is The Open Group Open Agile Architecture™ Standard, Version 2.0, also known as The Open Group O-AA™ Standard. It has been developed and approved by The Open Group.

This document provides guidance for organizations seeking to evolve toward agility at scale while simultaneously leveraging digital technologies to drive innovation, enhance customer experience, and develop competitive advantages. It enables enterprises to accelerate learning cycles, shorten time-to-market, and create environments where Agile and Digital capabilities continuously co-create one another. Through its modular structure, this document provides fundamental concepts, practical guidance, and detailed perspectives on experience design, product architecture, operations, and technical systems to support sustainable organizational transformation.

This document is organized as follows:

- Part 1: The Agile Way of Thinking establishes the fundamental concepts of the dual Digital and Agile Transformation, demonstrating why organizational agility is essential as a key enabler for Digital Transformation
- Part 2: The Agile Enterprise outlines the key capabilities needed for an Agile organization, including organizational structures, strategic approaches, transformation methodologies, and governance models required to sustain agility at scale
- Part 3: The Agile Architecture Capability describes the ways of working with respect to architecture within an Agile enterprise, including Agile Architecture building blocks, intentional architecture, continuous architectural refactoring, and supporting techniques and deliverables
- Part 4: The Ways of Supporting details the techniques and methods that can be used to support architecture activities within an Agile enterprise

Examples and case studies are provided as illustrations to foster understanding of the standard. Examples and case studies are not a normative part of the standard and therefore do not include requirements.

The target audience for this document includes:

- Agilists who need to understand the importance of architecture when shifting toward an Agile at scale model, and who want to learn architecture skills
- Enterprise Architects, solution architects, security architects, and software architects who want to stay relevant in an Agile at scale world and need to learn new architecture skills for the digital age
- Business managers, business executives, and technical leaders who need to learn the importance of the architecture discipline, and who need to influence architecture decisions

Changes from the Previous Version

Version 2.0 of the Open Agile Architecture™ Standard represents a substantial evolution from the previous version, reflecting new structural thinking, stronger alignment with dual transformation, and expanded guidance on organizational agility. Key enhancements include:

- Restructured core content: Version 2.0 reorganizes the standard into a clearer, four-part structure that aligns Agile thinking, organizational design, ways of working, and supporting techniques into one cohesive model (way of thinking, way of organizing, way of working, way of supporting)
- Explicit dual transformation foundation: Version 2.0 emphasizes dual transformation (simultaneous Digital and Agile Transformation) as the architectural starting point; highlighting the need for coordinated evolution across business and technology in a modern VUCA world, characterized by Volatility, Uncertainty, Complexity, and Ambiguity [Bennis & Nanus, 1985]
- Expanded review and refinement: Version 2.0 incorporates an extensive community review, resolving and integrating over 200 comments, showing substantial refinement over the previous version

Trademarks

ArchiMate, FACE, FACE logo, Future Airborne Capability Environment, Making Standards Work, Open Footprint, Open O logo, Open O and Check certification logo, Open Subsurface Data Universe, OSDU, Sensor Open Systems Architecture, SOSA, SOSA logo, The Open Group, TOGAF, UNIX, UNIXWARE, and X logo are registered trademarks and Boundaryless Information Flow, Build with Integrity Buy with Confidence, Commercial Aviation Reference Architecture, Dependability Through Assuredness, Digital Practitioner Body of Knowledge, DPBoK, EMMM, FHIM Profile Builder, FHIM logo, FPB, IT4IT, IT4IT logo, O-AA, O-DA, O-DEF, O-HERA, O-PAS, O-TTPS, O-VBA, Open Agile Architecture, Open FAIR, Open Process Automation, Open Trusted Technology Provider, and Sensor Integration Simplified are trademarks of The Open Group.

Agile Alliance is a registered trademark of Agile Alliance.
Amazon, Amazon Web Services, and AWS are trademarks of Amazon.com.
Apache Spark is a trademark of the Apache Software Foundation.
Azure, Excel, Microsoft, Microsoft Teams, and Skype are registered trademarks of Microsoft Corporation.
Calypso is a registered trademark of Calypso Technology, Inc.
Capital One and Auto Navigator are registered trademarks of Capital One.
ChemDraw is a registered trademark of Revvity Signals Software, Inc.
Compaq is a registered trademark of Hewlett-Packard Development Company, LP.
DEC is a trademark of Digital Equipment Corporation.
eBay is a registered trademark of eBay, Inc.
Facebook is a registered trademark of Facebook, Inc.
Fannie Mae is a registered trademark of Fannie Mae.
Flink is a registered trademark of the Apache Software Foundation.
Ford is a trademark of the Ford Motor Company.
Freddie Mac is a registered trademark of Freddie Mac.
Gartner is a registered trademark of Gartner, Inc.
General Electric is a registered trademark of General Electric Company.
Git is a trademark of Software Freedom Conservancy, Inc.
GitHub is a registered trademark of GitHub, Inc.
Google is a registered trademark and Tensorflow is a trademark of Google LLC.
IETF is a registered trademark of the IETF Trust.
Java is a registered trademark and JavaScript is a trademark of Oracle Corporation.
JPMorgan Chase is trademark of JPMorgan Chase & Co.
Kafka is a trademark of the Apache Software Foundation.
Li & Fung is a trademark of Li & Fung (BVI) Limited.
loanDepot is a registered trademark of loanDepot.com, LLC.
MQSeries is a registered trademark of International Business Machines (IBM) Corporation.
Murex is a registered trademark of Murex S.A.S.
Netflix is a registered trademark of Netflix, Inc.
Poiray is a registered trademark of Poiray International.
Pomodoro Technique is a registered trademark of Cirillo Consulting GmbH.

Acknowledgements

The Open Group gratefully acknowledges the contribution of the following people in the development of this document:

- Ruud De Wit
- Hans Van Rijs
- Andrew Missen
- Steve Nicholls

The Open Group gratefully acknowledges the following reviewers who participated in the Company Review of this document:

- Ken Block
- Sean Cantwell
- Glenn Char
- David Cretelli
- Andrew Davies
- Aristos Dimitriou
- Ruud De Wit
- Shannon Ellsworth
- Susan Gottschlich
- John Graham
- Daniel Greene
- Christopher Grounds
- Craig Hufault
- Daniel Levis
- Dale Lydigsen III
- John Mattingly
- Terence McKiernan
- Stephen Nicholls
- Kirk Rasmussen
- Joseph Ricci
- Christopher Runge
- Matt Thurman

- Hans van Rijs
- Tony Welch

The Open Group gratefully acknowledges the contribution of the following people in the development of the previous version of this document:

- Miguel de Andrade
- Jean-Marc Bunouf
- Paddy Fagan
- Jérémie Grodziski
- Peter Haviland
- Frédéric Le
- Jean-Pierre Le Cam
- Antoine Lonjon
- Eamonn Moriarty
- Jérôme Régnier

Referenced Documents

The following documents are referenced in this standard.

(Please note that the links below are good at the time of writing but cannot be guaranteed for the future.)

Normative References

This document does not contain any normative references at the time of publication. These may be added in a future release.

Informative References

[Adkins et al., 2020]	Building Secure and Reliable Systems, Best Practices for Designing, Implementing, and Maintaining Systems, by Heather Adkins, Betsy Beyer, Paul Blankinship, Ana Oprea, Piotr Lewandowski, and Adam Stubblefield, published by O'Reilly Media, March 2020
[Adler, 2020]	Bending the Law of Unintended Consequences: A Test-Drive Method for Critical Decision-Making in Organizations, by Richard M. Adler, published by Springer International Publishing, 2020
[Agile Alliance]	Agile Glossary, published by the Agile Alliance®; refer to: www.agilealliance.org/agile101/agile-glossary/
[Agile Manifesto]	Manifesto for Agile Software Development, 2001; refer to: www.agilemanifesto.org/
[Andreessen, 2011]	Why Software Is Eating The World, by Marc Andreessen, August 2011, published in the Wall Street Journal; refer to: www.wsj.com/articles/SB10001424053111903480904576512250915629460
[ANSI/IEEE]	Standard Glossary of Software Engineering Terminology, STD-729-1991, published by ANSI/IEEE
[Atwood, 2006]	The Last Responsible Moment, by Jeff Atwood, October 2006; refer to: www.blog.codinghorror.com/the-last-responsible-moment/
[Auto Navigator]	Capital One® Auto Navigator® App; refer to: www.capitalone.com/cars/
[Beaujean et al, 2006]	The "Moment of Truth" in Customer Service, by Marc Beaujean, Jonathan Davidson, and Stacey Madge, published by McKinsey & Company, February 2006; refer to: www.mckinsey.com/business-functions/organization/our-insights/the-moment-of-truth-in-customer-service
[Bennis & Nanus, 1985]	Leaders: Strategies for Taking Charge, by Warren G. Bennis and Burt Nanus, published by Harper Collins, September 1985

[Berdjag et al., 2019]	Automation Challenges of Socio-Technical Systems, by Denis Berdjag, Choubeila Maaoui, Mohamed Sallak, and Frederic Vanderhaegen, published by Wiley-ISTE, July 2019
[Beyer et al., 2016]	Site Reliability Engineering: How Google Runs Production Systems, by Betsy Beyer, Chris Jones, Jennifer Petoff, and Niall Richard Murphy, published by O'Reilly Media; refer to: landing.google.com/sre/sre-book/toc/index.html
[Beyer et al., 2018]	The Site Reliability Workbook: Practical Ways to Implement SRE, by Betsy Beyer, Niall Richard Murphy, David K. Rensin, Kent Kawahara, and Stephen Thorne, published by O'Reilly Media, July 2018; refer to: landing.google.com/sre/workbook/toc/
[Bezos, 2021]	The Bezos API Mandate: Amazon's Manifesto For Externalization, published by Nordic APIs, January 2021; refer to: nordicapis.com/the-bezos-api-mandate-amazons-manifesto-for-externalization/
[Blumberg et al., 2018]	Five Enterprise-Architecture Practices that Add Value to Digital Transformations, by Sven Blumberg, Olivier Bossert, and Jan Sokalski, published by McKinsey & Company, November 2018; refer to: www.mckinsey.com/business-functions/mckinsey-digital/our-insights/five-enterprise-architecture-practices-that-add-value-to-digital-transformations
[Bradley et al., 2018]	Strategy Beyond the Hockey Stick: People, Probabilities, and Big Moves to Beat the Odds, by Chris Bradley, Martin Hirt, and Sven Smit, published by John Wiley & Sons, March 2018
[Brandenburger, 2019]	Strategy Needs Creativity, by Adam Brandenburger, published in the Harvard Business Review, March-April 2019
[Brandolini, 2019]	Introducing EventStorming, by Alberto Brandolini, published as an ebook on Leanpub, last updated on August 2019; refer to www.leanpub.com/introducing_eventstorming
[Brosseau et al., 2019]	The Journey to an Agile Organization, by Daniel Brosseau, Sherina Ebrahim, Christopher Handscomb, and Shail Thaker, published by McKinsey & Company, May 2019
[Burton, 2014]	Leverage Business Capability Modeling to Integrate Strategy With Execution, by Betsy Burton, Gartner Vice President & Distinguished Analyst, 2014
[C182]	The TOGAF® Standard, Version 9.2, a standard of The Open Group (C182), published by The Open Group, April 2018; refer to: www.opengroup.org/library/c182
[C196]	The Digital Practitioner Body of Knowledge™ Standard (the DPBoK™ Standard), a standard of The Open Group (C196), January 2020, published by The Open Group; refer to: www.opengroup.org/library/c196

[C220]	TOGAF® Standard, 10th Edition, a standard of The Open Group (C220), published by The Open Group, April 2022 and updated May 2025; refer to: www.opengroup.org/library/c220
[C4 Model]	The C4 Model for Visualising Software Architecture, Context, Containers, Components and Code; refer to: c4model.com
[Cagan, 2018]	Inspired: How to Create Tech Products Customers Love, by Marty Cagan, January 2018, published by John Wiley & Sons
[Campbell et al., 2017]	Operating Model Canvas: Aligning Operations and Organization with Strategy, by Andrew Campell, Mikel Gutierrez, and Mark Lancelott, published by Van Haren Publishing, April 2017
[Charan & Yang, 2019]	The Amazon Management System: The Ultimate Digital Business Engine That Creates Extraordinary Value for Both Customers and Shareholders, by Ram Charan and Julia Yang, published by Ideapress Publishing, December 2019
[Christensen & Raynor, 2013]	The Innovator's Solution: Creating and Sustaining Successful Growth, by Clayton M. Christensen and Michael E. Raynor, published by Harvard Business Review Press, November 2013
[Christensen et al., 2016]	Know Your Customers' "Jobs-To-Be-Done", by Clayton M. Christensen, Karen Dillon, David S. Duncan, and Taddy Hall, published in the Harvard Business Review, September 2016
[CJCSM, 2005]	Operation of the Joint Capabilities Integration and Development System, published in the Chairman of the Joint Chiefs of Staff Manual, May 2005
[CloudEvents]	CloudEvents; refer to: www.cloudevents.io/
[Cobbler]	Cobbler Project; refer to: cobbler.readthedocs.io/en/latest/
[Cockburn, 2005]	Hexagonal Architecture, by Alistair Cockburn; refer to: www.alistair.cockburn.us/hexagonal-architecture/
[Colyer, 2020]	Meaningful Availability, a blog post by Adrian Colyer on a paper by Hauer et al., NSDI, February 2020
[Comella-Dorda et al., 2019]	Planning in an Agile Organization, by Santiago Comella-Dorda, Khushpreet Kaur, and Ahmad Zaidi, published by McKinsey & Company, February 2019; refer to: www.mckinsey.com/business-functions/mckinsey-digital/our-insights/planning-in-an-agile-organization
[Coplien & Bjørnvig, 2010]	Lean Architecture, by James Coplien and Gertrud Bjørnvig, published by Wiley, July 2010
[Crawley et al., 2016]	Systems Architecture: Strategy and Product Development for Complex Systems, by Edward Crawley, Bruce Cameron, and Daniel Selva, published by Pearson Education Limited, 2016
[Cruft]	Cruft, published by Wikipedia; refer to: www.wikipedia.org/wiki/Cruft

[Cusumano & Nobeoka, 1998]	Thinking Beyond Lean: How Multi-Project Management is Transforming Product Development at Toyota and Other Companies, by Michael A. Cusumano and Kentaro Nobeoka, published by Free Press, September 1998
[Cusumano et al., 2020]	The Future of Platforms, by Michael A. Cusumano, David B. Yoffie, and Annabelle Gawer, published by The MIT Press, February 2020
[Day & Schoemaker, 2019]	See Sooner, Act Faster: How Vigilant Leaders Thrive in an Era of Digital Turbulence, by George S. Day and Paul J. H. Schoemaker, published by The MIT Press, October 2019
[Dehghani, 2019]	How to Move Beyond a Monolithic Data Lake to a Distributed Data Mesh, by Zhamak Dehghani, May 2019; refer to: www.martinfowler.com/articles/data-monolith-to-mesh.html
[Dennis, 2006]	Getting the Right Things Done: A Leader's Guide to Planning and Execution, by Pascal Dennis, published by Lean Enterprise Institute, December 2006
[DevOps, 2015; 2017]	2015 State of DevOps Report; refer to: www.researchgate.net/publication/302566896_2015_State_of_DevOps_Report and 2017 State of DevOps Report; refer to: services.google.com/fh/files/misc/state-of-devops-2017.pdf
[De Weck et al., 2016]	Engineering Systems — Meeting Human Needs in a Complex Technological World, by Olivier L. de Weck, Daniel Roos, and Christopher L. Magee, published by MIT Press, September 2016
[DORA, 2019]	DevOps Research & Assessment (DORA) 2019 State of DevOps Report; refer to: services.google.com/fh/files/misc/state-of-devops-2019.pdf
[Erder & Pureur, 2015]	Continuous Architecture: Sustainable Architecture in an Agile and Cloud-Centric World, by Murat Erder and Pierre Pureur, Elsevier, published by Morgan Kaufmann, November 2015
[Evans, 2003]	Domain-Driven Design: Tackling Complexity in the Heart of Software, by Eric Evans, published by Addison-Wesley Professional, August 2003
[Event Storming]	Event Storming Workshop Format; refer to: www.eventstorming.com/
[Fielding, 2000]	Architectural Styles and the Design of Network-Based Software Architectures, by Roy Fielding; published by the University of California; refer to: roy.gbiv.com/pubs/ dissertation/fielding_dissertation.pdf
[Ford et al., 2017]	Building Evolutionary Architectures, by Neal Ford, Patrick Kua, and Rebecca Parsons, published by O'Reilly, September 2017
[Foreman]	Foreman Project; refer to: theforeman.org/introduction.html.
[Forsgren et al., 2018]	Accelerate: The Science of Lean Software and DevOps: Building and Scaling High Performing Technology Organizations, by Nicole Forsgren, Kim Humble, and Gene Kim, published by Trade Select, April 2018

[Fountaine et al., 2019]	Building the AI-Powered Organization: The Main Challenge Isn't Technology, It's Culture, by Tim Fountaine, Brian McCarthy, and Tamim Saleh, published in the Harvard Business Review, July-August 2019
[Fowler]	ExpositionalArchitecture, by Martin Fowler; refer to: www.martinfowler.com/bliki/ExpositionalArchitecture.html
[Fowler, 2004]	StranglerFigApplication, by Martin Fowler, June 2004; refer to: www.martinfowler.com/bliki/StranglerApplication.html
[Fowler, 2013]	Continuous Delivery, by Martin Fowler, May 2013; refer to: www.martinfowler.com/bliki/ContinuousDelivery.html
[Fowler, 2014]	Sacrificial Architecture, by Martin Fowler, October 2014; refer to: www.martinfowler.com/bliki/SacrificialArchitecture.html
[Fowler, 2015]	Making Architecture Matter — Martin Fowler Keynote, by Martin Fowler, July 2015, uploaded by O'Reilly Media; refer to: www.youtube.com/watch?v=DngAZyWMGR0
[Fowler, 2019]	Refactoring: Improving the Design of Existing Code, by Martin Fowler, published by Addison-Wesley, January 2019
[Friis Dam & Siang, 2020]	Personas — A Simple Introduction, by Rikke Friis Dam and Teo Yu Siang, published by the Interaction Design Foundation, 2020; refer to: www.interaction-design.org/literature/article/personas-why-and-how-you-should-use-them
[Furr & Shipilov, 2019]	Digital Doesn't Have to Be Disruptive: The Best Results Can Come From Adaptation Rather Than Reinvention, by Nathan Furr and Andrew Shipilov, published in the Harvard Business Review, July-August 2019
[G178]	TOGAF® Series Guide: Value Streams (G178), published by The Open Group, April 2022; refer to: www.opengroup.org/library/g178
[G20F]	TOGAF® Series Guide: Enabling Enterprise Agility (G20F), published by The Open Group, April 2022; refer to: www.opengroup.org/library/g20f
[Gartner]	Gartner® Glossary, Customer Journey; refer to: www.gartner.com/en/articles/customer-journey
[George et al., 2005]	Fast Innovation: Achieving Superior Differentiation, Speed to Market, and Increased Profitability, by Michael George, James Works, and Kimberly Watson-Hemphill, published by McGraw-Hill Education, July 2005
[George & Ting, 2018]	Integrating Around the Consumer: A Path Forward for the Global Apparel Manufacturing Supply Chain, by Jon George and Peter Ting, published by the Christensen Institute, November 2018; refer to: www.christenseninstitute.org/wp-content/uploads/2019/03/Integrating-around-the-consumer-1.pdf
[Gilbreth & Gilbreth, 1921]	Process Charts: First Steps in Finding the One Best Way to Do Work, by F. B. Gilbreth and L. M. Gilbreth, December 1921, presented at The Annual Meeting of The American Society of Mechanical Engineers

[GoF, 1994]	Design Patterns: Elements of Reusable Object-Oriented Software, by Erich Gamma, Richard Helm, Ralph Johnson, and John Vlissides, published by Addison-Wesley, October 1994
[Greyser & Urde, 2019]	What Does Your Corporate Brand Stand For?, by Stephen A. Greyser and Mats Urde, published in the Harvard Business Review, January-February 2019
[Groenfeldt, 2018]	Get Car Price And Finance Info Before Even Talking To A Car Salesman, by Tom Groenfeldt, published by Forbes, March 2018; refer to: www.forbes.com/sites/tomgroenfeldt/2018/03/13/get-car-price-and-finance-info-without-ever-talking-to-a-car-salesman/#43e794ba196a
[Harrington, 1991]	Business Process Improvement: The Breakthrough Strategy for Total Quality, Productivity, and Competitiveness, by H. James Harrington, published by McGraw-Hill Education, May 1991
[Hodgson, 2017]	Feature Toggles (aka Feature Flags), by Peter Hodgson, published in martinfowler.com, October 2017; refer to: www.martinfowler.com/articles/feature-toggles.html
[Holland, 2012]	Signals and Boundaries: Building Blocks for Complex Adaptive Systems, by John H. Holland, published by MIT Press, January 2014
[Holland, 2014]	Complexity: A Very Short Introduction, by John H. Holland, published by Oxford University Press, July 2014
[Hoshin Kanri]	Hoshin Kanri, published by Wikipedia; refer to: en.wikipedia.org/wiki/Hoshin_Kanri
[Humble & Farley, 2010]	Continuous Delivery: Reliable Software Releases through Build, Test, and Deployment Automation, by Jez Humble and David Farley, published by Addison-Wesley, July 2010
[IETF, 2017]	Uniform Resource Names (URNs), by P. Saint-Andre and J. Klensin, published by the Internet Engineering Task Force (IETF®), April 2017; refer to: www.tools.ietf.org/html/rfc8141
[Ishikawa, 1985]	What is Total Quality Control? The Japanese Way, by Kaoru Ishikawa, published by Prentice Hall, March 1985
[ISO/IEC 9126-1]	ISO/IEC 9126-1: Software Engineering — Product Quality — Part 1: Quality Model, published by ISO (now withdrawn), 2001; refer to: www.iso.org/standard/22749.html
[ISO/IEC 25002]	ISO/IEC 25002: Systems and Software Engineering — Systems and Software Quality Requirements and Evaluation (SQuaRE) — System and Software Quality Models, published by ISO, 2024; refer to: www.iso.org/standard/78175.html
[ISO/IEC/IEEE 42010]	ISO/IEC/IEEE 42010: Systems and Software Engineering — Architecture Description, published by ISO, 2022; refer to: www.iso.org/standard/74393.html

[Johnson et al., 2008]	Reinventing your Business Model_, by Mark W. Johnson, Clayton M. Christensen, and Henning Kagermann, published in the Harvard Business Review, December 2008
[Kalbach, 2016]	Mapping Experiences: A Guide to Creating Value through Journeys, Blueprints, and Diagrams, by James Kalbach, published by O'Reilly Media, December 2016
[Kellogg]	Kellogg School of Management; refer to: www.kellogg.northwestern.edu/
[Kent, 2012]	Data and Reality: A Timeless Perspective on Perceiving and Managing Information in Our Imprecise World, Third Edition, by William Kent, published by Technics Publications, LLC, February 2012
[Kersten, 2018]	Project to Product: How to Survive and Thrive in the Age of Digital Disruption with the Flow Framework, by Mik Kersten, published by IT Revolution Press, November 2018
[Kim et al., 2013]	The Phoenix Project: A Novel about IT, DevOps, and Helping your Business Win, by Gene Kim, Kevin Behr, and George Spafford, published by IT Revolution Press, January 2013
[Kim et al., 2016]	The DevOps Handbook: How to Create World-Class Agility, Reliability, and Security in Technology Organizations, by Gene Kim, Patrick Debois, and John Willis, published by Trade Select, December 2016
[Kniberg, 2019]	Spotify: A Scrum@Scale Case Study, by Henrik Kniberg, published by Scrum Alliance®, August 2019
[Korzybski, 1958]	Science and Sanity: An Introduction to Non-Aristotelian Systems and General Semantics, by Alfred Korzybski, published by the Institute of General Semantics, 1958
[Krafcik, 1988]	Triumph of the Lean Production System, by John F. Krafcik, MIT International Motor Vehicle Program, published in the Sloan Management Review, 1988; refer to: www.lean.org/downloads/MITSloan.pdf
[Leffingwell, 2011]	Agile Software Requirements, by Dean Leffingwell, published by Addison-Wesley, 2011
[LEI]	The Lean Enterprise Institute; refer to: www.lean.org/
[LEIa, 2004]	Strategy Deployment, The Lean Lexicon, Fifth Edition, by Chet Marchwinski, Alexis Schroeder, and John Shook, published by the Lean Enterprise Institute, April 2004; refer to: www.lean.org/lexicon/strategy-deployment
[LEIb, 2004]	True North, The Lean Lexicon, Fifth Edition, by Chet Marchwinski, Alexis Schroeder, and John Shook, published by the Lean Enterprise Institute, April 2004; refer to: www.lean.org/lexicon/true-north
[Levitt, 1960]	Marketing Myopia, by Theodore Levitt, first published in 1960 and reprinted in the "Best of HBR", published in the Harvard Business Review, July-August 2004; refer to: www.hbr.org/2004/07/marketing-myopia

[Levitt, 1962]	Innovation in Marketing: New Perspectives for Profit and Growth, by Theodore Levitt, published by McGraw-Hill, June 1962
[Liker & Ross, 2017]	The Toyota Way to Service Excellence: Lean Transformation in Service Organizations, by Jeffrey K. Liker and Karyn Ross, published by McGraw Hill Education, March 2017
[LSP]	Liskov Substitution Principle; refer to: en.wikipedia.org/wiki/Liskov_substitution_principle
[MacCormack et al., 2007]	Exploring the Duality between Product and Organizational Architectures: A Test of the "Mirroring" Hypothesis, Working Paper 08-039, by Alan MacCormack, John Rusnak, and Carliss Baldwin, published by the Harvard Business School, 2007; refer to: www.hbs.edu/faculty/Publication%20Files/08-039_1861e507-1dc1-4602-85b8-90d71559d85b.pdf
[Mandelbaum & Reed, 2006]	Value Engineering Handbook, by Jay Mandelbaum and Danny L. Reed, published by the Institute for Defense Analysis, 2006
[Marcuson Consulting, 2025]	UK Motor Insurance Market 2024: Updated Market-Wide Analysis; refer to: marcuson.co/wp-content/uploads/2025/08/Marcuson-Consulting-UK-Motor-Insurance-Market-2024-Updated-Market-Wide-Analysis.pdf
[Martin, 1995]	The Great Transition: Using the Seven Disciplines of Enterprise Engineering to Align People, Technology, and Strategy, by James Martin, published by Amacom, January 1995
[Martin, 2014]	The Big Lie of Strategic Planning, by Roger L. Martin, published in the Harvard Business Review, January-February 2014; refer to: www.hbr.org/2014/01/the-big-lie-of-strategic-planning
[McChrystal et al., 2015]	Team of Teams: New Rules of Engagement for a Complex World, by General Stanley McChrystal, Tantum Collins, Chris Fussell, and David Silverman, published by Penguin, November 2015
[Merriam-Webster]	Merriam-Webster Dictionary; refer to: www.merriam-webster.com/
[Mintel & Mordor Intelligence, 2024]	Germany Motor Insurance Market Analyses, including Aggregator Usage, Digital Adoption, and Premium Growth Trends; refer to: store.mintel.com/report/germany-car-insurance-market-report and marketresearch.com/Mordor-Intelligence-LLP-v4018/Germany-Motor-Insurance-Share-Trends-37689333/
[Miraglia, 2014]	Systems Architectures and Innovation: the Modularity-Integrality Framework, by Stefano Miraglia, a Working Paper, published by the University of Cambridge, 2014
[MITa]	Decision Rights and Governance; refer to: www.cisr.mit.edu/content/classic-topics-decision-rights
[MITb]	Mastering Design Thinking; refer to: www.executive-ed.mit.edu/mastering-design-thinking

[MIT OCW, 2010] Operations Strategy, MIT Course Number 15.769, published by Massachusetts Institute of Technology Open Courseware, 2010; refer to: www.ocw.mit.edu/courses/sloan-school-of-management/15-769-operations-strategy-fall-2010/

[Morgan & Liker, 2019] Designing the Future: How Ford™, Toyota™, and Other World-Class Organizations Use Lean Product Development to Drive Innovation and Transform their Business, by James M. Morgan and Jeffery K. Liker, November 2018, published by McGraw-Hill Education

[Murman et al., 2002] Lean Enterprise Value: Insights from the MIT's Lean Aerospace Initiative, by Earll M. Murman, Joel Cutcher-Gershenfeld, and Tom Allen, May 2002, published by AIAA

[Norman, 2013] The Design of Everyday Thing, by Don Norman, published by MIT Press, December 2013

[Northrop & Clements, 2012] A Framework for Software Product Line Practice, Version 5.0, by Linda M. Northrop and Paul C. Clements, published by the Software Engineering Institute (SEI), December 2012

[Nygard, 2015] Documenting Architecture Decisions, Michael Nygard Blog, 2015; refer to: www.thinkrelevance.com/blog/2011/11/15/documenting-architecture-decisions

[Nygard, 2018] Release It! Design and Deploy Production-Ready Software, by Michael Nygard, published by The Pragmatic Bookshelf, January 2018

[Nygard, 2020] Architecture Decision Record Template; refer to: www.github.com/joelparkerhenderson/architecture-decision-record

[Ohno & Bodek, 1988] Toyota Production System: Beyond Large-Scale Production, by Taiichi Ohno and Norman Bodek, published by Productivity Press, March 1988

[Olsen, 2015] The Lean Product Playbook: How to Innovate with Minimum Viable Products and Rapid Customer Feedback, by Dan Olsen, published by John Wiley & Sons, July 2015

[Parker et al., 2016] Platform Revolution: How Networked Markets are Transforming the Economy — and How to Make them Work for You, by Geoffrey G. Parker, Marshall W. Van Alstyne, and Sangeet Paul Choudary, published by W. W. Norton and Company, March 2016

[Parnas, 1972] On the Criteria to be Used in Decomposing Systems into Modules, by S. L. Parnas, published by Carnegie Mellon University, 1972

[Pasmore et al., 2019] Reflections: Sociotechnical Systems Design and Organization Change, by William Pasmore, Stu Winby, Susan Albers Mohrman, and Rick Vanasse, published in the Journal of Change Management, Vol. 19, 2019

[Patton, 2014] User Story Mapping: Discover the Whole Story, Build the Right Product, by Jeff Patton, published by O'Reilly Media, September 2014

[Paulchell, 2016]	Evolution of a Data Streaming Architecture: Enabling the Business to Turn Data into Insight, by Joseph Paulchell, Principal Software Engineer, published by Capital One Digital Engineering, 2016
[Porter, 1996]	What Is Strategy?, by Michael E. Porter, published in the Harvard Business Review, November-December 1996
[Prehofer et al., 2007]	Compositionality in Software Platforms, by Christian Prehofer, Jilles van Gurp, and Jan Bosch, published by Nokia Research, 2007
[Raft]	The Raft Consensus Algorithm; refer to: www.raft.github.io/
[Rezai, 2016]	When is Software Goods?, by Arezou Rezai, published by Paris Smith LLP, September 2016; refer to: www.parissmith.co.uk/blog/when-is-software-goods/
[Richards, 2015]	Software Architecture Patterns, by Mark Richards, published by O'Reilly Media, February 2015
[Richardson, 2010]	Understanding Customer Experience, by Adam Richardson, published in the Harvard Business Review, October 2010
[Ries, 2009]	Sharding for Startups, by Eric Ries, January 2009; refer to: www.startuplessonslearned.com/2009/01/sharding-for-startups.html
[Ries, 2011]	The Lean Startup: How Constant Innovation Creates Radically Successful Businesses, by Eric Ries, published by Portfolio Penguin, October 2011
[Rigby at al., 2018]	Agile at Scale, by Darrell K. Rigby, Jeff Sutherland, and Andy Noble, published in the Harvard Business Review, May-June 2018
[Ross, 2019]	Why Hypotheses Beat Goals, by Jeanne Ross, published by MIT Sloan Management Review, April 2019; refer to: www.sloanreview.mit.edu/article/why-hypotheses-beat-goals/
[Ross et al., 2019a]	Designed for Digital: How to Architect your Business for Sustained Success, by Jeanne W. Ross, Cynthia M. Beath, and Martin Mocker, published by MIT Press, September 2019
[Rossman, 2019]	Think Like Amazon: 50 1/2 Ideas to Become a Digital Leader, John Rossman, published by McGraw-Hill Education, May 2019
[Rother & Shook, 2003]	Learning to See — Value Stream Mapping to Create Value and Eliminate Muda, Version 1.3, by Mike Rother and John Shook, published by the Lean Enterprise Institute, June 2003
[Rozanski & Woods, 2005]	Software Systems Architecture: Working with Stakeholders using Viewpoints and Perspectives, by Nick Rozanski and Eoin Woods, published by Addison-Wesley, April 2005
[Samaras & Willis, 2013]	Capabilities-Based Planning for Energy Security at Department of Defense Installations, by Constantine Samaras and Henry H. Willis, published by RAND Corporation, 2013

[Sawhney, 2016] Putting Products into Services, by Mohanbir Sawhney, published in the Harvard Business Review, September 2016; refer to: www.hbr.org/2016/09/putting-products-into-services

[Scaled Agile, Inc.] Scaled Agile, Inc. The Provider of SAFe®; refer to: www.scaledagile.com

[Scheiber, 2017] How Uber Uses Psychological Tricks to Push Its Drivers' Buttons, by Noam Scheiber and graphics by Jon Huang, published by the New York Times Company, April 2017

[Schema.org] Schema.org is a collaborative, community activity with a mission to create, maintain, and promote schemas for structured data on the Internet, on web pages, in email messages, and beyond; refer to: www.schema.org/

[Schoemaker & Day, 2009] How to Make Sense of Weak Signals, by Paul J. H. Schoemaker and George S. Day, April 2009, published by Massachusetts Institute of Technology (MIT) Sloan Management Review (SMR); refer to: www.sloanreview.mit.edu/article/how-to-make-sense-of-weak-signals/

[Seddon & Lewis, 2003] Strategy and Business Models: What's the Difference?, by Peter B. Seddon and Geoffrey P. Lewis, published in the Pacific Asia Conference on Information Systems (PACIS), 2003

[Seite et al., 2010] The Concept of Modularisation of Industrial Services, by Fabrice Seite, Oliver Schneider, and Andreas Nobs, published by IFIP International Federation for Information Processing, 2010, and printed in Advances in Production Management Systems: New Challenges, New Approaches: International IFIP WG 5.7 Conference, APMS 2009, by B. Vallespir and T. Alix, November 2014, published by Springer

[Sen, 1992] Inequality Re-Examined, by Amartya Sen, published by Clarendon Press, 1992

[Shoup, 2014] From the Monolith to Micro-Services, by Randy Shoup, published by slideshare.net, October 2014; refer to: www.slideshare.net/RandyShoup/monoliths-migrations-and-microservices

[Simon, 1962] The Architecture of Complexity, by Herbert A. Simon, published in the Proceedings of the American Philosophical Society, Volume 106, December 1962

[Simon et al., 2018] Liquid Software: How to Achieve Trusted Continuous Updates in the DevOps World, by Fred Simon, Yoav Landman, Baruch Sadogursky, published by CreateSpace Independent Publishing Platform, May 2018

[Singh & Bhadani, 2020] Mobile Deep Learning with TensorFlow Lite, ML Kit, and Flutter, by Anubhav Singh and Rimjhim Bhadani, published by Packt Publishing, April 2020

[Skelton & Pais, 2019] Team Topologies: Organizing Business and Technology Teams for Fast Flow, by Matthew Skelton and Manuel Pais, published by IT Revolution Press, September 2019

[Spear & Bowen, 1999]	Decoding the DNA of the Toyota Production System, by Steven Spear and H. Kent Bowen, published in the Harvard Business Review, September-October 1999; refer to: www.hbr.org/1999/09/decoding-the-dna-of-the-toyota-production-system
[Stanford, 2010]	An Introduction to Design Thinking — Process Guide, by the Hasso Plattner Institute of Design, Stanford
[Steiglitz, 2019]	The Discrete Charm of the Machine: Why the World Became Digital, by Kenneth Steiglitz, published by Princeton University Press, February 2019
[Sull et al., 2015]	Why Strategy Execution Unravels — and What to Do About It, by Donald Sull, Rebecca Homkes, and Charles Sull, published in the Harvard Business Review, March 2015
[Sutcliff et al., 2019]	The Two Big Reasons That Digital Transformations Fail, by Mike Sutcliff, Raghav Narsalay, and Aarohi Sen, published by the Harvard Business School, October 2019
[TFX User Guide]	TFX User Guide; refer to: www.tensorflow.org/tfx/guide
[Ton et al., 2010]	Zara: Managing Stores for Fast Fashion, by Zeynep Ton, Elena Corsi, and Vincent Dessain, revised edition, published by Harvard Business School, January 2010
[Traynor, 2016]	Focus on the Job, Not the Customer, by Des Tranor, published by Inside Intercom, 2016; refer to: www.intercom.com/blog/when-personas-fail-you/
[Trist & Bamforth, 1951]	Some Social and Psychological Consequences of the Longwall Method of Coal-Getting, by E. L. Trist and K. W. Bamforth, published by The Tavistock Institute, 1951
[Ulrich, 1993]	The Role of Product Architecture in the Manufacturing Firm, by Karl Ulrich, Research Policy, final version received by MIT, Sloan School of Management, December 1993
[Ulrich et al., 2020]	Product Design and Development, Seventh Edition, by Karl T. Ulrich, Steven D. Eppinger, and Maria C. Yang, published by McGraw-Hill, 2020
[Unicorn (Finance)]	Unicorn (Finance); refer to: en.wikipedia.org/wiki/Unicorn_(finance).
[Van Mieghem & Allon, 2015]	Operations Strategy: Principles and Practice, Second Edition, by Jan A. Van Mieghem and Gad Allon, published by Dynamic Ideas, January 2015
[Vanderhaegen et al., 2019]	Automation Challenges of Socio-Technical Systems, by Frederic Vanderhaegen, Choubeila Maaoui, Denis Berdjag, and Mohamed Sallak, published by Wiley-ISTE, July 2019
[Vandermerwe & Rada, 1988]	Servitization of Business: Adding Value by Adding Services, by Sandra Vandermerwe and Juan Rada, published in the European Management Journal, Volume 6, Issue 4, Winter 1988
[Vernon, 2013]	Implementing Domain-Driven Design, by Vaughn Vernon, published by Addison-Wesley Professional, February 2013

[W178]	World-Class EA: Governors' Approach to Developing and Exercising an Enterprise Architecture Governance Capability (W178), published by The Open Group, July 2017; refer to: www.opengroup.org/library/w178
[Ward & Sobek, 2014]	Lean Product and Process Development, Second Edition, by Allen C. Ward and Durward K. Sobek II, published by the Lean Enterprise Institute, February 2014
[Weill & Ross, 2005]	How Effective is Your IT Governance?, Research Briefing, by Peter Weill and Jeanne Ross, published by MIT CISR, 2005
[Wikipedia®]	List of System Quality Attributes, published by Wikipedia®; refer to: en.wikipedia.org/wiki/List_of_system_quality_attributes
[Wind & Hays, 2015]	Beyond Advertising: Creating Value Through All Customer Touchpoints, by Yoram (Jerry) Wind and Catharine Findiesen Hays, published by Wiley, 2015
[Wind & Hays, 2016]	Beyond Advertising: Creating Value through All Customer Touchpoints, by Yoram (Jerry) Wind and Catharine Findiesen Hays, published by John Wiley & Sons, February 2016
[Womack & Jones, 1996]	Lean Thinking: Banish Waste and Create Wealth in Your Corporation, by James P. Womack and Daniel T. Jones, published by Simon & Schuster, 1996
[Wu et al., 2010]	Operational Capabilities: The Secret Ingredient, by Sarah Jinhui Wu, Steven A. Melnyk, and Barbara B. Flynn, published in Decision Sciences, Volume 41, No. 4, November 2010

[This page is intentionally blank]

Chapter 1. Introduction

1.1. Objective

This document is The Open Group Open Agile Architecture™ Standard, Version 2.0, also known as the O-AA™ Standard. The objective is to provide guidance for enterprises conducting both Digital Transformation and Agile Transformation. This document establishes the Open Agile Architecture Body of Knowledge, providing modular building blocks that can be configured and assembled to support various architecture development styles across the enterprise. It does not require the adoption of any particular process-oriented Agile framework. Instead, it is designed to complement whichever approach an organization chooses to use.

1.2. Overview

This document addresses the dual Digital Transformation and Agile Transformation of the enterprise. It applies to enterprises of all sizes and sectors seeking to evolve toward agility at scale while simultaneously leveraging digital technologies to drive innovation, enhance customer experience, and develop competitive advantages.

This document is organized into four parts:

Part 1: The Agile Way of Thinking covers the fundamental concepts of why the enterprise needs to conduct a dual Digital and Agile Transformation and establishes the foundation of the Open Agile Architecture Body of Knowledge. It defines a basic Agile Maturity Model and provides guidance on the need for Agile Architecture, the dual Digital and Agile Transformation, why organizational agility matters, and how business agility can be achieved through organizational agility.

Part 2: The Agile Enterprise addresses the characteristics of an Agile organization and the supporting ecosystem necessary for developing and maintaining an Agile Architecture capability. This includes detailed guidance on an Agile organization (incorporating learnings from socio-technical systems, autonomy and self-organization, team taxonomy, product teams, and organizational transformation), Agile strategy (addressing strategy tenets, unintended consequences, and strategy deployment), architecting the Agile Transformation (covering accountability, incremental transformation, organizational architecture rationale, new organizational culture, and leadership-driven change), and Agile governance (examining classical IT governance limitations, governance challenges in Agile contexts, hybrid delivery styles, and evolved governance models).

Part 3: The Agile Architecture Capability provides guidance on developing, delivering, and managing architecture within Agile enterprises. This part addresses both architectural development approaches (Part 3A) and architecture techniques and deliverables (Part 3B).

Part 3A covers intentional architecture, continuous architecture, and architecture refactoring.

Part 3B covers:

- Product architecture: Managing trade-offs between modularity and integration, including product platforms
- Operations architecture: Leveraging operational capabilities and digital technology platforms for competitive advantage
- Software architecture: System decomposition, event-driven architecture, hexagonal architecture, and non-functional requirements (security, reliability, performance, operability, maintainability)
- Software management of computing resources: Infrastructure as Code, DevOps practices (four key metrics, principles, capabilities), and Site Reliability Engineering (SRE) practices focused on availability, performance, and capacity planning

Part 4: The Ways of Supporting examines the techniques and methods that can be used to support Agile Architecture development:

- Experience design combines customer research using jobs-to-be-done analysis with product discovery through experience mapping to define products, features, outcomes, and benefits
- Journey mapping bridges outside-in and inside-out thinking, identifying moments of truth and automation roles
- Lean value stream mapping models and improves value streams by visualizing current conditions, identifying waste unevenness, and overburden then creating future state mappings
- Event storming provides collaborative brainstorming using domain events to discover domains. Domain-driven design addresses problem space (domains/sub-domains) and solution space (bounded contexts) with context maps organizing upstream, midway, and downstream integration patterns
- Data information and Artificial Intelligence (AI) addresses data streaming architectures, modular data models, Machine Learning (ML) pipelines, and deep learning for mobile applications

1.3. Conformance

Refer to The Open Group website for conformance requirements for this document.

1.4. Normative References

None.

1.5. Terminology

For the purposes of this document, the following terminology definitions apply:

Can

Describes a possible feature or behavior available to the user or application.

May

Describes a feature or behavior that is optional. To avoid ambiguity, the opposite of "may" is expressed as "need not", instead of "may not".

Shall

Describes a feature or behavior that is a requirement. To avoid ambiguity, do not use "must" as an alternative to "shall".

Shall not

Describes a feature or behavior that is an absolute prohibition.

Should

Describes a feature or behavior that is recommended but not required.

Will

Same meaning as "shall"; "shall" is the preferred term.

1.6. Future Directions

It is expected that this document will be revised from time to time to remain current with both practice and technology.

Chapter 2. Definitions

For the purposes of this document, the following terms and definitions apply. Merriam-Webster's Collegiate Dictionary should be referenced for terms not defined in this section.

2.1. Accountability

The obligation to demonstrate task achievement and take responsibility for performance in accordance with agreed expectations; the obligation to answer for an action. (Source: Vanderhaegen et al., 2019)

2.2. Alignment Diagram

Any map, diagram, or visualization that reveals both sides of value creation in a single overview. It is a category of diagram that illustrates the interaction between people and organizations. (Source: Kalbach, 2016)

2.3. Allowable Lead Time

The time available between starting a product development initiative or process and finishing it in order to satisfy customers.

2.4. Architectural Runway

Consists of the existing code, components, and technical infrastructure needed to implement near-term features without excessive redesign and delay. (Source: Scaled Agile, Inc.)

2.5. Architecture

1. The fundamental concepts or properties of a system in its environment embodied in its elements, relationships, and in the principles of its design and evolution (Source: ISO/IEC/IEEE 42010)
2. (System Engineering Context) The embodiment of concept, and the allocation of physical/informational function (process) to elements of form (objects) and definition of structural interfaces among the objects (Source: Crawley et al., 2016)

2.6. Architecture Principle

A qualitative statement of intent that should be met by the architecture. (Source: C220)

2.7. Architecture Style

A coordinated set of architectural constraints that restricts the roles/features of architectural elements and the allowed relationships among those elements within any architecture that conforms to that style. (Source: Fielding, 2000)

2.8. Capability

1. An ability that an organization, person, or system possesses (Source: C220)
2. The ability to achieve a desired outcome (Source: CJCSM, 2005)

2.9. Catchball

A dialogue between senior managers and project teams about the resources and time both available and needed to achieve the targets. (Source: LEIa)

NOTE	Once the major goals are set, planning should become a top-down and bottom-up process involving a dialogue. This dialogue is often called catchball (or nemawashi) as ideas are tossed back and forth like a ball.

2.10. Continuous Architecture

An architecture with no end-state that is designed to evolve to support the changing needs of the digital enterprise.

2.11. Customer Experience

The sum-totality of how customers engage with a company and its brand, not just in a snapshot in time, but throughout the entire arc of being a customer. (Source: Richardson, 2010)

2.12. Customer Journey

The series of interactions between a customer and a company that occur as the customer pursues a specific goal. (Source: Gartner®)

2.13. Design Thinking

A methodology for creative problem-solving that begins with understanding unmet customer needs. (Sources: Stanford, 2010; MITb)

2.14. Digital Platform

A software system composed of application and infrastructure components that can be rapidly reconfigured using DevOps and cloud-native computing.

2.15. Digital Practices

A synthesis of methods and guidance from a wide variety of practitioners and professional communities active in digital technology (Lean, Agile, DevOps, etc.) designed to create and manage products with an increasing digital component, or lead their organization through Digital Transformation.

2.16. Digital Technology

A powerful, accessible, and potentially game-changing technology (social, mobile, cloud, analytics, Internet of Things (IoT), cognitive computing, and biometrics) often used in combination and usually characterized by its ability to positively impact an enterprise's business model, customer experience, product, or operating system to enable innovation and growth.

2.17. Digital Transformation

A strategy and an operating model change, in which technological advancements are leveraged to improve human experiences and operating efficiencies, and to evolve the products and services to which customers will remain loyal. (Source: C196)

2.18. Domain Model: Domain-Driven Design

The representation of a selected abstraction of domain knowledge that is rigorously organized. (Source: Evans, 2003)

NOTE	It is not necessarily a particular diagram; it can also be captured in carefully written code or in a well-written text.

2.19. Ecosystem

A group of interconnected resources that can function as a unit to drive the creation and delivery of information technology products. (Source: Wind & Hays, 2015)

NOTE	In the mathematics of dynamic ecosystems, a common result is that the more aligned the objectives of the various components of the system, the healthier the system.

2.20. Epic

1. (Classical Agile) A large user story that cannot be delivered as defined within a single iteration, or is large enough that it can be split into smaller user stories (Source: Agile Alliance®)

NOTE	There is no standard form to represent epics. Some teams use the familiar user story formats (as a, I want, so that or in order to, as a, I want), while other teams represent them with a short phrase.

2. (Scaled Agile) The highest-level expression of a customer need; development initiatives that are intended to deliver the value of an investment theme and are identified, prioritized, estimated, and maintained in the portfolio backlog (Source: Leffingwell, 2011)

2.21. Event Storming

The identification of domain events, commands, persona, or entities to facilitate a structured conversation about the domain.

2.22. Evolutionary Architecture

An architecture that supports guided, incremental change across multiple dimensions. (Source: Ford™, 2017)

2.23. Evolvability

A meta-non-functional requirement that aims to prevent the architecture from degrading and/or aging out over time.

2.24. Feature

The functional characteristic of a product (goods or services).

NOTE	It provides a factual description of how a product delivers its outcomes.

2.25. Hardware

Tools, machines, wiring, and other physical components of a system.

2.26. Information Security

The protection of information and Information Systems (ISs) from unauthorized access, use, disclosure, disruption, modification, or destruction in order to provide integrity, confidentiality, and availability.

> **NOTE**
>
> - Integrity, which means guarding against improper information modification or destruction, and includes ensuring information authenticity and non-repudiation
> - Confidentiality, which means preserving authorized restrictions on access and disclosure, including the means for protecting personal privacy and proprietary information
> - Availability, which means ensuring timely and reliable access to, and use of information

2.27. Integrality

The system's property of being made up of elements that behave consistently as a whole. (Source: Miraglia, 2014)

2.28. Intentional Architecture

A purposeful set of statements, models, and decisions that represent some future architectural state.

2.29. Job-To-Be-Done

What the customer hopes to accomplish. (Source: Christensen et al., 2016)

> **NOTE**
>
> "Job" is shorthand for what an individual really seeks to accomplish in a given circumstance.

2.30. Journey Mapping

Laying out the entire end-to-end customer experience.

2.31. Lead Time

The time between the initiation and completion of a process.

2.32. Lean Value Stream

A technique developed from Lean manufacturing that visualizes all the steps necessary to deliver a product or service, with the goal of optimizing business processes. (Source: LEI)

> **NOTE** These include actions to process information from the customer and actions to transform the product on its way to the customer.

2.33. Modularity

The system's property of being made up of elements that present a high level of independence from other elements. (Source: Miraglia, 2014)

2.34. Modularization

A design approach in which a complex system is broken down into smaller independent units, called modules, with well-defined interfaces, enabling independent development, testing, and replacement over time. (Source: Parnas, 1972)

> **NOTE** Every module is characterized by its assigned function(s) and interface(s).

2.35. Obeya Room

A Japanese term that translates to "big room". An Obeya room is a structured, collaborative space that uses visual management to align strategy with execution, enabling cross-functional teams to make decisions quickly and transparently.

2.36. Operating System

The foundational layer of assets and processes necessary to develop and deliver a product or service to the end user. The Operating System acts as the organization's foundation, providing the intermediary connections to all its resources, people, and processes needed to run efficiently and securely. (Source: Van Mieghem & Allon, 2015)

> **NOTE**
>
> - Assets: Main processing resources utilized by the firm, including human resources and capital resources that either add value or are necessary for the processing and delivery of the product
> - Processes: Flows through a network of activities that transform the product or service from input to output

2.37. Persona

A fictional character which is created based upon research in order to represent the different user types that might use a service, product, site, or brand in a similar way. (Source: Friis Dam & Siang, 2020)

2.38. Platform Business Model

A business model that is based on the two-sided market theory. Multi-sided (n-sided) markets may also be considered.

2.39. Process

Any activity or group of activities that takes an input, adds value to it, and provides an output to an internal or external customer. (Source: Harrington, 1991)

NOTE There is no product and/or service without a process. Likewise, there is no process without a product or a service.

2.40. Product

A bundle of services and/or goods offered to customers.

NOTE Products have features, which are the functional attributes that define how the products work and deliver benefits to customers. Agile product architecting focuses on segmenting products, so they:

- Meet the needs of customers (product/market fit)
- Offer differentiated features to customer segments
- Can be delivered incrementally by an Agile team or team of teams

2.41. Product Backlog

A list of the new features, changes to existing features, bug fixes, infrastructure changes, or other activities that a team may deliver in order to achieve a specific outcome. (Source: Agile Alliance)

2.42. Product-Centric Organization

An organization composed of cross-functional Agile teams which are responsible for developing products and operating them.

> **NOTE** In an Agile context, product-centricity refers to the shift from temporary organizational structures (projects) to permanent ones. The DevOps principle "you build it, you run it" is core to product-centricity.

2.43. Refactoring

The process of changing a software system in a way that does not alter the external behavior of the code yet improves its internal structure. (Source: Fowler, 2019)

> **NOTE** Refactoring is a disciplined way to clean up code that minimizes the chances of introducing bugs. It may be undertaken for a variety of reasons, such as to improve readability and maintainability, reduce technical debt, make it simpler to incorporate new features, or even improve performance or efficiency.

2.44. Responsibility

The obligation to carry forward a task to its successful conclusion. (Source: Vanderhaegen et al., 2019)

> **NOTE** With responsibility goes the authority to direct and take the necessary action to ensure success.

2.45. Service

1. (Business context) An act performed for the benefit of another

NOTE	Services involve at least two parties. One applies competence (a provider) and another experiences an outcome (a consumer). For example, a taxi ride is a service used by a person for traveling (outcome) and is delivered by a taxi driver (provider). Audio typing is a service used by a person to produce a written document based on their speech (outcome), and is delivered by an audio-typer (provider).

2. (Software context) An encapsulated component that delivers its outcomes through well-defined interfaces

NOTE	Well-designed services are self-contained and provide Application Program Interfaces (APIs) that shield their consumers from their implementation details. Web services are a popular kind of software service, in which interface calls occur over the Internet using standard Internet protocols.

2.46. Social System

People, their behavior, cultural beliefs, skills, and expertise, and how work teams are forming and interacting, as well as organizational leadership, strategy, structure, policy, and procedures.

2.47. Software

Something used or associated with, and usually contrasted with, hardware, such as a program for a computer [Merriam-Webster].

NOTE	Software can be used to automate almost anything, ranging from IT infrastructure to decision-making; e.g., prescriptive analytics.

2.48. System

A set of entities and their relationships whose functionality is greater than the sum of the individual entities. (Source: Crawley et al., 2016)

2.49. User Story

A brief statement of intent that describes something the system needs to do for the user. (Source: Patton, 2014)

NOTE	A simple story template is as follows: • As a [type of user] • I want to [do something] • So that I can [get some benefit]

2.50. Value Stream

Represents a sequence of activities that creates an overall result (value) from the customer's (stakeholder's) perspective. (Source: G178)

2.51. Weak Signal

A seemingly random or disconnected piece of information that at first appears to be background noise but can be recognized as part of a significant pattern by viewing it through a different frame or connecting it with other pieces of information. (Source: Schoemaker & Day, 2009)

2.52. Work System

Human participants or machines, or both, performing processes and activities using software, hardware, and other resources to deliver products or experiences.

Part 1: The Agile Way of Thinking

This part defines the fundamental concepts of shifting to an Agile organization as a key enabler for Digital Transformation.

It is recognized that enterprises are at various stages of the adoption of Agile methodologies. Figure P-1 represents a basic Agile Maturity Model that should help the reader to make an assessment of where they are, and ideally helps to frame the key concepts that follow.

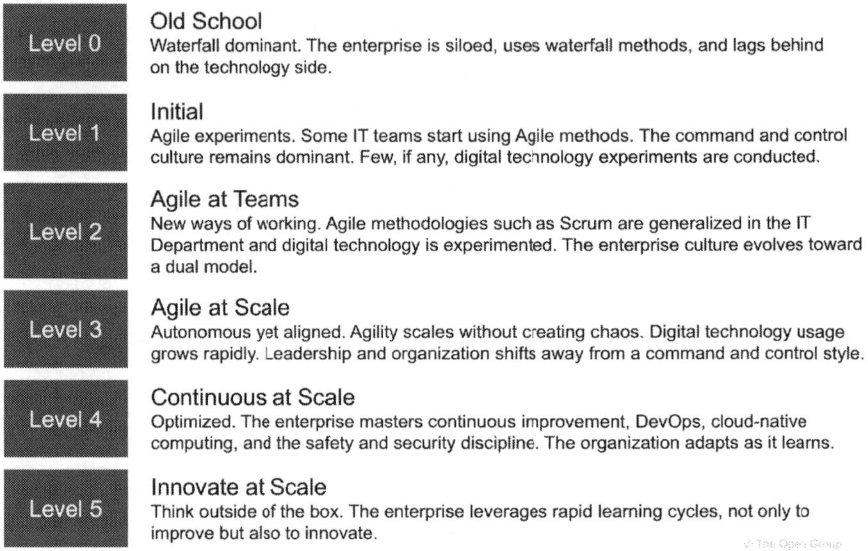

Figure P-1: Agile Maturity Model

Chapter 3. A Dual Transformation

> *"According to Darwin's Origin of Species, it is not the most intellectual of the species that survives; it is not the strongest that survives; but the species that survives is the one that is able best to adapt and adjust to the changing environment in which it finds itself."*
>
> — Leon C. Megginson, Lessons from Europe for American Business

3.1. The Need for Agile Architecture

Agile Architecture is required to enable adaptability in the enterprise to meet emerging product needs while maintaining the enterprise integrity to deliver value in the least constrained way. This document builds upon that statement. In the modern VUCA world, characterized by Volatility, Uncertainty, Complexity, and Ambiguity [Bennis & Nanus, 1985], where change is constant at an ever-increasing speed and impact, it is essential for organizations to be adaptable to this change. The focus here is on the required transformation coming from the introduction of new and emerging technology. The need for **dual transformation** is taken as the starting point (see Chapter 1), referring to *the parallel Digital and Agile Transformation*; see Figure 3-1.

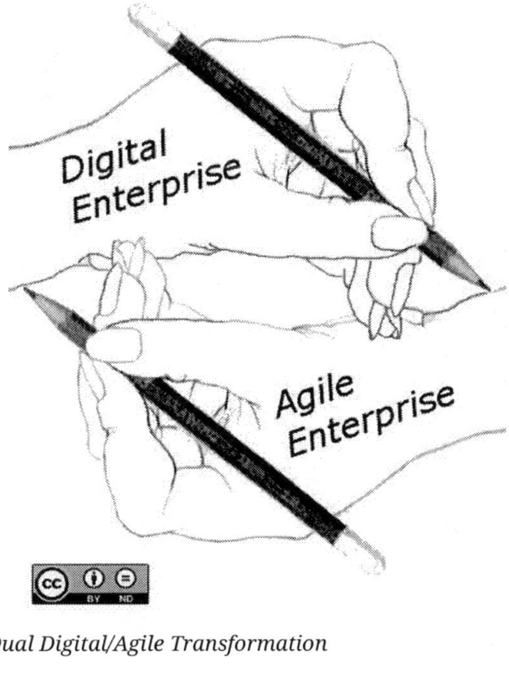

Figure 3-1: Architecting the Dual Digital/Agile Transformation

It is acknowledged that VUCA is not only about new and emerging technology; it is about the four aspects a modern organization is facing. Although the focus is on dual transformation, the transformation toward an Agile organization is also shown to be an enabler for addressing the VUCA aspects.

The Digital Practitioner Body of Knowledge™ Standard [C196] defines Digital Transformation as: *"A strategy and an operating model change, in which technological advancements are leveraged to improve human experiences and operating efficiencies, and to evolve the products and services to which customers will remain loyal"*.

In order for Digital Transformation to be successful, an organization needs to address several topics as part of that transformation. One of them is **organizational agility**.

3.2. Why Organizational Agility Matters

Mike Sutcliff and his co-authors conducted a survey among 1,350 executives to discover why Digital Transformations fail [Sutcliff et al., 2019]. The number one reason given for failure is the unspoken disagreements between top managers about goals. The recommendation is to *"define and articulate not only the opportunity but also the problem it solves, and how the company will build the organization around the desired solution before investing"*.

Tim Fountaine and his co-authors show that technology is not the biggest challenge when building the AI-powered organization [Fountaine et al., 2019]: *"Cutting-edge technology and talent are not enough. Companies must break down organizational and cultural barriers that stand in AI's way"*.

These articles and surveys show that:

- Organizational agility is required to support scaling beyond the pilot stage
- Addressing the organizational and soft aspects of Digital Transformation is a key success factor

In order to become Agile, the organization must:

- Shift from siloed work to interdisciplinary collaboration, because digital technology has the biggest impact when leveraged by cross-functional teams aligned on outcomes
- Empower decentralized decision-making, because **business agility** requires vigilant organizations capable of seeing risks and opportunities sooner, and positioning themselves to act faster to address them [Day & Schoemaker, 2019]

3.3. Developing Business Agility through Organizational Agility

Business agility is the ability to quickly identify and respond to market and environment changes. Enterprises develop business agility when they sense changes in their environment early and act upon them decisively and rapidly.

> *"Employees deep down in the organization may be closer to weak signals at the edge of the organization and must believe they will receive an open hearing when raising concerns or suggesting ideas."* [Day & Schoemaker, 2019]
>
> — George S. Day, Think Sooner Act Faster

When Agile teams are vigilant and empowered to act, they are better at navigating digital turbulence than those at head office. When weak signals reach head office, they are filtered and cascaded down the organization. This increases the likelihood that weak signals (represented by the triangles on Figure 3-2) will not be seen, or that no one will respond to them. This explains why head office can be slow to identify and act upon potential threats and opportunities.

Figure 3-2 illustrates that Agile teams close to the field have enough autonomy to modify products or journeys in response to weak signals. This autonomy means that Agile teams do not have to seek permission from head office before experimenting with responses to weak signals.

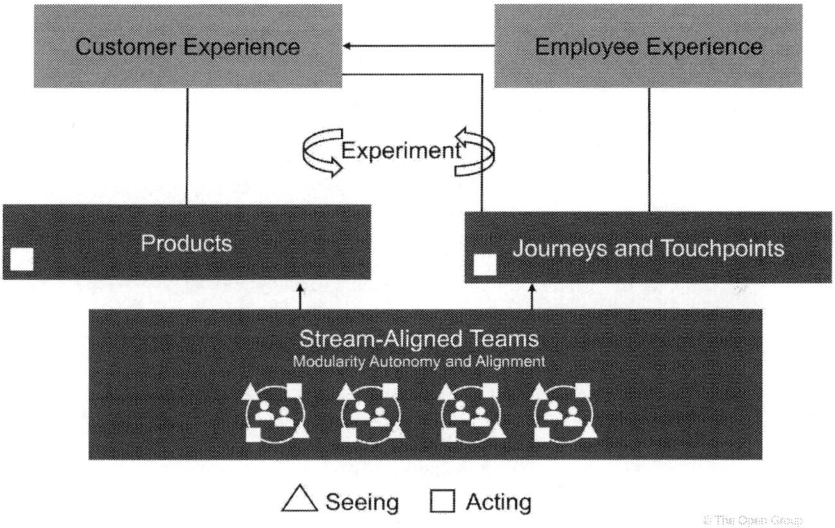

Figure 3-2: Business Agility

Business agility is facilitated by **organizational agility** because:

- Agile teams are cross-functional, which brings diverse perspectives when analyzing weak signals
- They share a common purpose and vision, which helps to put weak signals in perspective
- Most of them are stream-aligned, which means Agile teams are directly responsible for delivering products or journeys, facilitating rapid experimentation

Digital Transformation does not have to be disruptive [Sutcliff et al., 2019]. Business agility is about organizations learning to be capable of evolving rapidly. This evolution toward a **digital enterprise** is about applying **digital technology** to adapt or change:

- The **strategy** of the enterprise
- The **product** or **service** it markets
- The **experience** it delivers to customers, employees, and other stakeholders
- Its **operating system**

The operating system is the combination of assets and processes required to deliver a product or a service; for a more detailed definition of operating system, see Section 2.36.

New operating systems are required to create real-time, personalized experiences. One of their key functions is to enable **touchpoint** orchestration.

3.4. Connecting Touchpoints to the Operating System

Every interaction with a brand, from the first time awareness is established to every touchpoint encountered in daily life, has an impact: "*From the customer perspective, touchpoints with a brand or product are not differentiated: it is the seamless experience that matters.*" Figure 3-3 illustrates the variety of touchpoints that a brand has to orchestrate to deliver a positive customer experience.

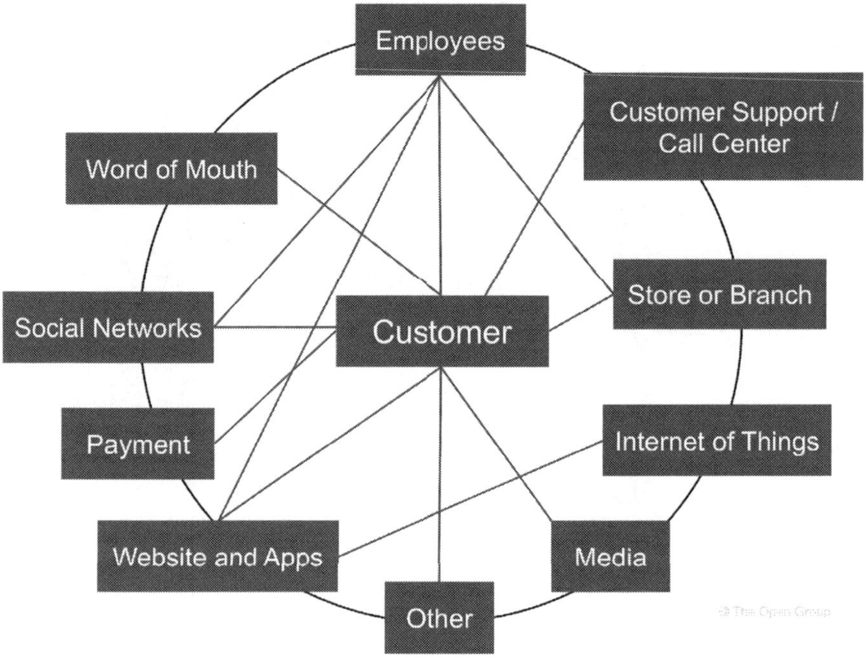

Figure 3-3: Touchpoints

Decomposing the enterprise operating system into a suite of value streams for these touchpoints is a useful way to help to better understand the value to the customer and reduce the overall complexity; see the *TOGAF® Series Guide: Value Streams* [G178].

It can be predicted that: "*Touchpoints will continue to multiply in an era where every object has the potential to become connected and interactive*".

This evolution impacts the enterprise as a whole: "*New structures and processes will need to allow for agility and reaping the benefits both from decentralization and, when needed, the power that leveraging through centralization facilitates*".

Part 2: The Agile Enterprise

This part outlines some key capabilities of an Agile organization. It addresses the organizational characteristics, strategy, transformation architecture, and governance required to develop and maintain an Agile Architecture capability.

Chapter 4. Agile Organization

The main purpose of an Agile at scale organization is to scale while keeping the agility and flexibility (like a startup) to adjust and change quickly while still complying with any industry, safety, and regulatory constraints it must observe. Scaling is important for a startup that may be on track to becoming a unicorn [Unicorn (Finance)] as well as for an established enterprise competing in the digital world.

Agility at scale can be achieved when the enterprise is driven by autonomous, stream-aligned, and cross-functional teams:

- An autonomous team is empowered to make decisions and manages a minimum set of dependencies with other teams
- A stream-aligned team is aligned to a single, valuable stream of work; this might be a single product or service, a single set of features, or a single user journey [Skelton & Pais, 2019]
- A cross-functional team is composed of people from different areas of the enterprise, who together bring the range of competencies and skills required to deliver a product, feature, or journey

The ideas that drive the design of Agile at scale organizations are not new. They date back to the birth of socio-technical systems thinking.

4.1. Learnings from Socio-Technical Systems

Eric Trist and Ken Bamforth studied the consequences of introducing new technology, coal-cutters, and mechanical conveyors in English coal mines [Trist & Bamforth, 1951].

4.1.1. Example: English Coal Mines

NOTE	This example is presented here for illustrative purposes only, to support the text and to enable a clearer understanding for the reader.

Before the introduction of new technology, work organization was based upon pair-based units, which contained the full range of coal-face skills; each collier was an all-round workman. He was usually able to substitute for his workmate. The choice of workmates was made by the men themselves.

Leadership and supervision was internal to the group, which enjoyed a responsible autonomy. This organization had the advantage of placing responsibility for the complete coal-getting task onto the shoulders of a single small group. Work was meaningful and colliers could relate it to clearly identified outcomes.

When pair-based teams encountered hazardous conditions, they had enough skills and autonomy to respond in an appropriate way. The capacity of these small teams for self-regulation and self-adaptation was a function of the wholeness of their work task.

Trist and Bamforth [Trist & Bamforth, 1951] make it clear that the new technology was incompatible with the old work system: *"With the advent of coal-cutters and mechanical conveyors, the degree of technological complexity of the coal-getting task was raised to a different level. Mechanization made possible the working of a single long face in place of a series of short faces"*.

The organizational construct of a "longwall" production unit was based upon a series of shifts with cycle groups of 40-50 men, their shot-firer, and the shift deputies responsible for the working as a whole. The introduction of the new system disturbed the social balance: *"It was impossible for the methods to develop as a technological system without bringing into existence a work relationship structure radically different ..."*.

In many coal mines, the consequence of the introduction of new technology was disorganization and waste: *"Disorganization on the filling shift disorganizes the subsequent shifts, and its own disorganization is often produced by the bad preparation left by these teams. Every time the cycle is stopped, some 200 tons of coals are lost. So close is the task interdependence that the system becomes vulnerable from its need for one hundred percent performance at each stop"*.

Autonomy and trust was replaced by blame and lack of accountability: *"Since bad conditions and bad work interact so closely, it is usually difficult to pin blame specifically. Mutual scapegoating is a self-perpetuating system, in which nothing is resolved and no one feels guilt"*, the authors of the study observe.

Not all coal mines that deployed new technology suffered from these problems. The mines that let teams of multi-skilled workers form spontaneously and take on responsibility for the entire mining operations cycle did much better [Pasmore et al., 2019]. The new form of organization that emerged features men who allocated themselves to tasks and shifts. Although the tasks are those of conventional mechanized systems, management and supervisors do not monitor, enforce, or reward single task execution. The multi-skilled group takes over some of the managerial tasks as it had in the pre-mechanized organization, such as the selection of group members and the informal monitoring of work. Problems are solved by teams as they are encountered, resulting in operations running more smoothly and safely.

4.1.2. Principles

Pasmore and his co-authors identify the following socio-technical systems design principles:

- **Wholeness**: The work system should be conceived as a set of activities that make up a functioning whole, rather than a collection of individual jobs
- **Teams**: The work group should be considered more central than individual contributors
- **Process**: Variance or deviation should be identified and handled as close to its point of origin as possible
- **Self-direction**: Internal regulation of the work system is preferable to external regulation by supervisors when the teams and individuals understand the overall goals; utilization of a skilled product owner, who can translate the needs of the overall project goals into a vision and requirements for the product team, provides a critical success enabler for the Agile organization

- **Multi-skilling**: Job and team design should be based on polyvalence or multi-skilling rather than single-skilling
- **Slack**: The work system should preserve some room for slack
- **Joint-optimization**: The individual should be viewed as complementary to the machine rather than as an extension of it
- **Incompletion**: Since the context of the organization will continue to evolve over time, no organizational design can be considered "finished"

To this day, these principles remain valid and should influence the enterprise that deploys agility at scale.

4.2. Autonomy and Self-Organization

Autonomous teams are capable of self-organization. They are more resilient when they face adverse conditions, and can adapt when circumstances change.

Self-organization refers to the emergence of an order that results from the collective interactions of the system's components. Self-organization is central to the formation of numerous structures, including biological ones. For example, there is no centralized control in a neural network. All the nodes are connected directly or indirectly to each other, but none is in control. Yet, together, they learn from complex patterns of inputs.

Self-organization cannot happen in an enterprise that:

- Has a centralized command and control culture
- Distributes the work in a piecemeal manner, the pieces being too small to self-organize

Team autonomy, which is a precondition to agility, is hard to achieve at scale. First, the enterprise needs to trust its people, otherwise they will not enjoy the freedom to act. Second, effective alignment mechanisms are necessary to avoid chaos; see the four alignment levers in Section 7.4. Third, the work system should be designed to regroup activities that together make a functioning whole, otherwise the work will lack meaning.

4.3. Team Taxonomy

Agile teams can be classified into three categories: stream-aligned, platform, and competency teams.

Figure 4-1 summarizes the ideas developed in this section. Further details on alignment and feedback can be found in Chapter 7.

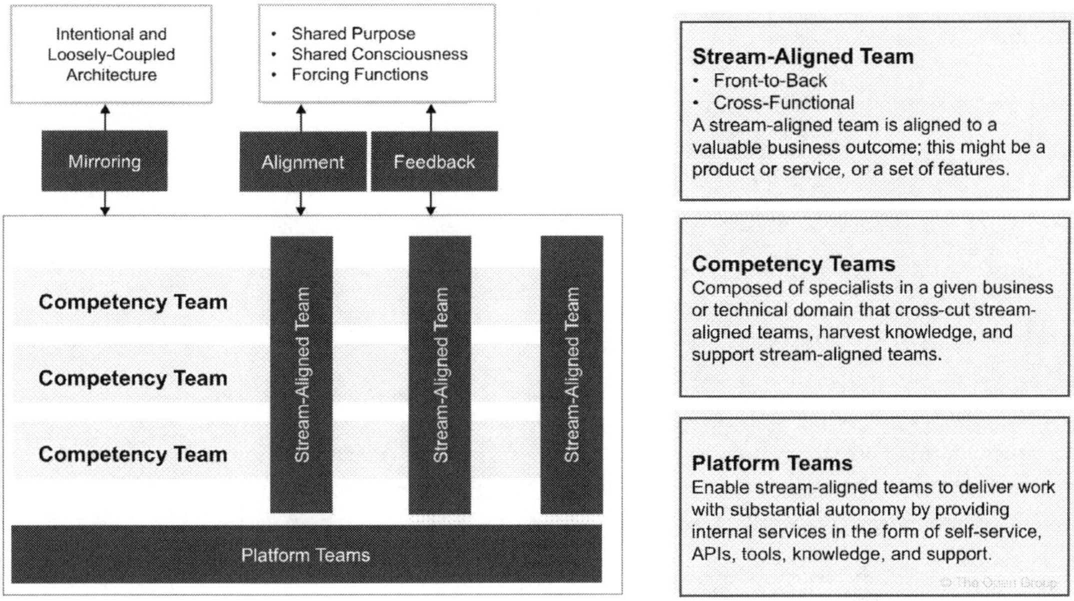

Figure 4-1: Agile Organization at Scale

4.3.1. Stream-Aligned Teams

Stream-aligned teams make a functioning whole because they are responsible for all the activities necessary to deliver valuable streams of work. They are closer to external or internal customers because they deliver value to them. Stream-aligned teams usually interact with customers and are able to quickly integrate their feedback.

A great number of streams exist in an Agile at scale organization. The intentional architecture defines a modular decomposition of the architecture at all levels of the enterprise. Stream-aligned teams are assigned the responsibility of segments of the enterprise at different levels of granularity. For example, a "team of teams" can be entrusted the responsibility of lending products that target small businesses. At a lower level of granularity, a small "two-pizza" team can be entrusted with the responsibility of the customer appointment management feature.

When assigning responsibilities to a team, it is critical to ensure the resulting cognitive load will not be too high [Skelton & Pais, 2019]. When the capacity of a team is spread too thin over a scope that is too large, it affects team morale and work quality. Taking cognitive load into consideration when defining the scope of Agile teams is critical.

Another consideration is the "Dunbar number", which is a limit to the number of people with whom a person can maintain stable social relationships. Robin Dunbar found a correlation between a primate's brain size and the average social group size. Extrapolating this result to humans, the Dunbar number estimates that the size of a stable and cohesive human group should not exceed 150 to 200 people.

When the architecture of a system and the structure of the organization that is responsible for that system are at odds, the likelihood that the structure of the organization will win is high. This is why the Inverse Conway Maneuver (see Axiom 12. *Organization Mirroring Architecture*) recommends shaping the organization so that communication lines mirror intentional architecture boundaries.

This document recommends the decomposition of the enterprise into segments that are:

- Orthogonal, to prevent teams from working on the same things
- Loosely-coupled, to minimize inter-team dependencies

4.3.2. Platform Teams

Platform teams deliver an architecture and a set of integrated components to internal customers.

For example, the automotive industry develops platforms that consist of the floor panels, suspension system, firewall, and rocker panels. It constrains the architecture of the product. It provides a structure for major components by determining the body size and type of engine and transmission [Cusumano & Nobeoka, 1998].

In software engineering, a software product line is equivalent to an automotive platform. It is a *"set of software-intensive systems that share a common, managed set of features satisfying the specific needs of a particular market segment or mission and that are developed from a common set of core assets in a prescribed way"* [Northrop & Clements, 2012].

4.3.3. Competency Teams

Stream-aligned and platform teams are at risk of becoming silos if they are not completed by another type of organizational construct: competency teams.

Competency teams regroup people from the same discipline or competency area. Competencies can be of various types, ranging from "hard" engineering disciplines to "soft" disciplines such as anthropology or psychology.

Competency teams can take various forms, ranging from a virtual organization, such as the Chapters or Guilds for Spotify™ [Kniberg, 2019], to a functional department which regroups similarly-skilled people to manage their career and develop specialized knowledge.

Competency teams can also take the form of enabling teams, as described by Matthew Skelton and Manuel Pais [Skelton & Pais, 2019].

4.4. Product Teams

In technology companies, Marty Cagan reports that a product team is generally composed of a product manager, a product designer, and somewhere between two and about 10 to 12 engineers [Cagan, 2018]. Product teams fall into the category of stream-aligned teams. Product teams are stream-aligned.

A product team is composed of highly skilled people who work together for an extended period. True collaboration between product, design, and engineering roles resembles the type of collaboration described in the experience report of Section 4.1. A product team is not a hierarchy. Product team members typically continue to report to their business unit; for example, engineers may report to an engineering manager.

Product teams have the responsibility for all product-related work, including the full customer experience. When the scope of the product is too large, a product team can be composed of sub-teams. Each sub-team is then responsible for a smaller but meaningful piece of that experience, and for the features that deliver it.

4.4.1. Product Manager *versus* Product Owner

A product manager leads a product team. This is not a management role, but a true leadership role that requires those assigned to be among the strongest talent in the enterprise. Marty Cagan claims that a product manager who operates according to the Silicon Valley model must, like a CEO, have the following characteristics:

- Possess a deep knowledge of customers, the market, and the industry
- Understand enough of the design and engineering disciplines to elicit meaningful design conversations and make architecture decisions when consensus cannot be reached
- Be personally credible with key stakeholders such as general management, sales, marketing, engineering, finance, legal, customer support, etc.

The product owner role definition differs depending on the Agile framework:

- The Scrum product owner is responsible for ensuring Agile teams build a product of the highest possible value

  If the product responsibility is shared between several Agile teams, the product owner manages only one product backlog.

- The SAFe product owner is no longer responsible for ensuring a product of the highest possible value is built; the SAFe product owner is now responsible for the Agile Team's backlog and maximizing the value the Agile team produces [Scaled Agile, Inc.]

  The responsibility for delivering value moves to the product management team. Product backlog gets replaced with program backlog. Program backlog gets broken down into team backlogs, for which product owners are responsible.

Marty Cagan compares and contrasts the product owner role with the product manager role [Cagan, 2018]. He observes that product owners tend to be less qualified than product managers. Too often, a product owner is a "recycled" project manager or Project Management Officer (PMO) who does not possess enough experience, competencies, and skills to truly play a product manager role. When a true product manager is appointed, it is critical that they play a product owner role too.

Unlike most product owners who prioritize features, successful product managers prioritize outcomes rather than product features.

Unlike the project-oriented model, which is all about getting product features developed and deployed, a product team is accountable for business outcomes. The product manager should establish measures of success prior to the engagement based on the participant's contributions and business results. These measures should be designed to reward and motivate the participants.

4.4.2. Chief Engineer

The chief engineer is an entrepreneur and architect. They represent the voice of the customer and are accountable for the economic performance of the product; for example, a new car model. They have enough technology and business insight to solve cross-disciplinary problems.

The chief engineer has a passion for the new product and can inspire excellent engineers. Their primary focus is to guide product design and defining/modeling the value stream that will produce it. Functional departments manage personnel that will support the chief engineer, and capitalize upon knowledge from their respective engineering disciplines.

Figure 4-2 illustrates how the system works.

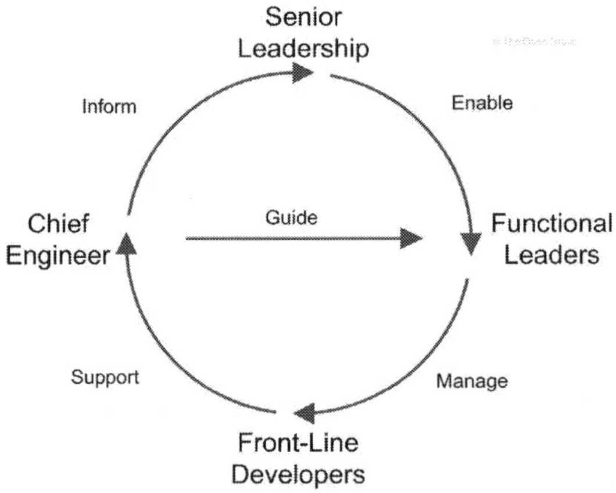

Figure 4-2: Chief Engineer Model

The Lean Product Development organization [Morgan & Liker, 2019] is quite similar to Marty Cagan's product team model; a similarity worth acknowledging as these practices come from different industries and were developed independently. Both models also differ from the way Agile frameworks usually define the product owner role.

4.5. Shifting to an Agile Organization

A capital management example is used here to compare and contrast a siloed command and control organization with an Agile one. This section shows how the wholeness and multi-skilling (see Section 4.1.2) from socio-technical systems characterize the new Agile capital management organization.

Regulators issue minimum capital requirement regulations. Banks are mandated to compute the amount of liquid capital they need to cover for credit, market, and operational risks. The capital requirement numbers matter because they set a cap on growth and impact returns on equity. Because the bank was not managing its capital to the satisfaction of regulators and shareholders, the executive committee decided to launch a program to fix it; see Figure 4-3.

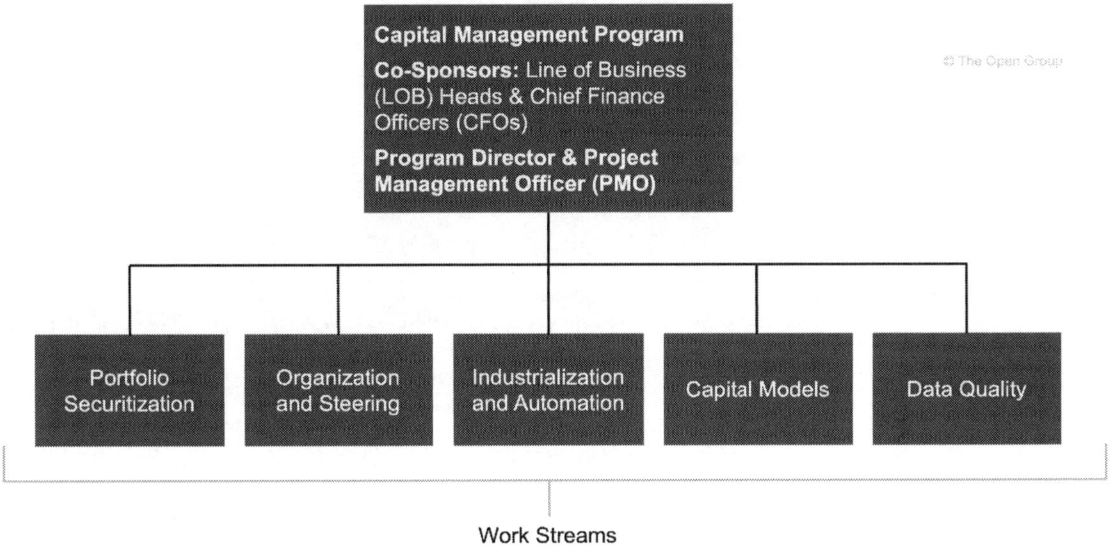

Figure 4-3: Initial Program Organization

This is a classical program structure run by a program director assisted by a project manager. The co-sponsors of the program are Line of Business (LOB) heads and their Chief Finance Officers (CFOs). The scope is huge; it covers all businesses such as retail banking, Corporate & Investment Banking (CIB), global markets, and consumer finance in all geographies.

Work streams are functionally aligned; for example, capital management models to improve the Risk-Weighted Asset (RWA) calculation, or the data quality to generate more accurate data. Each work stream regroups experts in a domain. For example, portfolio securitization experts are knowledgeable enough to decide which securitization structure is better to reduce the RWA.

After six months of operation, the program delivered few, if any, results. Why?

- True cross-functional work did not happen: Work streams were optimized from the perspective of their own discipline; cross-functional issues discussed in steering committees were not properly investigated; and decisions were influenced by internal politics rather than facts
- The cognitive load of functional work streams was too big; having to understand all of the business lines and all of the products
- It was difficult for work stream leaders to develop trust relationships with key people across all business lines, product groups, and geographies; i.e., the Dunbar number limit

Since the bank had been successful at deploying agility on the IT side, business executives decided to radically change the capital management setup; see Figure 4-4.

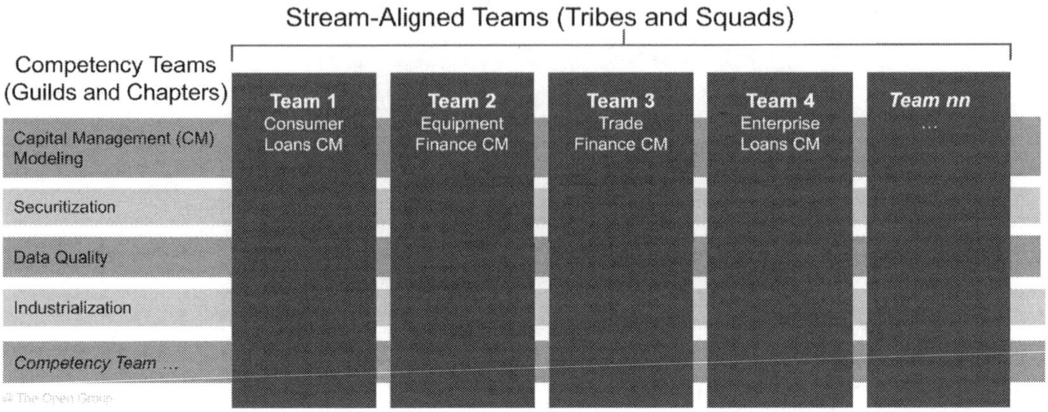

Figure 4-4: Agile Capital Management

Though the topic was regulatory, program sponsors identified two client constituencies; regulators and shareholders. Two expected outcomes were defined:

- Strict adherence to rules for regulators
- Improved return on equity for shareholders

Capital management shifted from a temporary program structure to a set of permanent and cross-functional teams. The scope of each team was bounded by their business line and their products.

New capital management teams were now stream-aligned. The front line became responsible and accountable for the quality of capital management numbers. For example, the "Consumer Loans Capital Management" team took ownership of the regulatory capital consumed by the consumer lending business.

The cognitive load of stream-aligned teams is reduced compared to the former program streams. Each capital management team only needs to know their own business and products; not all of the bank's businesses and products. Team members can remain capital management generalists because they get the support of the experts who staff competency teams.

Functional experts, such as "Capital Management Modeling" specialists or "Securitization" specialists, were regrouped into competency teams to provide support to stream-aligned capital management teams.

How this model works is illustrated here using the securitization example. Securitization is about creating composite financial instruments, real or synthetic, by pooling various financial assets. The issuer sells this financial instrument to investors. Securitization offers the bank an opportunity to free up capital.

The CFO defines the overall securitization strategy. However, it does not have enough operational knowledge to study the feasibility of securitizing enterprise loans. In this example, the "Enterprise Loans Capital Management" team is responsible for defining the specific enterprise loans securitization strategy and is accountable for the outcomes: compliance with regulations and reduction of regulatory capital consumption.

The new Agile organization helped improve the quality of regulatory capital management Key Performance Indicators (KPIs), accelerate RWA production lead time, and reduce operating costs. Far fewer issues are reported and regulatory capital consumption decreased by 15% on a like-for-like basis.

Chapter 5. Agile Strategy

The Agile enterprise needs to balance autonomy with effective alignment mechanisms. Agile strategy provides key alignment mechanisms:

- Formulate a vision or "true north" [Dennis, 2006] that exerts a magnetic *pull*
- Identify and select the big bets or breakthrough objectives that drive cross-silo collaboration
- Cascade objectives down the organization to allocate responsibilities and accountabilities
- Monitor strategic measures and KPIs to correct course when results differ from expectations

As described in Section 8.2.1, the enterprise strategy will not be effective if it is not communicated, well understood, and deployed. To benefit from strategy, the Agile enterprise must address the issues below:

- Strategy that is disconnected from field realities, because thinking is separated from doing
- Social dynamics that favor superficial consensus over honest conversations
- Unrealistic growth plans leveraged by executives to compete for resources and influence
- Strategy formulation that ignores uncertainty or treats it as an afterthought
- Inflexible strategic planning cycles that freeze priorities and budget allocation decisions for a year
- Planning systems that emphasize strategic decision-making over strategy deployment

Agile strategy shall follow the tenets described in Section 5.1.

5.1. Agile Strategy Tenets

5.1.1. Tenet 1. Situational Awareness

Strategy formulation is often done behind closed doors in a "strategy room" supported by the corporate strategy function and/or strategy consultants. The world of market studies and operational/financial numbers must be complemented by real-world experience. *"Going to the Gemba"* is a powerful Lean management practice that must inform the strategy formulation process. It means visiting the place (Gemba) where value is created; for example, when clients interact with the enterprise or when employees deliver products or services. *"Gemba walks"* are comparable to the Management by Walking Around (MBWA) practice popularized by Tom Peter. Data provides a model of the world; it must be completed by real-world experience. The map is not the territory.

Real-world experience can help executives to challenge the mental models that shape their view of competition and of their enterprise. Talking to clients and to employees who are closer to the front line helps to sense weak signals sooner. Asking the right questions helps executives discover the limits of their current knowledge.

Situational awareness is about seeing what is actually happening, unfiltered by existing mental models. It is also referred to as "sense-making". Design thinking helps to discover and formulate the big problems that challenge the enterprise. It provides a structured process to help executives reflect on the situation and discover what it means.

5.1.2. Tenet 2. Frame Strategy Around "Hard-to-Reverse" Choices

Agile strategy is a problem-solving approach that focuses on the enterprise's big problems and breakthrough objectives. It requires opening up the solution space to study different options. It uses design thinking to help inform difficult and challenging problems. Instead of creating strategic plans that are distant from the field, design thinking helps bring together multi-disciplinary teams with different points of view.

The authors of *Strategy Beyond the Hockey Stick* recommend identifying and debating real alternatives [Bradley et al., 2018]. They also suggest framing strategy around "hard-to-reverse" choices, which are Type 1 decisions; see Section 10.2: *"Think of it this way: real strategy is about making your hard-to-reverse choices about how to win. Planning is about how to make those choices happen. But the first step is being skipped too often, even if we try to make ourselves feel okay by labeling the plan* ***strategic****"*.

5.1.3. Tenet 3. Managing Strategy Implementation

When Type 1 decisions are made, the enterprise needs to factor in emergence, which is introduced in Section 8.5.1. When undesirable functions or outcomes are not anticipated and managed, Type 1 decisions are likely to result in poor or even disastrous consequences. This phenomenon is generally known as the "law of unintended consequences".

In order to improve the outcome of Type 1 decisions, leaders should follow an explicit method that takes into account the complexity of the enterprise and its environment, the uncertainty of future events, and the cognitive processes of leaders who make those decisions. Section 5.2 describes a method that enterprises can follow to improve the outcomes of Type 1 decisions.

5.1.4. Tenet 4. Strategy is a Journey

The annual strategy cycle tends to freeze strategy decisions into an annual budget that changes when revenue or profitability targets are not met. Budgets are rarely modified during a fiscal year for strategic reasons. Instead, Agile architecting shall hold regular strategy dialogues.

Chris Bradley et al. recommend decoupling big strategy conversations from the strategic planning cycle: *"In fact, trying to solve your big strategic questions and lock down an agreed plan at the same time can be near impossible. You can be sure the urgent will dominate the important, and those big questions won't get the airtime. Besides, those messy non-linear and uncertain strategic issues don't fit into the linear world of the 3 to 5-year plan"* [Bradley et al., 2018].

5.1.5. Tenet 5. Balance Stability and Dynamism

Holding regular strategy dialogues should not result in strategy volatility. Strategy should evolve for good reasons. When market conditions change, the enterprise should be Agile enough to adjust its objectives and budgets to consider the new situation. Most of the time, this dynamism equates to battlefield mobility, to use a military metaphor. When more fundamental changes are sensed, the Agile enterprise should not hesitate to immediately start the necessary strategic conversations.

Agile strategy shall decouple strategic priorities conversations from Agile planning, which evolves at a faster pace: *"The elements that lend stability to Agile planning are setting clear strategic priorities and defining closely related objectives for teams ... The dynamism in Agile planning comes from holding quarterly planning sessions, in which funding is redistributed among business units, and providing teams with support to use funding as they see fit"* [Comella-Dorda et al, 2019].

The stable part of the strategy continues to align Agile teams until it has to change due to new circumstances.

5.1.6. Tenet 6. Do Not Deploy Strategy in Silos

The first recommendation of Donald Sull and his co-authors to prevent strategy execution from unraveling is to foster coordination across units [Sull et al., 2015]. This should become a focus of attention to strategy deployment approaches, such as Hoshin Kanri [Hoshin Kanri] or Objectives and Key Results (OKR).

Before cascading down objectives or goals, big problems and breakthrough objectives should be analyzed by cross-functional teams. When root cause analysis identifies hypotheses to be verified and countermeasures to be experimented, it becomes possible to assign objectives down through the organization. This is a recursive process that not only improves the odds of strategy deployment success, it will also likely improve the quality of strategy formulation.

5.2. Bending the Law of Unintended Consequences

The law of unintended consequences states that decisions to intervene in complex situations create unanticipated and often undesirable outcomes.

In her article, *Why Hypotheses Beat Goals* [Ross, 2019], Jeanne Ross recommends the development of a culture of evidence-based decision-making by promoting hypothesis generation: *"A hypothesis emerges from a set of underlying assumptions. It is an articulation of how those assumptions are expected to play out in a given context. In short, a hypothesis is an intelligent, articulated guess that is the basis for taking action and assessing outcomes"*.

In a complex situation, hypothesizing simple causal relationships may not be sufficient. It is also not practical to experiment with "hard-to-reverse" decisions. The Agile strategist needs new methods to frame critical decisions and prevent unanticipated and undesirable outcomes. Richard Adler proposes a well-articulated and comprehensive method to help bend the law of unintended consequences [Adler 2020].

One of the central ideas of this method is to test-drive decisions, much like consumers road test vehicles to get a better sense of how they satisfy wants and needs before choosing which one to buy. Test-driving a decision provides insight into its consequences for a business and other parties of interest. This is accomplished by projecting the likely outcomes of implementing that decision over time under a range of plausible future conditions. Test-drives for decisions, much like cars, are admittedly limited in scope and offer insights into the future that are imperfect. That said, they offer far better chances for identifying (and improving) a Type 1 decision than the alternative of blindly choosing a Type 1 option without testing it. Encompassing a mix of external human input as well as models where possible can make the results more representative.

Richard Adler's method combines:

- Scenario planning
- "What-if" simulations and analyses
- A decision rule for selecting a preferred decision option

Its key differentiators are:

- Capturing scenarios as detailed, scalable, and easy to navigate software models rather than broad narratives
- Inserting decision options into scenarios (so that they are actionable)
- Projecting the consequences of decision options against the dynamic background of events and evolving conditions with simulations

The mechanical details of modeling and simulating dynamic scenarios are fairly complicated. Richard Adler indicates that: *"Fortunately, these details are left to programming and simulation experts; the test-drive method insulates analysts and decision-makers from most of the underlying technology"*.

Simulations must be instrumented with relevant business and technical performance metrics to drive comparative analytics of outcomes. The decision rule identifies an option that is robust in the face of the law of unintended consequences, namely the one that avoids "train wrecks" and which performs better than the alternatives across a spectrum of plausible futures.

Simulations can also be used during execution to periodically re-project outcomes of the chosen decision given the results to date, and scenarios updated to reflect the current situation. In this mode, the method detects emerging problems, prompting and allowing for mid-course corrections to ensure success.

This iterative process drives decision options experimentation — testing and validation, or refinement — in a virtual world. This is similar to conducting Agile experiments, without the high cost associated with a real experiment, such as a Minimum Viable Product (MVP).

In summary, this method does not replace Agile experiments, but adds a new way of evaluating — and iteratively refining — decision options, which is well suited to Type 1 decisions.

5.3. Succeeding Strategy Deployment

To improve the odds for the success of strategy implementation, the Agile enterprise shall define an effective system of objectives.

In alignment with the strategic vision, the deployment process starts with the definition of the few top-level objectives which will be further decomposed recursively into sub-objectives. The objectives tree shall contain objectives:

- That are result-oriented, expressed as OKRs
- Can guide breakthrough actions by opposition to incremental improvements
- Are federative and deployable along the management line
- To which teams and individuals are able to commit

An example is used here to illustrate a policy deployment anti-pattern. An enterprise wishes to change its positioning toward the high-end market. In order to satisfy high-end customers, it must dramatically improve service reliability.

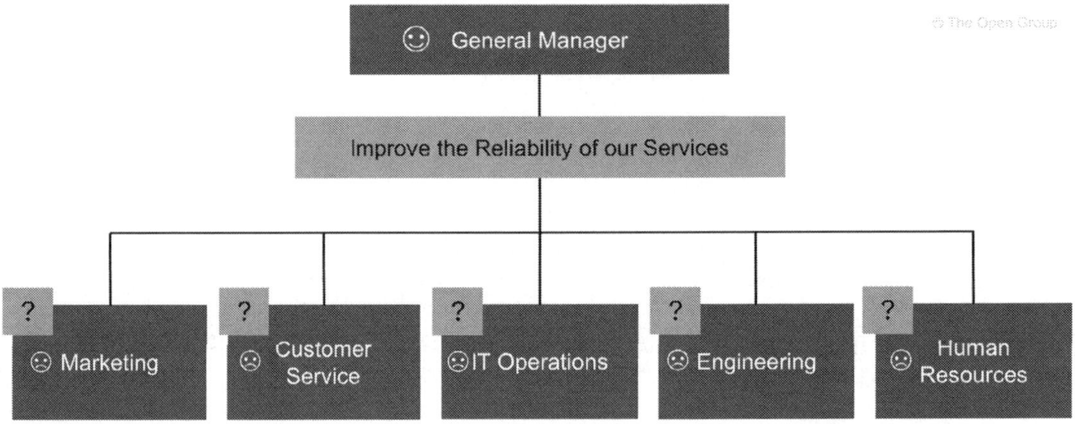

Figure 5-1: Objectives Deployment Anti-Pattern

It is not good enough to assign the same objective down through an organization, as illustrated in Figure 5-1. Why? Because when the strategic objective reaches a lower level of the organization:

- The assignee may lack the competencies required to act on the assigned objective
- The scope of the objective may far exceed the scope of responsibility of the assignee
- The objective may not be specific enough to be actionable at a lower level

The Agile strategist will decompose objectives using the approach below:

- Investigate the performance gap
- Formulate a causality hypothesis

- Conduct experiments to verify causality
- Develop scenarios and run simulations to analyze complex situations
- Identify and experiment with countermeasures

Figure 5-2 illustrates how the "Improve the Reliability of Our Services" objective can be decomposed.

Some of the sub-objectives can be assigned to one team. For example, "Monitor Distributed Systems Effectively" could be assigned to "IT Operations". Being responsible and accountable for an objective may require a team to manage dependencies with other teams. In this example, "IT Operations" needs inputs and buy-in from "Engineering".

Other objectives, such as "Shift Toward an Open and Blameless Culture", are too broad to be assigned to a single team. In this example, the objective will be shared by several teams.

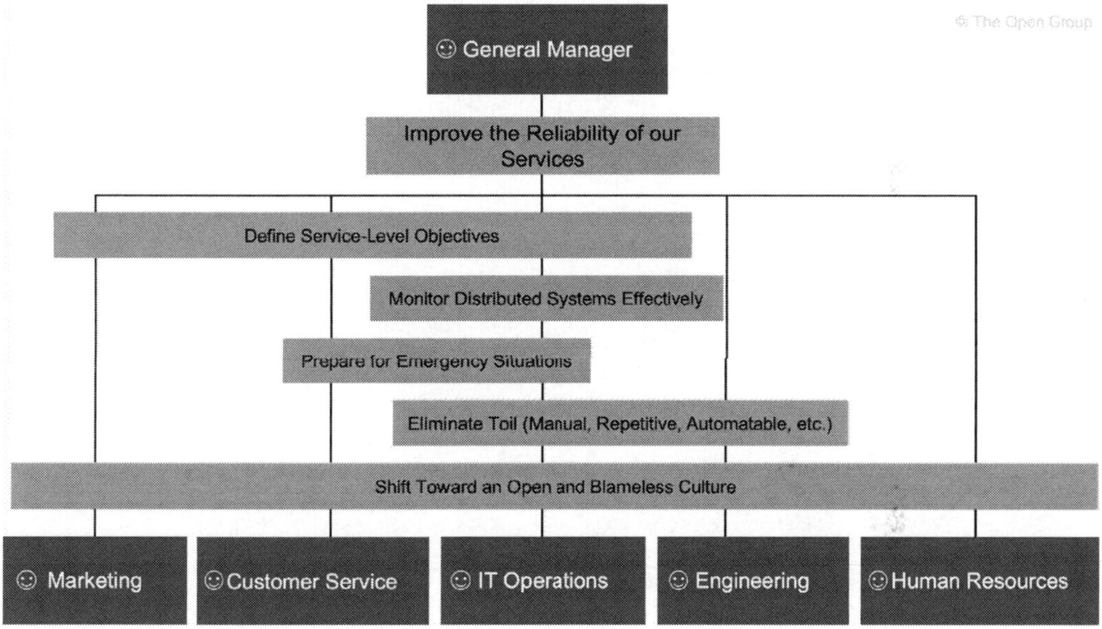

Figure 5-2: Objectives Deployment Example

When the objectives decomposition tree is stabilized, two things need to happen:

1. The definition of the OKRs
2. A "catchball" process, to gain consensus on the objectives and the target results that are assigned

An OKR spells out the company's priorities in terms of specific accomplishments and performance improvements. The **Objective** consists of a clearly defined qualitative change, while the **Key Result** is a specific, often quantitative performance target that must be met. Agile organizations should set OKRs annually and assess progress against them on a quarterly basis [Comella-Dorda et al., 2019].

KPIs can help the enterprise measure progress toward key results.

Strategy deployment is both top-down and bottom-up. When the vision of leaders is translated into concrete OKRs throughout the enterprise, the "catchball" process entails frank, reality-based discussions between and within management levels. Leaders normally define required results; the team members the means [Dennis, 2006].

Chapter 6. Architecting the Agile Transformation

In Chapter 3, the recommendation was to conduct the Digital and Agile Transformations of the enterprise concurrently. This chapter covers the change management dimension of this dual transformation, and zooms in on the Agile side of the overall enterprise transformation.

TheAgile Transformation of the enterprise covers three areas:

- Adopting new ways of working
- Deploying new management systems
- Changing the organizational structure

The new ways of working promote the practices below:

- Rapid iteration and experimentation, which promotes continuous learning
- Fact-based decision-making
- Information sharing and transparency
- Cohesive cross-functional teams coached by "servant" leaders
- Performance orientation driven by peer pressure

Management systems evolve toward more autonomy for Agile teams, balanced by clear accountability. Freedom is required to empower teams to rapidly make decisions closer to the field. Accountability in an Agile organization is not about controlling people; it is about a two-way exchange where it is agreed to deliver something to another person.

6.1. Accountability

In an Agile organization, employees are accountable to their peers, their manager, and their clients. Managers are accountable to their teams, the board of directors, and the broader community and stakeholders. The management system cascades goals at all levels of the organization and promotes a constructive dialogue to help set up accountability relationships between employees and managers. The reward system recognizes individual performance while promoting collaboration.

The organizational structure is flattened. Autonomous cross-functional teams, often named "feature teams" or "squads", are formed. Cross-functional roles emerge to help construct robust communities of practice, often named "chapters" or "guilds". Resource allocation is flexible and driven by the evolution of demand or activity level.

The left part of Figure 6-1 represents the three transformation dimensions already introduced, with the addition of the "Enterprise Culture" dimension. Having the right supportive culture is imperative to the success of an Agile enterprise. Culture evolution results from changes in the three dimensions. For a culture change to take hold, people have to experience success operating in the new Agile organization.

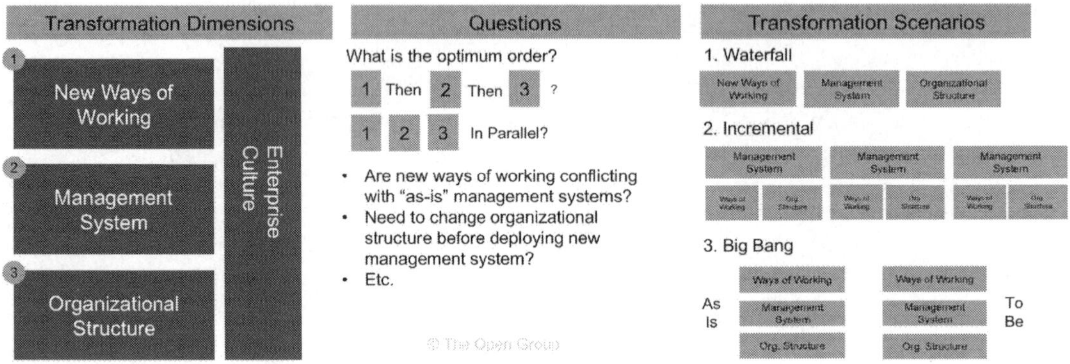

Figure 6-1: Agile Transformation

The middle part of the figure lists a few important questions that the enterprise needs to address. For example, the waterfall scenario is likely to create intermediary stages that are suboptimal. New ways of working may conflict with the existing management system. The enterprise that deploys a new management system on top of an existing organizational structure will have to redeploy it at a later time.

Due to the interdependencies that link the transformation dimensions, it is tempting to conduct change on the three dimensions in parallel. This leads to either a big bang scenario or an incremental deployment. In the case of an incremental deployment, the challenge is to define the scope of each increment.

6.2. Incremental Agile Transformation

Figure 6-2 shows that each transformation increment should cover the entire hierarchical line. Why? Because if the way one level of the organization operates is changed while the hierarchical line continues to operate the old way, the enterprise runs the risk of submitting its employees and managers to a double bind; i.e., employees and managers becoming at risk of being confronted with two irreconcilable demands or a choice between two undesirable courses of action. For example, re-prioritize the backlog but stick to established budgets and product plans.

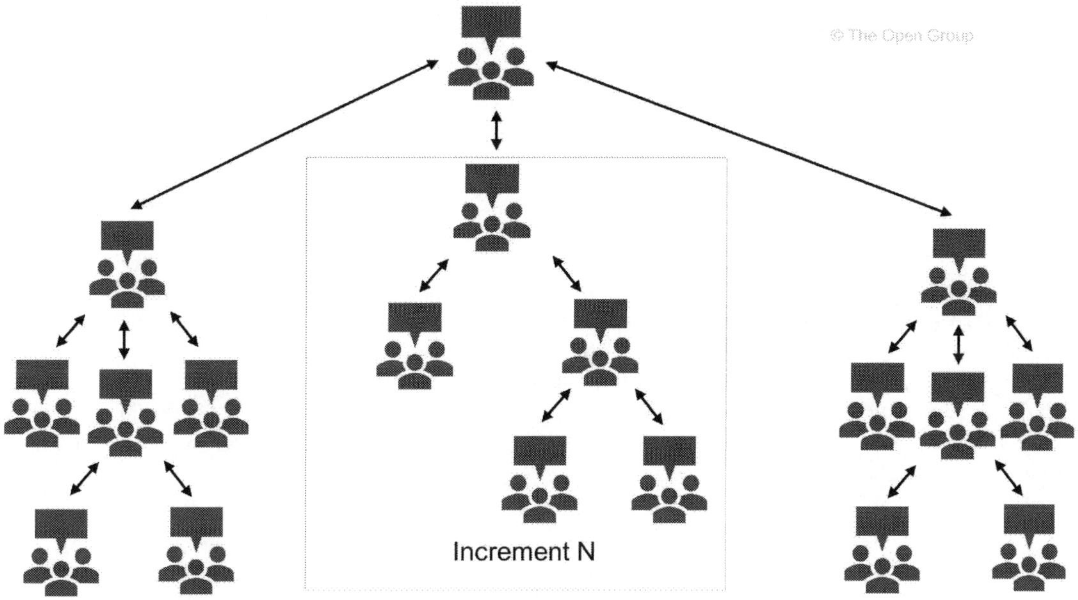

Figure 6-2: Transformation Increment

Incremental transformation deployment is easier when two conditions are met:

- Dependencies that link organizational units are minimal
- The business and IT organizational structures are well-aligned

When those conditions are not met, it is better to change the organizational structure before deploying new ways of working and a new management system. The new organizational structure reflects an architectural intent, which is either implicit or explicit.

6.3. Why Architect the Organization?

This document illustrates the need to re-architect the organization with the example of an IT organization that evolved to become more Agile.

The legacy IT organization was structured by process/function (front-office, middle-office, finance, risk) rather than by product families (plain vanilla swaps, equity derivative, commodities, etc.). Two powerful central functions controlled operational teams:

- Budgeting and financial control to rein in costs
- Architecture to ensure the coherence of the IS

Pools of software development resources were organized by technologies; for example, server-side Java® development or mobile front-end development. Software development projects would on-board required resources for the duration of the project and release them when done. Last but not least, IT operations and support was separate from application development.

Though the specialization of the legacy organization was supposed to help the IT organization to capture economies of skill and scale, several problems surfaced.

The level of inter-team dependency is high because of the multiplication of organizational entities that have to intervene on a project. Time-to-market is increasing due to the high level of inter-silo coordination required; for example, between development and IT operations teams. Alignment between business and IT is complicated because of the lack of simple mapping between organizational structures.

6.4. New Organizational Culture

The IT re-organization was inspired by the Spotify model. Small, cross-functional teams named " squads" replaced projects. The size of a squad does not exceed 10 to 15 people. Unlike a project, a squad is a stable team composed of dedicated resources that develops an end-to-end perspective. Squads are product-centric, meaning they develop, deploy, and operate a service. Squads adopt a DevOps culture, which translates into the mantra *"you build it, you run it"*.

Squads are grouped into tribes, which are no bigger, on average, than 150 people. In order to maintain and develop functional or technical competencies, chapters and guilds are created; for example, chapters that regroup mobile developers or NoSQL Database Management System (DBMS) experts.

As the number of Agile teams grows to a few hundred squads running in parallel, it is important to define a taxonomy of Agile teams that clearly specifies the scope of each one and minimizes inter-team dependencies. True Enterprise Architecture thinking is required to discover an effective way to decompose the organization, and to draw boundaries that minimize inter-team dependencies.

Figure 6-3 represents a simplified taxonomy.

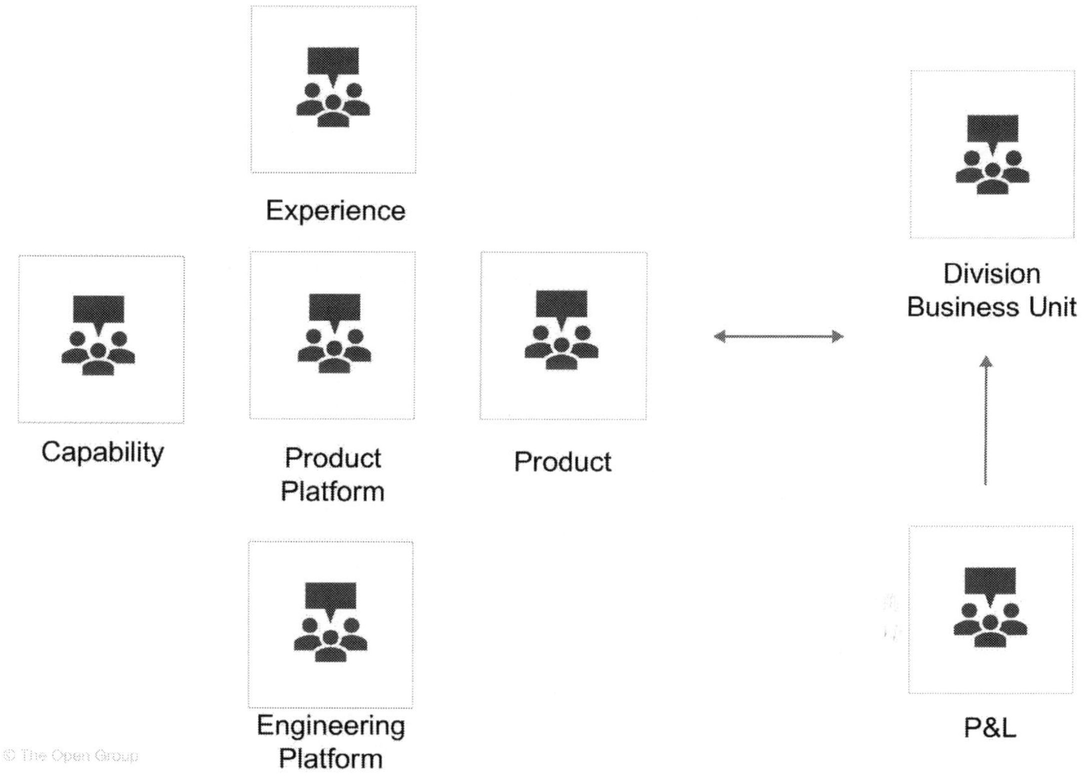

Figure 6-3: The Taxonomy of Agile Teams

The primary goal of an Agile team's taxonomy is to minimize redundancy and duplication [Rigby et al., 2018]. Because the taxonomy of Agile teams may be different from the formal Profit and Loss (P&L) structure of the enterprise, it is necessary to map it to the division, business unit, and P&L structure of the enterprise.

6.5. Leadership Drives Change

The Agile Transformation described in this chapter must be initiated by executives. Because Agile Transformation moves the organization from a siloed model to cross-functional cooperation, executives form coalitions to drive change across the enterprise.

Executives who drive change must be driven by an intrapreneurship mindset. Figure 6-4 shows how they propel change throughout the organization.

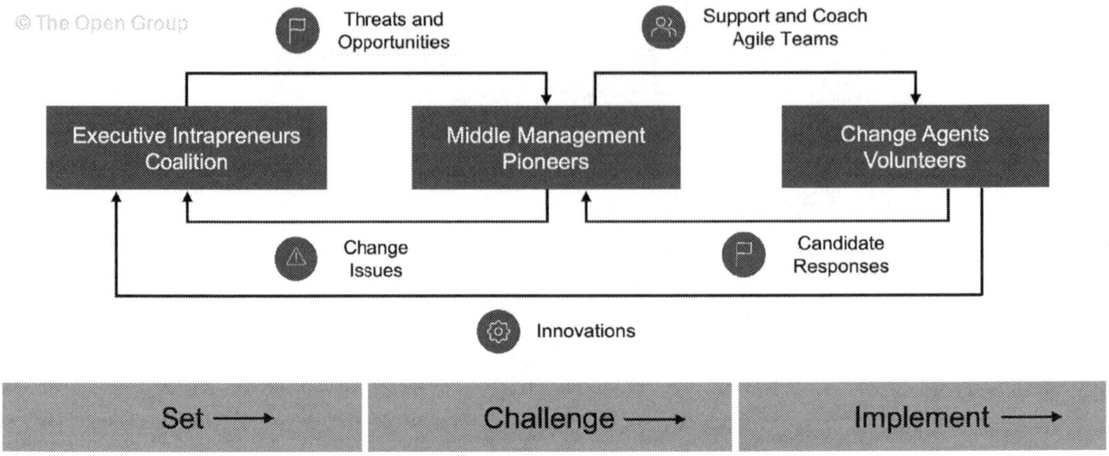

Figure 6-4: Leadership Drives Change

Coalitions of executive intrapreneurs adopt an outside-in perspective to identify threats and opportunities that justify change. Middle management pioneers play several major roles:

- Analyze threats and opportunities to determine possible responses to changes in the environment and market
- Identify change agents, drilling down to define candidate responses in more detail
- Report issues and problems to the executive intrapreneurs coalition
- Identify innovation opportunities that require executive support

Middle management pioneers collect feedback from touchpoints internally, including their leaders and external sources. The feedback is processed and analyzed to identify issues and opportunities for the executives. When change issues jeopardize successful implementation, middle managers initiate conversations that challenge executives when necessary. The change journey is incremental, inclusive, and experiment-driven. The change model moves away from classical command and control to engage all organizational levels.

Chapter 7. Agile Governance

The Digital and Agile Transformations of the enterprise each pose a challenge to classical IT governance frameworks. This chapter explores existing classical IT governance practices and new Agile governance models, and outlines how they can co-exist within an enterprise.

The typical organization chart for an enterprise defines hierarchical and functional reporting relationships, together with the scope of responsibilities for organizational entities. It does little to help understand how decision-making will happen. This is the scope of governance, which defines who has power and accountability, and who makes decisions. Governance is defined as: "*A company's allocation of decision rights and accountabilities: who has the authority to make — and is held accountable for — key decisions*" [MITa]. Good governance aligns decision-making authority with accountability. "Authority" is defined as *the power to act*, and "accountability" is defined as *being accountable or liable for the outcomes of decisions or activities.*

A lack of coherence between the allocation of responsibility, authority, and accountability results in dysfunctional organizations.

The established governance forms in the TOGAF Standard, 10th Edition — Enterprise Architecture Capability and Governance [C220] are:

- Corporate Governance
- Technology Governance
- IT Governance
- Architecture Governance

The way enterprises define IT governance is not uniform. Some IT governance models are centralized while others are decentralized. In some cases, *ad hoc* governance bodies are created to oversee large transformation initiatives.

The TOGAF Standard defines Architecture Governance as the practice and orientation by which Enterprise Architectures and other architectures are managed and controlled at an enterprise-wide level.

One of the key objectives of Architecture Governance is to ensure that business value is delivered in alignment with strategy, and follows the business and technical compliance criteria.

Architecture Governance has a number of dimensions per the TOGAF Standard definition:

- Guiding via controls and monitoring
- Compliance
- Supporting processes
- Ensuring accountability

7.1. Classical IT Governance

Most classical IT governance models:

- Appoint a decision-making body, for which names and composition vary; for example, an IT executive committee or a large project committee, which may include the Chief Executive Officers (CEOs) of operational entities
- Set rules to determine which projects or programs will be reviewed, and what happens when approval is denied
- Organize architecture reviews to inform IT governance committee decisions
- Set up architecture offices to conduct reviews, define standards, and drive compliance
- Set up focus groups to identify best practices in key areas, such as Application Architecture, testing, infrastructure, or security
- Consolidate IT budgets and manage an enterprise-wide IT investment portfolio
- Track the utilization of IT resources to verify that once projects are approved, they follow plans and comply with budget guidelines

7.2. Governance in the Face of Agile

Agile organizations shift from project to product, which is about replacing temporary teams with stable teams led by product owners. Most Agile teams are cross-functional and stream-aligned. Product owners are responsible and accountable for delivering product features or sub-journeys, which include software components. Because Agile teams are cross-functional and led by product owners who have business and technology acumen, the project manager role is becoming less relevant.

In this approach, decision-making and associated accountability are distributed across the organization to the lowest practical level of architecture. However, it is vital to understand that not all decisions are equal. As product and program teams do not operate in a vacuum, decisions that may have a higher level of impact must attract a higher level of consideration. This is covered in detail in Section 10.2.

In Agile organizations there are fewer standards and processes. Those that remain are defined differently. Instead of being specified as a set of tasks or activities to accomplish, standards are now used as guardrails, which express policy intent. For example, instead of mandating software engineers to select software products from a catalog of approved technologies, a standard could specify a set of operational and security requirements expressed as guardrails. In this example, the purpose is to develop software systems that can be operated reliably and securely. Candidate software products are assessed against guardrails by Agile teams in a bottom-up manner *versus* being defined and imposed top-down by an architecture office.

These guardrails flow down the layers from Enterprise to Segment to Capability while Type 1 decisions are escalated up to the appropriate higher level depending on the scope of the decision.

7.3. Hybrid Delivery Styles

It is important to consider that there will rarely be a pure Agile environment and that most enterprises work in a hybrid environment whether they accept that or not. It is important to understand these styles and constraints when considering how to apply the appropriate level of IT governance for a given engagement.

In *TOGAF® Series Guide: Enabling Enterprise Agility* [G20F], §4.7 Selecting Delivery Styles, three styles are defined: Rapid, Agile, and Robust. This document expands these to the following five styles:

- Rapid: Involves shaping requirements, addressing unclear goals, and creating vision

  Near immediate implementations of simple components will demonstrate value and prove out the approach. These include Proof of Concept, Proof of Value, and Prototypes that are potentially throwaway; e.g., Kanban, Skunk Works®. This is normally a stage to subsequent delivery rather than a full end-to-end delivery in its own right.

- Agile: Fast cycles of component delivery produce specific bounded functionality

  Goal is to deliver business value early and often. This may include Minimal Viable Products (MVPs) and unlikely to be throwaway. Normally there will be one to two Agile teams with minimal additional management overhead; e.g., Scrum, Kanban, Rapid.

- Scaled Agile: Delivery of complicated, large-scale components, interoperable across the breadth of a segment or an enterprise that can be broken down into discrete composable elements that can be worked on iteratively, independently, and concurrently; e.g., Scaled Agile Framework® [SAFe®]
- Accepted: Near immediate implementations of well-defined, simple components with clear goals and vision and firm set of requirements; e.g., Kanban, Waterfall
- Robust: Delivery of complicated, large-scale components, interoperable across the breadth of a segment or an enterprise which are constrained due to regulatory, legislative, architecture (monolithic/closely-coupled), and environment factors such that delivery must be consecutively planned and managed; e.g. Waterfall, PRINCE2®

  That said, key Agile principles may still be applied where appropriate; e.g., Kanban, sense/measure feedback, digital infrastructure, etc.

7.4. Agile Governance

Agile governance should not be conceived in isolation. It is part of a larger whole which includes the enterprise social system, its organization, and delivery styles. Agile governance, therefore, has to embrace a level of command and control usually managed at the Enterprise layer, where appropriate, while also supporting increased autonomy of products/programs at Segment/Capabilities layers. This is a delicate balancing act that has to focus on "just the right level of governance" to support development at scale and velocity.

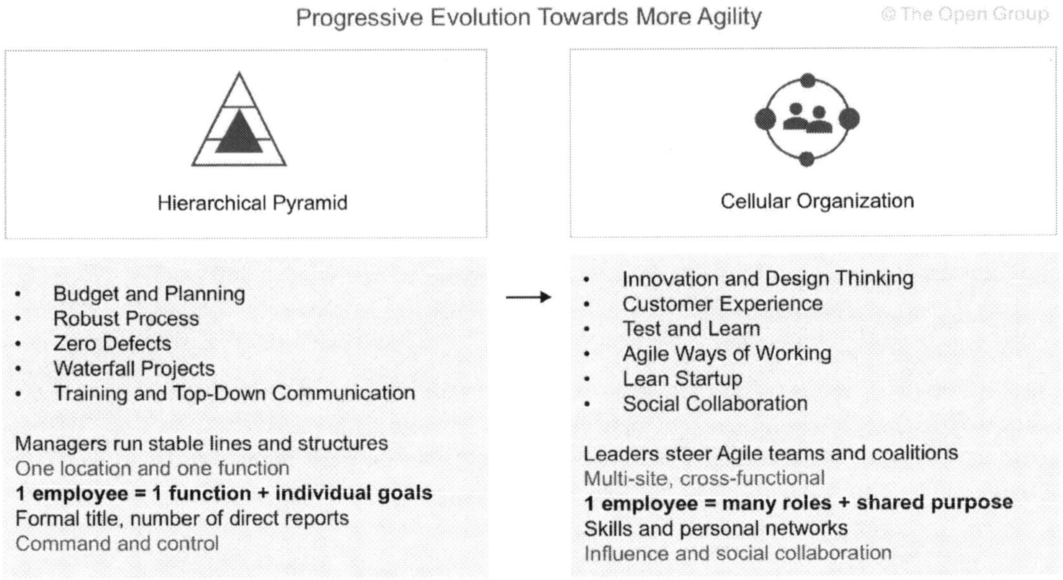

Figure 7-1: Towards the Agile Organization

Agile organizations promote both autonomy and alignment [Ross et al., 2019] by:

- Providing distinct goals and objectives to autonomous teams, and aligning them without introducing layers of hierarchy
- Setting formal sharing mechanisms that synchronize activities as the number of teams grows
- Defining architectural guardrails that facilitate autonomy by ensuring that individual components are compatible

Agile governance uses the four levers below to align autonomous teams:

- Shared purpose or "true north" [LEIb], defined as "*an organization's strategic and philosophical vision that may include "hard" business goals such as revenue and profits as well as "broadbrush" visionary objectives that appeal to the heart*"
- Shared consciousness, described by General Stanley McChrystal [McChrystal et al., 2015] as "*sharing a fundamental, holistic understanding of the operating environment and of our own organization while also preserving each team's distinct skill sets*"
- Forcing functions (or guardrails), described by John Rossman [Rossman, 2019] as a set of "*guidelines, restrictions, requirements, or commitments that "force", or direct, a desirable outcome without having to manage all the details of making it happen*"
- Feedback loops (including decision logs) that help to adjust the behavior of autonomous teams

As Agile teams become responsible for delivering and deploying software that impacts the quality of customer experience, the scope and size of the central IT organization decreases. What remains central mainly covers:

- Corporate functions, such as IT strategy or the architecture office
- Infrastructure and IT operations, which deliver services to Agile teams
- Cross-cutting services, ranging from federated identity management to collaboration services
- Systems with high compliance or investor obligations

In addition to infrastructure platforms, the digital enterprise develops and operates business platforms. Platforms need governance as a set of rules concerning who gets to participate, how to divide cost and value, and how to resolve conflicts. For example, a large financial services organization has created a service marketplace governed by a Design and Operations Authority (DOA).

The DOA creates its governance framework based on the four levers (to align the autonomous teams) using the following mission objectives:

- Support the shift toward an "as-a-service" model, by ensuring services are built and used consistently across the enterprise
- Define and maintain service development and exposition guardrails to bring together service consumers, providers, and operators
- Define forcing functions to ensure that every service meets minimum quality requirements before being published in the marketplace
- Ensure the timely publication of services in the Market Place Catalog

As more and more IT capabilities are moving under the responsibility of cross-functional Agile teams, business and IT governance are merged into an integrated model; as illustrated in Figure 7-2 and described in Points 1 to 4 below.

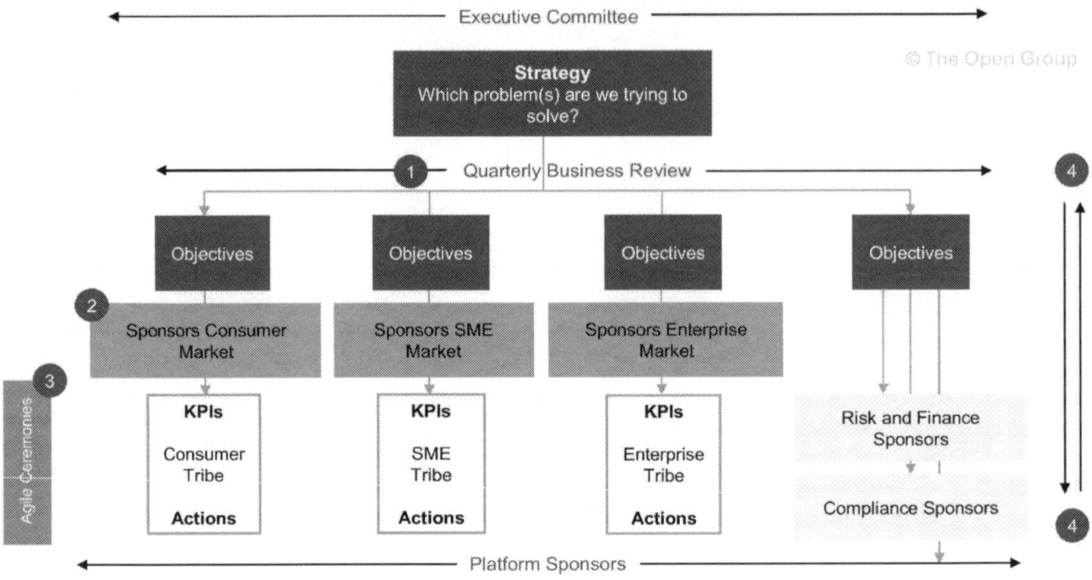

Figure 7-2: Integrated Business/IT Governance

1. Quarterly Business Reviews (includes key decisions) verify that tribes fulfill their commitments
2. Tribes are monitored by their sponsors, who progressively release resources to match market growth needs
3. Tribes evolve autonomously, paced by Agile ceremonies
4. Postmortems are conducted during business reviews; resource reallocation decisions take team performance and business situations into account

The integrated governance model does not isolate IT investment decisions anymore. IT investments are a subset of the investments made by the business to develop new products or journeys. Investment decisions are evaluated against business outcome metrics.

The Agile governance features described in this chapter need to be adapted to fit the context, culture, and maturity level of each enterprise.

7.5. What Can Lead to IT Governance Failures

IT governance does not always prevent large projects or programs from failing. Large enterprises have experienced project or program failures resulting in several hundred million dollar write-offs. For example, a large financial services firm had to “kill” a new securities handling system that was supposed to be deployed in several European countries, or a bank that failed to consolidate two core banking systems derailing the Mergers & Acquisitions (M&A) business case.

Among the root causes of these failures, governance issues represent a fair share; for example:

- Governance committee members who break their commitments without facing consequences
- Decisions tainted by power struggles or territory battles
- *Ad hoc* governance which weakens established IT governance
- Too little cross-silo cooperation before IT governance bodies make decisions
- Committee members who influence decisions despite not being accountable for outcomes
- Unbalanced Agile adoption with a lack of enterprise level vision and guardrails leading to suboptimal integrations, reduced interoperability, and increased costs

A governance model alone cannot fix problems that are rooted in the social system or culture of the enterprise; for example, when:

- Committee members do not respect their commitments
- Enterprise silos use governance committees as a political battleground rather than cooperating upstream
- Leaders find "good reason" to avoid respecting IT governance decisions

Governance deployment will not be effective if it does not address social system or organizational culture issues.

Part 3: The Agile Architecture Capability

This part outlines the ways of working in respect to architecture within an Agile enterprise. It provides guidance on developing, delivering, and managing architecture within Agile enterprises. This part addresses both architectural development approaches (Part 3A) and architecture techniques and deliverables (Part 3B).

Chapter 8. Architecture Development

This chapter defines the O-AA approach to Agile Architecture development. It is based on a set of modular building blocks (see Chapter 9) that can be configured and assembled in a variety of manners. It supports several architecture development styles.

The scope of this document covers the enterprise *as a whole*, not just the alignment of business and IT; see Figure 8-1. It includes designing the enterprise business, organization, and operating models, which is the responsibility of senior executives who can be assisted by management consultants or Enterprise Architect profiles. Along with the authors of *Designed for Digital: How to Architect your Business for Sustained Success*, there is reluctance to use the term *Business Architecture* because in many companies architecture is seen as the IT unit's responsibility: "*Right now, if you have a Business Architecture function, it's probably buried in your IT organization (and having limited impact)*" [Ross et al., 2019].

Enterprise Architecture in this context will become more like an internal management consultancy, which implies that Enterprise Architects must develop their management consulting skills to include relationship building, problem-solving, coaching, and negotiation as well as specialty skills, such as product management, design thinking, and Lean management.

The range of skills that should be considered part of the Enterprise Architect role includes the disciplines needed for management consultants who design business and operating models. This document incorporates these disciplines. It borrows concepts and methods from:

- Strategic marketing and marketing research
- User Experience (UX)
- Design thinking
- Lean Product and Process Development (LPPD)
- Socio-technical systems
- Organizational sociology
- Operations strategy
- Software architecture

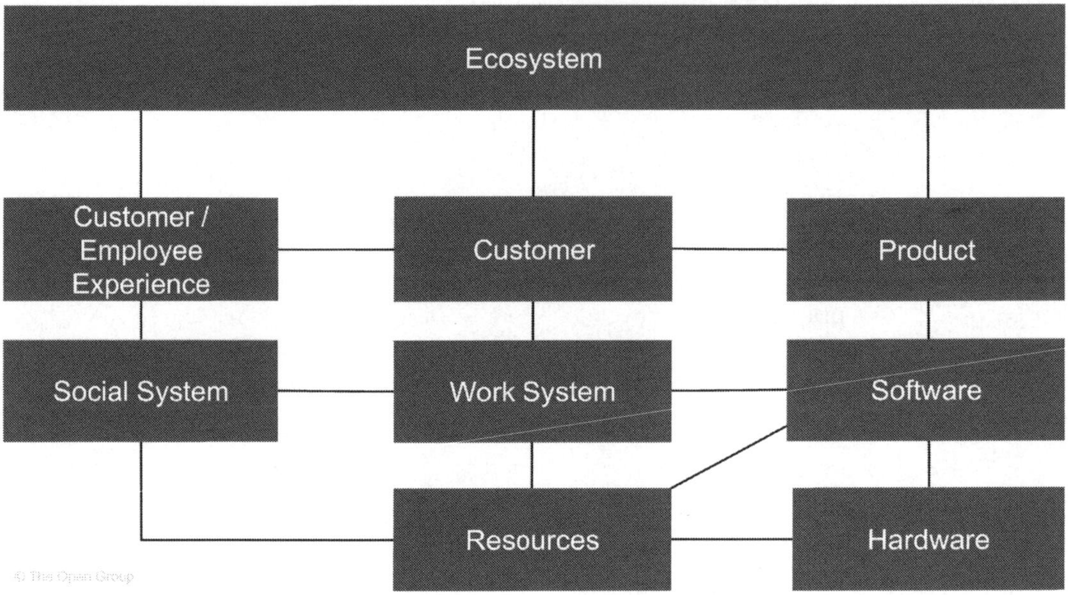

Figure 8-1: The Scope of the O-AA Standard

Figure 8-1 illustrates the scope of this document; see Chapter 2.

8.1. Architecture

Martin Fowler wrote: *"There is no such thing as a universally accepted definition of architecture"* [Fowler]. His view of architecture is aligned with that of Ralph Johnson, who defines architecture as "*the important stuff (whatever that is)*" [Johnson et al., 2008]. The lack of a universally accepted architecture definition justifies why this document borrows from three different sources to analyze what architecture means.

Most architecture definitions, such as these examples from IEC/IEC/IEEE 42010 [ISO/IEC/IEEE 42010] and the TOGAF Standard [C220], adopt a systems thinking view that models the enterprise as a set of interrelated elements:

> "The fundamental concepts or properties of a system in its environment embodied in its elements, relationships, and in the principles of its design and evolution."
>
> — ISO/IEC/IEEE 42010

> "The structure of components, their interrelationships, and the principles and guidelines governing their design and evolution over time."
>
> — The TOGAF Standard

Both of these definitions focus on *"what the enterprise is"*, its elements of form, rather than *"what the enterprise does"*, its functions; thus positioning architecture as a discipline which guides the design and evolution of the enterprise modeled as a *system*.

To paraphrase Alfred Korzybski's famous sentence [Korzybski, 1958]: *"a map is not the territory it represents, but if correct, it has a similar structure to the territory, which accounts for its usefulness"*; the architecture model of the enterprise is not the enterprise. The enterprise makes architecture decisions that are reflected in the way it does business and operates. Architecture decisions may be implicit and are not necessarily documented or modeled.

The systems engineering discipline [Crawley et al., 2016] adds two important ideas:

- The allocation of functions or activities to the system's elements or components
- The definition of the structural interfaces that link the system's elements or components

> "Architecture is the embodiment of concept, and the allocation of physical/informational functions (processes) to elements of form (objects) and definition of structural interfaces among the objects."
>
> — Crawley et al., 2016

8.2. Development Building Blocks

As shown in Figure 8-2, the O-AA development is structured along two axes that represent:

- *The function-form axis*: What the Enterprise "Does", What the Enterprise "Is"
- *The perspective axis*: Experience Perspective, Work System Perspective, Technical System Perspective

The "Experience Perspective" is in the problem space, while the "Work System Perspective" is in the solution space, as well as the "Technical System Perspective".
The O-AA building blocks are positioned along the two axes, with the exception of: "Strategy", "Value", and "Data/Information and AI".
The "Corporate Brand Identity" and "Corporate Culture" building blocks influence what the enterprise does.

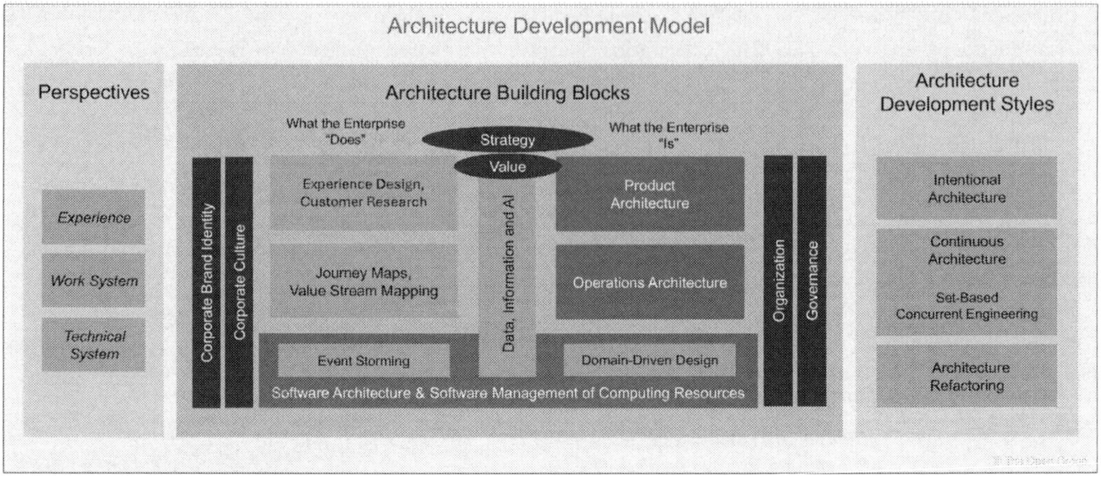

Figure 8-2: O-AA Building Blocks

8.2.1. Strategy

Michael Porter recommends distinguishing operational effectiveness from strategy [Porter, 1996]. Strategy is about developing sustainable differentiation based upon strategic positioning.

> "Strategic positioning means performing different activities from rivals' or performing similar activities in different ways."
>
> — Porter 1996

Porter's strategy formulation helps to connect strategic intent with execution. Mapping *activity systems* helps to verify interactivity, consistency, and identify when activities are reinforce each other.

Strategy formulation is also influenced by the Agile culture, which insists on the importance of experimentation. Strategy is seen as a set of strategic assumptions that need to be experimentally verified. Strategy professor, Adam Brandenburger, observes: *"the assumptions underlying your business model are embedded in all your processes"*. Therefore, he recommends challenging these assumptions when formulating strategy [Brandenburger, 2019]:

- Precisely identify the assumptions that underlie conventional thinking within the company or industry
- Think about what might be gained by proving one or more of them false
- Deliberately disturb an aspect of a normal work pattern to break up ingrained assumptions

The digital era has seen the rise in popularity of the concept of the **business model**. Sometimes the use of the words "strategy" and "business model" are interchangeable. Peter Seddon and Geoffrey Lewis examine in detail the meaning of two frequently used — and misused — terms, namely, "business model" and "strategy". They argue that as used by leading thinkers these two terms might reasonably be interpreted as having roughly equivalent meanings [Seddon & Lewis, 2003].

A business model describes the rationale of how an organization creates, delivers, and captures value. It provides an analytical way of connecting strategy to execution. A business model has three components [Johnson et al., 2008]:

- A customer value proposition, which models how customers perform a specific "job" that alternative offerings do not address
- A profit formula, which models how to generate value for the enterprise through factors such as revenue model, cost structure, margins, and inventory turnover
- Key resources and processes, including the people, technology, products, facilities, equipment, and brand required to deliver the value proposition

Regardless of their quality, the odds that implementing the strategy and associated business model(s) will fail are high. Why?

> "Culture eats strategy for breakfast."
>
> — attributed to Peter Drucker

Donald Sull [Sull et al., 2015] and his co-authors analyzed why strategy execution unravels. They acknowledge that strategy alignment processes are fine; the issues are due to unreliable commitments from colleagues. Furthermore, strategic plans are just a set of assumptions that need to be verified.

> "No plan survives first contact with the enemy."
>
> — attributed to Helmuth van Moltke, Prussian military commander

Other strategy execution issues are:

- Strategy is often not well understood, even at the executive level
- Past performance is over-valued at the expense of experimentation and agility
- Execution should be driven by leaders who know the field, which is rarely the case when only driven by top executives

To overcome these issues the Agile strategy should follow the tenets described in Section 5.1.

8.2.2. Corporate Brand Identity, Culture

A clear and unified corporate identity can be critical to competitive strategy. It serves as a "*north star providing direction and purpose*" [Greyser & Urde, 2019]. Corporate brand identity starts from the enterprise mission and vision. It must be consistent with the culture and capabilities of the enterprise.

Jez Frampton believes that great brands are "*business strategy brought to life*" [Wind & Hays, 2016]. The authors of *Beyond Advertising: Creating Value Through All Customer Touchpoints* point out that brands never had more ways to reach and engage people. The image of the brand is now the result of the experience of people across all channels.

In a digital world, brand experience depends on the effective bridging of the enterprise strategy with its operating model. Marketing can no longer manage brands in silos, relying on classical marketing and advertising tools. Marketing people must now become members of multi-disciplinary teams that manage brand experience holistically.

8.2.3. Value

Agile architecting borrows concepts from Value Engineering (VE), which was pioneered by L. D. Miles from General Electric®. VE is an approach directed at *"analyzing the function of systems, equipment, facilities, services, and supplies for the purpose of achieving their essential functions at the lowest lifecycle cost consistent with required performance, reliability, quality, and safety"* [Mandelbaum & Reed, 2006].

In the digital age, value cannot be reduced to functional benefits. Value definition includes the emotional dimension; for example, reducing anxiety, providing fun, or a sense of affiliation.

The central idea is to provide benefits to clients and other stakeholders at the lowest reasonable cost. The value of a product can be increased either by maintaining its functions and features while reducing its cost, or by keeping the cost constant while increasing the functionality of the product.

8.2.4. Perspectives

The **Experience** perspective defines value from a client perspective. It analyzes a client's job-to-be done; their pain points and gains. It also covers the emotional dimension of the experience, starting from an outside-in view that places customer needs and problems at the center. Design thinking and market research are incorporated into the broader Agile architecting discipline.

The **Work System** perspective defines the ability of the enterprise to deliver client benefits efficiently. It starts with analyzing capabilities across value streams; this helps to identify activities that could be shared, thus contributing to architecting the operating model.

The **Technical System** perspective covers the software and hardware parts of the enterprise. It starts from analyzing domains such as payments, mortgage lending, or federated identity management and also includes architecting the physical world. The software architecture discipline is part of the broader Agile architecting discipline.

8.2.5. What the Enterprise "*Is*"

Analyzing *what the enterprise "is"* starts by defining the boundaries that connect:

- The enterprise to its environment
- The enterprise parts to each other and to the environment

Defining boundaries covers:

- **Product architecture**, which is driven by the questions:
  - How should products be broken down into components?
  - Which interfaces should link product components?
  - Which modularity–integrality trade-off is appropriate?
  - Which product platform, if any, would bring value?
- **Operations architecture**, which is driven by the questions:
  - Are economies, skills, and scale being leveraged?
  - What is the platform strategy, if any?
  - Are the right resources, skills, and technologies deployed in the right facilities and locations?
- **Organization**, which is driven by the questions:
  - What is the right organizational structure and culture?
  - How should organizational levels be defined, and the group, entity, team, and team of teams levels be articulated?
  - How should authority, responsibility, and accountability be distributed?
  - Which teams and teams of teams should be stream-aligned?
- **Domain-driven design** segmentation, which is driven by the questions:
  - What are the enterprise domains and sub-domains?
  - How to decompose sub-domains into bounded contexts?
  - What are the upstream/downstream dependencies that link bounded contexts?
  - How to minimize inter-bounded context dependencies?

When modeling the enterprise as a Complex Adaptive System (CAS), architects should pay attention to leveling, boundaries, dependencies, and interactions: a CAS "*is characterized by intricate hierarchical arrangements of boundaries and signals*" [Holland, 2012]. The definition of levels, boundaries, and interactions is a lever used in Agile Architecture to influence the evolution of the enterprise.

8.2.6. What the Enterprise "*Does*"

Experience design combines customer research and product discovery during a set of **design thinking** iterations. This is not a linear process; it alternates between divergent and convergent thinking. Customer research borrows from marketing research, anthropology, and design thinking to capture and analyze customer needs and desires. Product discovery applies divergent and convergent thinking in the solution space to discover which products and features could satisfy customers. Customer research and product discovery apply outside-in thinking and aim at framing problems and solutions through the lens of the customer.

Journey maps bridge outside-in thinking with inside-out thinking by defining which activities deliver the experience customers expect.

Value streams complement the outside-in view by representing all the activities, both value and non-value creating, required to bring a product from concept to launch (also known as the development value stream) and from order to delivery or provisioning (also known as the operational value stream). More detail about value streams can be found in Section 2.50. These value streams should be regularly reviewed to ensure they are still fit for purpose.

These value streams define the what and are decomposed into stages and capabilities that describe the how [G178].

Event storming helps Agile teams to explore the domain. The identification of domain events, commands, persona, or entities facilitates a structured conversation about the domain. The participants of an event storming workshop share knowledge of the domain to establish a common vocabulary or ubiquitous language. Domain events help to identify boundaries. Commands help to identify responsibilities to be allocated to services or components.

8.3. Data, Information, and AI

The digital enterprise collects and processes vast amounts of data. **Data** describes a portion of "reality" that is of interest to the enterprise. Data becomes **information** when it is interpreted, when it has meaning. Data can be interpreted by humans or algorithms. **AI** transforms data into predictions, prescriptions, and automation capabilities.

The combination of data and AI is having a transformational impact on industries. For example, predictive maintenance can improve service quality while lowering costs. Vast numbers of images can teach machines how to recognize faces or interpret chest x-rays.

Architecting systems that handle data at scale is critical. Non-functional requirements, such as compliance (e.g., privacy) or security requirements, influence Data Architecture decisions. The move from batch processing to real-time data flows is having a profound impact on Data Architecture.

8.4. Software and Hardware Architecture

> "Software is eating the world."

Marc Andreessen explained in a famous Wall Street Journal article why software is eating the world [Andreessen 2011]. The rapid evolution of software technology has fueled the growth of digital business. Following the lead of Internet giants, some enterprises from the old economy are framing themselves as tech companies; for example, Banco Bilbao Vizcaya Argentaria (BBVA): *"If you want to be a leading bank, you have to be a technology company"*.

In 2002, Amazon™ was facing a complexity barrier. The size of its home page reached 800MB and it took 8 to 12 hours to compile. Jeff Bezos issued a mandate [Bezos, 2021] that profoundly changed the way software is created and how the enterprise is organized.

By shifting toward modularity and APIs, Amazon became well-positioned to open its distribution and logistics capabilities to third-party vendors. The self-service nature of the platform made it easy for vendors to sell and distribute their products in a frictionless manner. This helped Amazon to compete against eBay®, leveraging a business model which is different.

Software and hardware represents an increasing part of products and their supporting operations. Software architecture, product architecture, and operations architecture must be developed in a concurrent manner.

8.5. Architecture Development Styles

Except when they are in their creation phase (e.g., startups), enterprises have an *"as-is"* architecture, which may be explicit or implicit, documented or in the mind of employees.

This document distinguishes an architecture from its model; the map is not the territory. Architecture evolves due to emergence, which refers to what appears when the parts that compose a system come together and operate. An architecture model does not emerge; it is a representation of an *"as-is"* architecture or it is designed.

8.5.1. Emergence

Emergence refers to what appears, materializes, or surfaces when a complex system operates; desired or undesirable functions or outcomes emerge. An example of an undesirable outcome is the pollution that results from operating cars. Architecture aims to develop systems that deliver predictable and desirable outcomes.

However, as enterprise complexity grows, unpredictable and sometimes undesirable outcomes appear. Agile architecting aims at benefiting from emergence while minimizing unnecessary complexity and undesirable outcomes.

John Holland observes that *"emergent properties often occur when coevolving signals and boundaries generate new levels of organization. Newer signals and boundaries can then emerge from combinations of building blocks at this new level of organization"* [Holland, 2012]. The more complex a system becomes, the more emergence is likely to appear.

As enterprises grow in complexity, they increase in resilience, become more capable of handling complex ecosystems, and are less likely to be imitated by competitors. However, complexity has a cost and can threaten the future of an enterprise if it gets out-of-hand.

To mitigate undesirable complexity growth, Agile architecting recommends using the controls below:

- Modularity, to facilitate team autonomy and increase resilience
- Standardization, to facilitate product or operating model reconfiguration
- Architecting for a built-in responsiveness to change

Relaxing control favors emergent over designed or micromanaged solutions, which are often inferior. Favoring emergence does not mean it is impossible to steer the evolution of the enterprise.

John Holland suggests steering complex systems by modifying their signal/boundary hierarchies. The components of complex systems are bounded sub-systems or agents that adapt or learn when they interact. Defining the boundaries of sub-systems and their rules of interaction has a major influence on the evolution of the system [Holland, 2014].

Agile architecting steers the evolution of the enterprise by modifying its organization and changing the allocation of authority, responsibility, and accountability.

8.5.2. Intentional Architecture

Does emergence mean that intentional architecture is no longer needed? This document makes the case that intentional architecture brings value. However, the architecture discipline needs to evolve. A shift from a Big Design Up Front (BDUF) to continuous architecture is necessary. As James Coplien and Gertrud Bjørnvig [Coplien & Bjørnvig, 2010] argue:

- Some upfront intentional architecture prevents waste and accelerates decision-making
- Driving architecture from requirements is a mistake
- Intentional architecture should focus on the essence of the system without being unduly influenced by the functionality it provides
- Partitioning (segmentation) allows each part of the system to evolve as autonomously as possible

This document views architecture development as a combination of intentional and emergent architecture. It promotes enterprise segmentation to facilitate concurrent development and architecture refactoring.

Lessons learned from the strategy field apply to intentional architecture too. The success of intentional architecture depends on the reliability of commitments, which is covered in Chapter 6.

Intentional architecture should be simple, focused, and compact because:

- It is likely to evolve, so investing in a detailed model would be wasteful
- It is guided by guardrails imposed by governance
- Concentrating on the "*important stuff*" is likely to make the architecture model easier to understand

Chapter 10 will cover this topic in more detail and show how intentional architecture can be combined with continuous architecture.

8.5.3. Concurrent, Continuous, and Refactored

Agile architecting adopts Set-Based **Concurrent** Engineering (SBCE) practices from Lean Product Development [Ward & Sobek, 2014]:

- Simultaneously explore multiple solutions for every sub-system
- Aggressively explore them with rapid, low-cost analysis, and tests, progressively eliminating weak solutions
- Converge on a solution only after it has been proven

SBCE requires architecture thinking to decompose the product or the product platform into sub-systems.

When weak solutions are eliminated, architecture has to evolve. **Continuous architecture** facilitates incremental changes to the product or platform architectures.

Architecture refactoring refers to the architecture restructuring that occurs when architecture evolves.

In an Agile world, **evolvability** is becoming a top-quality attribute. The objective should be to architect a system in such a way that will allow change without damaging any non-functional qualities.

8.5.4. Tailoring Architecture Development

The modularity of this document enables the formulation of specific architecture development approaches tailored to solve specific enterprise problems. Chapter 10 describes patterns that can guide the definition of tailored approaches that use and combine the O-AA building blocks.

A description of building blocks, their links, and how to segment the enterprise can be found in Chapter 9.

Chapter 9. Building Blocks Overview

The perspectives introduced in Figure 8-2 are not layers; they are views that translate into the concerns of Figure 9-1. The concerns are focused upon:

- **Experience**, to target the right customers and identify unserved needs
- **Product**, to deliver the value proposition and the customer experience
- **Operations**, to define/model the value stream and operating model that produces or operates the product
- **Software and hardware**, to automate the product and the operations that support it

9.1. Building Blocks Logic

Figure 9-1 also highlights a fifth concern, **Organization**, which is related to the other concerns via the Inverse Conway Maneuver; see Axiom 12. *Organization Mirroring Architecture*.

The Experience concern provides an outside-in view that informs product development. “Value-Driven” implies that unlike some Agile methods that prioritize features, this document prioritizes business objectives and outcomes. Features must solve business objectives, measured by KPIs.

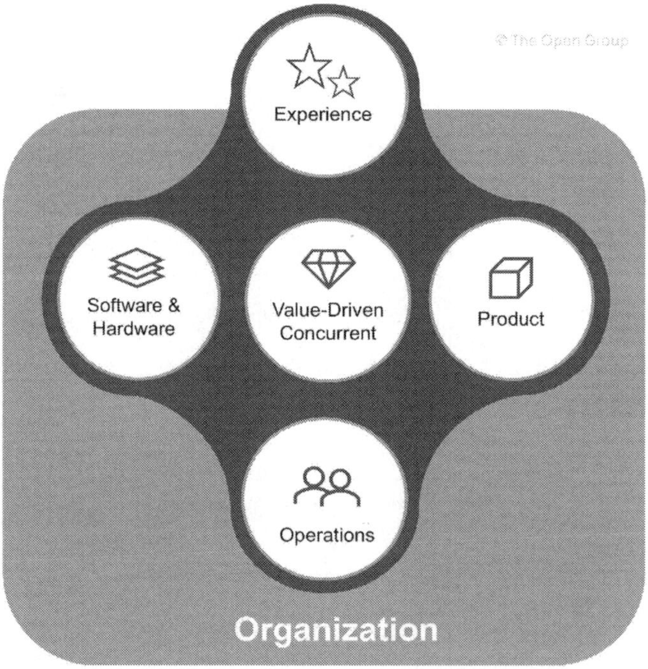

Figure 9-1: Building Blocks Logic

In alignment with Section 4.1, this document recommends developing concurrently the technical and social systems of the enterprise. This document is not about aligning the "Information System" layer with the "Business" layer. Business decisions impact all concerns, including software and hardware concerns. For example, when Jeff Bezos issued his mandate [Bezos, 2021], he made a software architecture decision and a business decision to impact the organization and strategy of Amazon:

- All teams will henceforth expose their data and functionality through service interfaces
- Teams must communicate with each other through these interfaces
- There will be no other form of inter-process communication allowed: no direct linking, no direct reads of another team's data store, no shared-memory model, no back-doors whatsoever
- The only communication allowed is via service interface calls over the network
- All service interfaces, without exception, must be designed from the ground up to be externalizable

By prohibiting any form of inter-process communication other than a service call, Jeff Bezos laid the foundation of what would become "microservices" (Technical System Perspective). He also created the conditions for increased team autonomy by reducing inter-team dependencies (Work System Perspective). By requesting that all service interfaces be externalizable, Jeff Bezos enabled the creation of a third-party vendors market. This was instrumental in helping Amazon compete against eBay based on a two-sided market business model.

Now that it is clear that building blocks do not represent layers, the relationships that link them will be reviewed; see Figure 9-2.

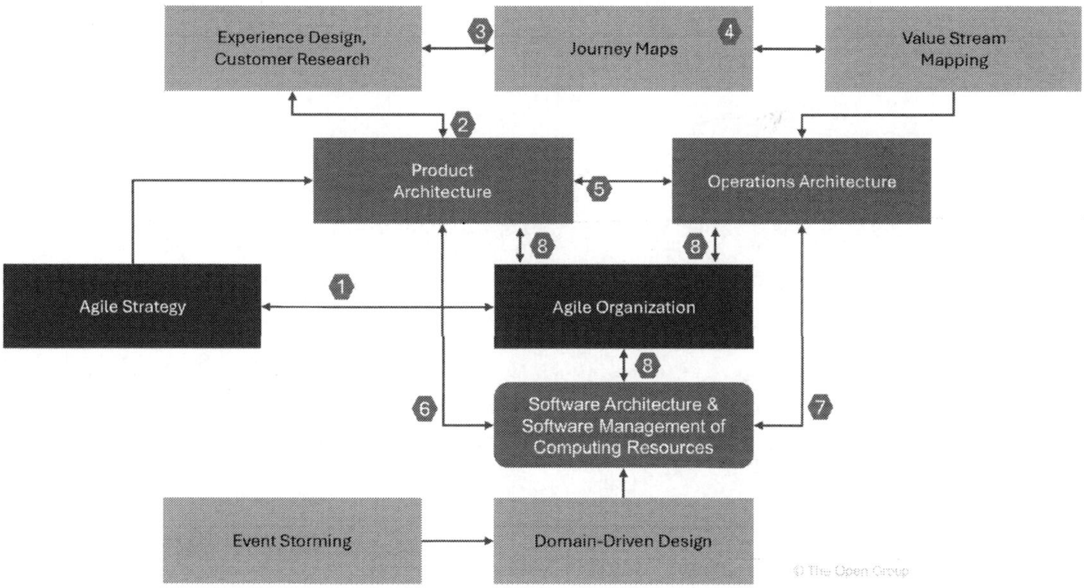

Figure 9-2: Building Blocks Dependencies

The arrows in the diagram represent preconditions. For example, the arrow that links "Experience Design" to "Product Architecture" represents that the outcome of "Experience Design" is a precondition to starting "Product Architecture".

1. "Agile Strategy" is deployed within the "Agile Organization", which also influences strategy in a bottom-up manner
2. "Experience Design" feeds "Product Architecture"
3. "Experience Design" creates experience maps, which are then translated into journey maps by "Journey Mapping"
4. "Value Stream Mapping" models and improves the value streams that deliver products

   When value streams have steps with customer interactions, they are mapped to the corresponding journey maps.

5. "Product Architecture" may require new operational capabilities that "Operations Architecture" should deliver
6. "Product Architecture" is developed concurrently with "Software Architecture", and incorporates software functionalities
7. "Operations Architecture" is developed concurrently with "Software Architecture", and incorporates software functionalities
8. Applying the Inverse Conway Maneuver (see Axiom 12. *Organization Mirroring Architecture*), the organization is shaped to mirror the enterprise's intentional architecture

The building blocks are generic. They are applied at different levels of granularity.

9.2. Enterprise Decomposition

How to decompose an enterprise is a key architecture decision.

> "Hierarchy, I shall argue, is one of the central structural schemes that the architect of complexity uses."
>
> — Herbert Simon

Simon observes that the word "hierarchy" usually refers to situations in which each of the sub-systems is subordinated by an authority in relation to the system it belongs to: *"We shall want to consider systems in which the relations among sub-systems are more complex than the formal organizational hierarchy just described"* [Simon, 1962].

This can be illustrated with a banking example. At the top level, this universal bank is composed of three business lines: retail banking, wholesale banking, and global markets.

At the second level, the retail bank could be decomposed along a customer segment logic: consumer, small business, and enterprise.

Figure 9-3 represents a third level of decomposition that mixes customer segments and product logic. This example illustrates that levels should not be confused with layers.

How retail banking is decomposed matters. Each *rectangle* represents a modular part of the business which can operate in relative autonomy *vis-à-vis* other parts of the business. The fewer dependencies that remain are identified, standardized, and managed. For example, "Consumer Prospect On-Boarding" will order credit cards for new customers.

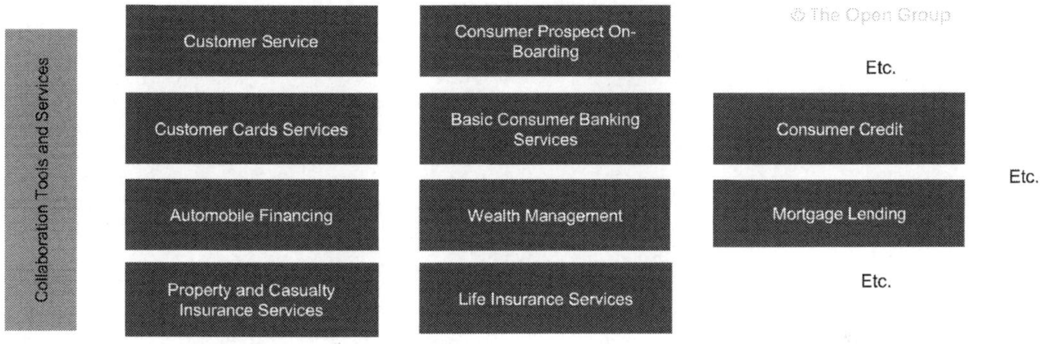

Figure 9-3: Retail Banking Segmentation Example

9.3. Segmentation Approach

This section describes the O-AA segmentation approach; see Figure 9-4.

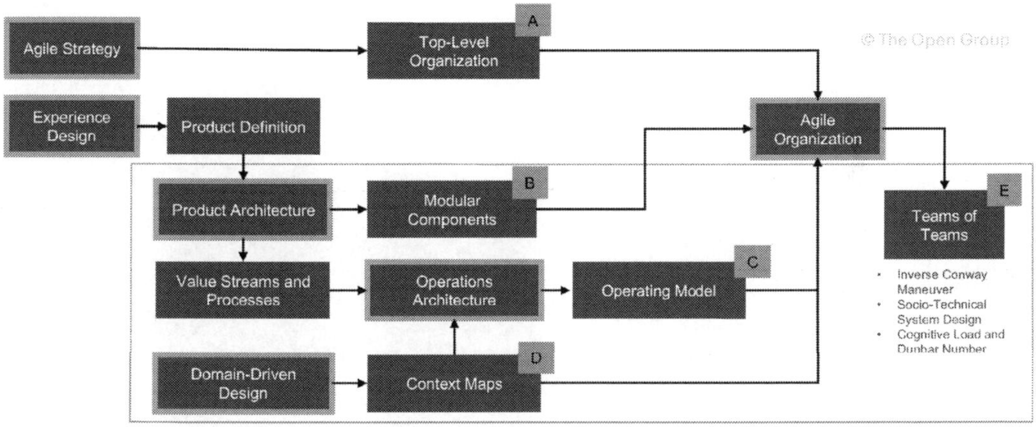

Figure 9-4: Enterprise Segmentation Approach

The highlighted rectangles represent building blocks, and the arrows represent direct links between the building blocks and work products.

"Agile Strategy" influences the definition of the enterprise's "Top-Level Organization" (A). Business lines and corporate functions are defined or adjusted to support the enterprise's strategic direction.

"Experience Design" discovers the products that meet the needs of client segments. "Product Architecture" explores the modularity–integrality trade-off, defines how to decompose products into "Modular Components" (B), and identifies product platforms.

"Operations Architecture" from the defined value streams, identifies the "Technology & Processes" that realize them and in turn designs the target "Operating Model" (C).

"Domain-Driven Design" drives the decomposition of the domain into bounded contexts which are organized into "Context Maps" (D). Context maps (see Section 20.3) define the patterns that link bounded contexts; see Figure 20-1, Figure 20-2, and Figure 20-3.

The "Modular Components" that compose products, the "Operating Model", and the "Context Maps" are inputs to "Agile Organization", which decompose the top-level organization into a "Teams of Teams" (E); guided by:

- The "Inverse Conway Maneuver", which advocates shaping the organization so that communication lines mirror intentional architecture boundaries; see Axiom 12. *Organization Mirroring Architecture*
- "Socio-Technical System Design", which advocates designing the technical and social sub-systems concurrently
- Cognitive limits to the number of people with whom stable social relationships can be maintained ("Dunbar Number"), and the amount of information that working memory can hold at one time ("Cognitive Load")

9.4. Mental Model Shifts

Figure 9-5 lists the shifts that Agile Architecture requires.

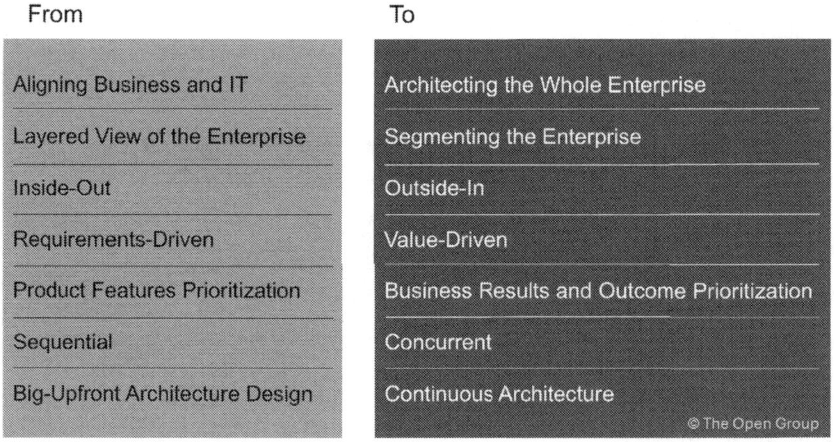

Figure 9-5: Summary of Mental Shifts

Part 3A — Architecture Development Style

This part describes the two key architecture development styles, namely continuous architectural refactoring and intentional architecture.

Chapter 10. Intentional Architecture

This document defines **intentional architecture** as a purposeful set of statements, models, and decisions that represent some future architectural state. This document recommends balancing intentionality and emergence. Though BDUF is incompatible with Agile ways of working, this document recognizes the need and value for intentional architecture. Agile Architecture is leaner and combines intentionality and emergence (see Section 8.5).

The scope of intentional architecture is defined by the three axes of Figure 10-1. It is equivalent to Figure 3-1, Summary Classification Model for Architecture Landscape, in the TOGAF Standard, 10th Edition — Applying the ADM [C220].

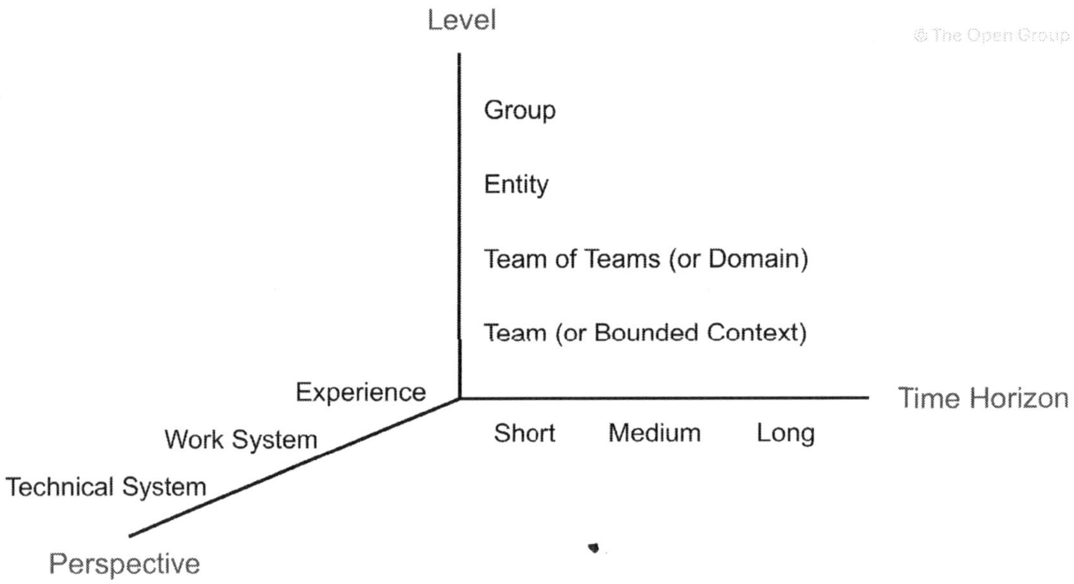

Figure 10-1: Roadmap Space

10.1. Enterprise Architecture *versus* Solution Architecture

Sometimes, and depending on the approach used, Enterprise Architecture frameworks distinguish Enterprise Architecture from solution architecture. Enterprise Architecture is at the entity level and has a medium to long time horizon. In contrast, the scope of solution architecture is sometimes limited to a project. For example, the TOGAF Standard [C182] notes solution architecture as typically applying to "*a single project or project release, assisting in the translation of requirements into a solution vision, high-level business and/or IT system specifications, and a portfolio of implementation tasks*". The time horizon of solution architecture is therefore contingent to the time horizon of projects. This does not imply, however, that the approach could not be adapted to cover a solution that does not depend on, or is not tied to, a specific project.

To echo this, Murat Erder and Pierre Pureur observe that *"solution architects focus on providing project-level architectures, but Enterprise Architects attempt to create strategies, architecture plans, architecture standards, and architecture frameworks for the whole enterprise"* [Erder & Pureur, 2015].

When the definition of solution architecture refers to a project or an application, the following points of attention need to be addressed:

- A project time horizon may not match the time horizon of other solutions or products; therefore, they may impact other teams with different time horizons
- When Agile organizations shift from project to product, the definition of solution architecture evolves to become the product architecture
- The boundary between architecture work and project work is blurred; for example, it is not obvious that implementation tasks qualify as architecture work

As Murat Erder and Pierre Pureur recommend, *"architecting products, not just solutions for projects, because architecting products is more efficient than just designing point solutions to projects and focuses the team on its customers"*.

10.2. Architecturally Significant Decisions

Architecturally significant decisions fall into the following categories. They define or modify:

- The way the enterprise is segmented
- The allocation of functions or activities to segments
- The structural interfaces that link segments
- The standards or guardrails that facilitate interoperability and composability

They are classified according to:

- Their degree of reversibility
- The breadth of their scope

Think about decisions as one-way or two-way doors [Rossman, 2019]. When walking through a one-way door, if the outcome on the other side is unsatisfactory, it is not possible to return to the initial state. This type of decision, also referred to as a Type 1 decision, is difficult to reverse. For example, once an asynchronous architecture style has been adopted, it is difficult to revert to a synchronous architecture style.

When walking through a two-way door, if the outcome on the other side is unsatisfactory, it is possible to walk right back through the door and return to the previous state. This type of decision, also referred to as a Type 2 decision, is easy to reverse. Type 2 decisions should be delegated to the lowest reasonable organizational level.

The scope of a decision is the surface of its impacts along the *Level* and *Perspective* axes of Figure 10-1.

Table 10-1 formulates recommendations depending on the type and scope of decisions.

Table 10-1: Decisioning Patterns

Decision Type	Decision Scope	Decisioning Approach
Type 2	One team	Delegated to the team. Fast decision-making and experimentation.
Type 1	One team	Delegated to the team. Careful discussions. Delay the architecture decision until "*the last responsible moment*" [Atwood, 2006].
Type 2	One team of teams	Delegated to the team of teams. Cross-team coordination. Fast decision-making and experimentation.
Type 1	One team of teams	Delegated to the team of teams. Careful discussions and cross-team coordination. SBCE. Delay the architecture decision until "*the last responsible moment*" [Atwood, 2006].
Type 2	Several teams of teams	Cross-team coordination. Consensus or committee decision-making. Fast decision-making and experimentation.
Type 1	Several teams of teams	Cross-team coordination. Committee decision-making. SBCE. Delay the architecture decision until "*the last responsible moment*" [Atwood, 2006].

When combining intentional and emergent architecture, decisions that come from intentional architecture may change. New ones are added and past decisions can be reversed. Therefore, it is important to document the motivations behind past decisions. An Architecture Decision Record (ADR) provides an Agile and lightweight way of doing this.

10.3. Architecture Decision Record

Michael Nygard [Nygard, 2015] wrote a blog that explains why and how to document architecture decisions. When someone does not understand the rationale of a decision the choice must be made to either accept it, though it should be changed because the context has changed, or change it without understanding the consequences.

Michael Nygard has developed an ADR template that is accessible on GitHub® [Nygard] and outlined below:

ADR Title

- Status

  What is the status: proposed, accepted, rejected, deprecated, superseded, etc.?

- Context

  What is the issue being seen that is motivating this decision or change?

- Decision

  What is the change that is being proposed and/or done?

- Decision scope

  Which segments of the enterprise and its software systems are impacted?

- Decision type

  Is the decision easily reversible or not, and why?

- Consequences

  What becomes easier or more difficult to do because of this change?

10.4. Example: Car Sharing Platform (CSP)

NOTE	This fictional example is presented here for illustrative purposes only, to support the text and to enable a clearer understanding for the reader.

Intentional architecture will now be illustrated using a Car Sharing Platform (CSP) example, which began as a startup that connects drivers to passengers. Drivers publish their available seats and passengers reserve them online.

At the beginning, the connection between users was free of charge. The CSP needed to add a *profit formula* to its business model and has experimented with several economic models:

- Sell the car sharing service to other enterprises
- Offer a "for a fee" phone bridge that participants can use to talk to each other
- Offer a monthly subscription model
- Charge passengers for each ride (transactional model)

The transactional model is now the most frequent; the driver sets a price per passenger based on a recommendation from the platform of around €0.065 per kilometer. The price must not exceed the cost of the journey so that the driver cannot make a profit from it. The CSP adds a commission that changes depending on the country of operation. In France, it is around 18% to 21%.

In order to fund its international development, the CSP conducted a few massive fundraising events. Because the economic situation and culture of each country is different, the economic model was customized by each country. For example, in some countries, the CSP does not charge a commission. In Poland, the CSP has switched to subscription. The net is that few countries are profitable.

The rather unprofitable international development combined with increased competition forced the CSP to change. The number of employees was significantly reduced, and platform algorithms were improved; for example:

- To automatically define new points of contact between drivers and passengers, closer to their homes
- To enable a multi-modal platform that includes other modes of transportation than cars; for example, bus rides

On the organizational side, the CSP was initially divided into large teams. Then, little by little, the CSP broke down its organization into smaller teams aligned with outcomes. It effectively created small startups of 6 to 12 people, regrouped into tribes.

On the software side, the CSP adopted DevOps. This enabled the enterprise to make more than ten updates of its services a day.

10.5. From Intentional to Continuous

Figure 10-2 is a simplified representation of the CSP development stages, with the corresponding points (1) to (5) described in the text that follows. Architecturally significant decisions must be made at some development stages. Not all "Continuous Product Improvement" iterations require "Product Architecture Refactoring".

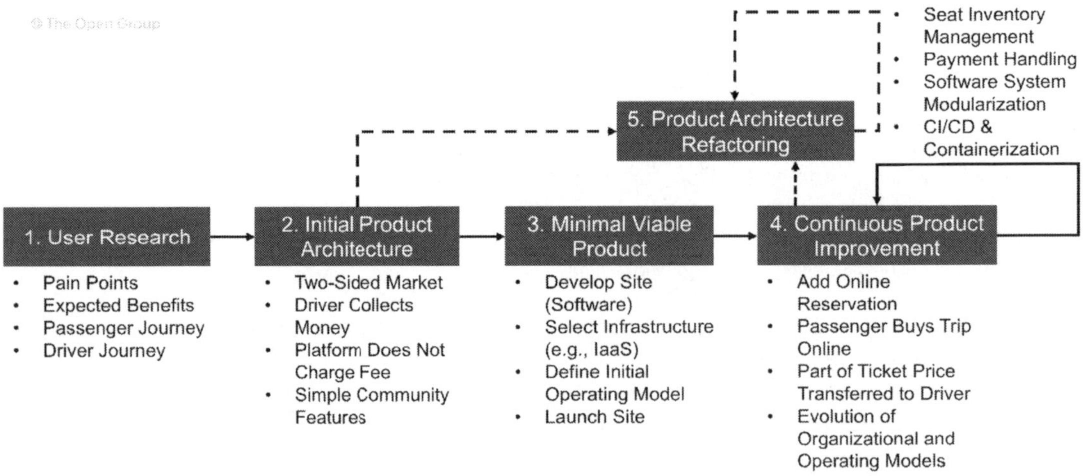

Figure 10-2: Startup Stages

"User Research" (1) helps to clarify driver and passenger needs. It provides inputs to segment the market. Passengers need to travel cheaply from Point A to Point B at some date and time. Drivers who have seats available can offer them. Passengers may work for enterprises that need to facilitate employee commuting.

The first architecturally important decision is about segmenting the market. Passengers and drivers are two obvious segments with complementary needs. Enterprises are a potential market segment, though less obvious to define.

The "Initial Product Architecture" (2) is simple. It is based on a two-sided market supported by a platform that connects passengers and drivers. The platform offers minimum community features to help better match passengers and drivers; for example, using social reputation. The key design objective is to balance the growth in demand for transportation with the growth of transportation offers. If the two are unbalanced, passengers or drivers will become frustrated.

The next stage is to develop a "Minimum Viable Product" (MVP) (3), which consists of:

- The website
- Client support
- A communication plan to boost usage

Because the MVP objective is to validate the product's market viability, the CSP opts for a sacrificial architecture for its initial website.

Martin Fowler coined the term "sacrificial architecture" [Fowler, 2014] to designate situations where a team deliberately chooses to throw away a codebase. He lists some examples of companies that have done this, such as eBay or Google®.

When fewer resources are allocated to developing the website, more can be spent:

- To improve quality, which directly impacts UX
- To boost communication, which is key to MVP success

In this example, a sacrificial architecture is risky should rapid traffic growth exceed the capacity of the website. This is one example of the trade-offs that must be analyzed. The sacrificial architecture decision should be documented using an ADR.

Architecting the support function is important too. One of the goals is to minimize fixed costs until the CSP can prove that the economic model works. Support primarily relies on self-care, which is complemented by a call center to handle cases that require human intervention.

The more sophisticated the self-care, the higher the software development costs. The more cases not solved by self-care, the higher the support costs. This is an example of an operating model decision that impacts architecture (4), (5). Architecturally important operating model decisions must be documented using ADRs.

Architecture evolution is also triggered by new ideas that emerge from the bottom up. For example, a new car rider's localization feature was invented during a "coding night". One hour before the scheduled departure time, the driver is asked to join Ride Map, and to indicate the exact starting point on that map. Passengers can then easily find their driver and are also invited to share their location, to facilitate the meeting.

This new feature requires updating the driver and passenger journeys and interfacing the platform with mapping software in real time. This impacts the existing platform architecture.

10.6. When Intentional Architecture is Recommended

Two CSP business development strategies require intentional thinking:

- The fast international expansion
- The shift toward a multi-modal transportation model

The fast international expansion requires a well-thought out operating model and platform architecture. Examples of architecture questions include:

- Which activities should remain centralized, or be decentralized?
- What should be the scope and setup of local country operations?
- Should the original website be cloned in each country, or should the CSP develop a multi-tenant platform that could be customized to meet individual country needs?

The shift toward a multi-modal transportation model requires a different approach. Instead of an iterative process, it is recommended to shift to a concurrent development process. Though the CSP "as-is" architecture is modular, unavoidable dependencies remain. For example, a new "multi-modal reservation" sub-system needs to interface with the "car-pooling seats reservation" sub-system. A new "multi-modal pricing" module aggregates the prices quoted by car-pooling drivers with prices provided by third-party reservation systems.

Because seats offered by third-party reservation systems cannot be blocked by a distributed transaction monitor, an event-driven architecture that implements a Saga transactional model is mandated. Section 14.4.7 introduces this architecture style and the concept of Saga.

10.7. Set-Based Concurrent Engineering (SBCE)

Waterfall processes often tend to identify the incompatibilities of architectural decisions too late, which is a major cause of rework. By contrast, SBCE delays architecture decisions until "the last responsible moment" [Atwood, 2006]. It is counterintuitive that delaying decisions actually shortens development time while improving quality.

When the solution space is constrained too early, it leads to suboptimal architecture decisions. In contrast, SBCE works like this:

- The product team breaks the system down recursively into sub-systems until the right level of granularity is reached
- It identifies a broad target for the system and each sub-system
- Multiple concepts for the system and each sub-system are created
- The team filters these concepts by thorough evaluation, eliminating concepts that are weak or do not fit with each other
- Failure information goes into a knowledge base that guides architecture design
- As filtering occurs, there is a rapid convergence toward a solution that is often more elegant and innovative than the one conventional point-based development would produce

The set of design alternatives shrinks as they are eliminated, knowledge accumulates, and the remaining alternatives are developed to increasing levels of fidelity. Simultaneously, target ranges narrow in corresponding stages, converging on values that provide the best set of trade-offs.

10.8. SBCE of the CSP

The starting point is the creation of a context map to help decompose the CSP platform into sub-systems. Chapter 20 introduces context maps.

Figure 10-3 represents a context map for the multi-modal reservation domain.

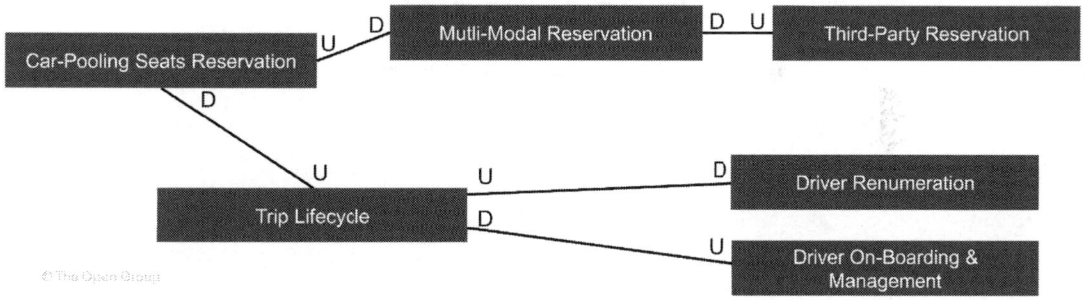

Figure 10-3: Simplified Context Map

Applying the Inverse Conway Maneuver, the CSP segments the organization into teams that:

- Deliver a product, a product feature, a journey, or a sub-journey
- Mirror the candidate sub-systems identified by the context map (the Inverse Conway Maneuver)
- Include business, software development, security, and IT profiles (cross-functional)
- Are led by product owners
- Measure success against OKRs

Agile teams work in parallel and follow a responsibility-based management style. Figure 10-4 illustrates the big picture and describes how all the pieces fit together.

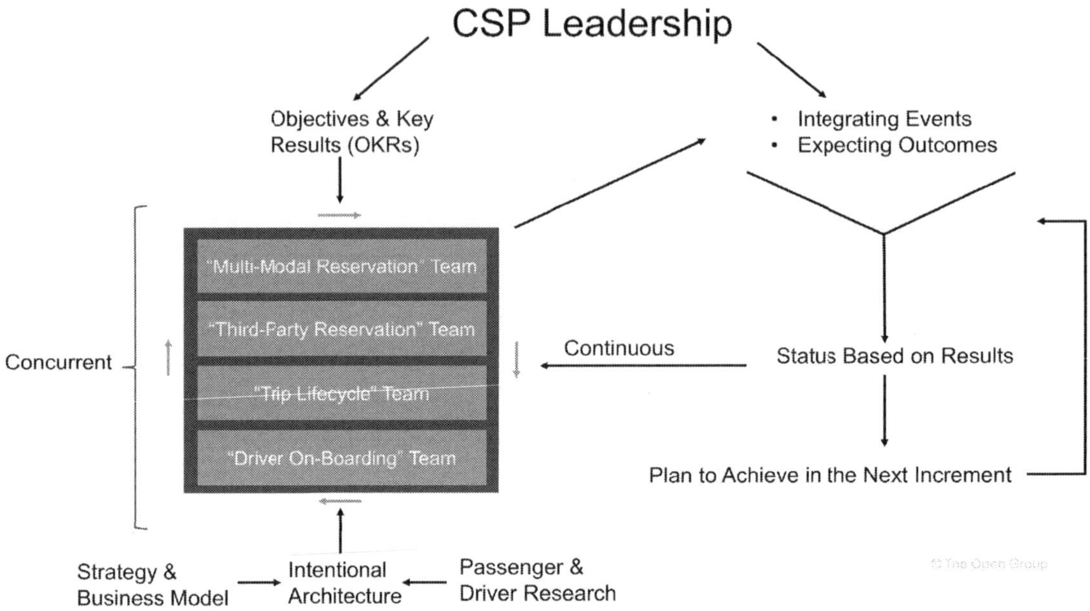

Figure 10-4: Responsibility-Based Management

Each team of teams (tribe) and team (squad) mirrors some piece of the intentional architecture model. Integration events are scheduled on a regular basis; for example, for integrating the "Multi-Modal Reservation" sub-system with the "Third-Party Reservation" sub-system. The Third-Party Reservation sub-system encapsulates access to third-party reservation sites; for example, Ouibus.

Design and architecture conversations between teams happen continuously. An Obeya room can be set up to facilitate coordination and cooperation. This is a room that contains visually engaging charts and graphs where teams meet to engage in meaningful design and architecture conversations.

Integration events are experiments that aim to verify how the pieces of the larger system work together. The status is based on results, not on progress reports processed by a project manager who does not understand design and architecture issues.

10.9. A Few Concluding Words

This document does not impose adopting a "process-oriented" Agile framework such as the Scaled Agile Framework (SAFe) or Large-Scale Scrum (LeSS). Its purpose is to complement them. A word of caution though; the Agile community is increasingly criticizing these frameworks because they promote practices that are sometimes inconsistent with Lean and Agile tenets. This chapter introduced the concept of continuous architecture in the context of intentional architecture. Chapter 11 will drill down further into continuous architecture in a software context.

Chapter 11. Continuous Architectural Refactoring

11.1. Introduction

This chapter discusses the topic of continuous architectural refactoring, a topic of increasing importance in today's Agile, DevOps-oriented software landscape. Here, the focus is on software architecture, as this is a particularly important focus for continuous architectural refactoring.

To properly discuss the concept, it is necessary to first adequately define it, and every word in the term is important. Each will be briefly discussed in turn (but not in order).

11.1.1. Refactoring

This discussion centers around the concept of taking a system architecture and changing its structure over time. Many reasons may exist for doing so: design debt or "cruft" [Cruft] which has inevitably accumulated; changes to the understanding of the important non-functional requirements; remedying suboptimal architectural decisions; changes to the environment; project pivots, etc. Whatever the reason, sometimes fundamental aspects of how a system is put together need to change.

Before continuing, a note on the choice of the word "refactoring". Martin Fowler [Fowler, 2019] would likely describe this topic as "restructuring"; he uses the term "refactoring" to describe small, almost impact-free changes to the codebase of a system to improve its design. The term is decorated with the word "architectural" to make it obvious that larger-scale, structural system changes are being described.

All of which leads to the next question — what does "architecture" actually mean in this context?

11.1.2. Architectural

There may be as many definitions of "architecture", in the context of software architecture, as there are software architects to define it. Ralph Johnson, of the Gang of Four [GoF, 1994], defined software architecture as: *"the important stuff (whatever that is)"*. This deceptively obvious statement highlights the need for an architect to identify, analyze, and prioritize the non-functional requirements of a system. In this definition, the architecture could be viewed as a plan to implement these non-functional requirements. Ford [Ford et al., 2017] provides a comprehensive list of such requirement types, or "-ilities". The TOGAF Standard [C220] provides a more concrete description of architecture, namely: *"the structure of components, their interrelationships, and the principles and guidelines governing their design and evolution over time"*.

This "evolvability" — the ability for architecture to be changed or evolved over time — is becoming critical. There are many reasons for this: the increasingly fast pace of the industry; adoption of Agile approaches at scale; the cloud-first nature of much new development; the failure of expensive, high-profile, and long-running projects, etc. System evolution has always been an important concept in architectural frameworks. Rozanski [Rozanski & Woods, 2005] had an "evolution" perspective; the

TOGAF Standard has the concept of "change management". There is an increasing reluctance to worry up front about five-year architecture plans or massive upfront architectural efforts, which is requiring organizations to consider building in "ease-of-change". This viewpoint is in harmony with that of Martin Fowler [Fowler, 2015], who argues that software architecture must address technical characteristics that are both important and hard to change.

Of course, not all architectural changes represent refactoring. Changes in functional and non-functional requirements (or an evolving understanding of the requirements) can all drive architectural change, but these kinds of architectural change are not the focus in this context.

11.1.3. Continuous

The industry has, over the past few years, revisited the "hard to change later" problem in a new light. Instead of looking at individual requirements from the perspective of how they will evolve in a system, what if "evolvability" was baked into the architecture as a first-class concept? Evolutionary architectures, as described by Ford [Ford et al., 2017], have no end-state. They are designed to evolve with an ever-changing software development ecosystem, and include built-in protections around important architectural characteristics — adding time and change as first-class architectural elements. Indeed, Ford describes such an architecture as one that "*supports guided, incremental change across multiple dimensions*". It is this incremental nature of change that facilitates making changes to the software architecture in a continuous manner, planning for such change from the outset and having, as part of the backlog, items which reflect the desired architectural evolution.

11.2. Planning for Continuous Architectural Refactoring

The remainder of this chapter discusses the key considerations in planning for the continuous architectural refactoring of a digital technology system; it answers the question of how organizations can position themselves to continuously evolve their architectures in response to changing requirements, architectural debt, and other change. These are detailed under three headings:

- Understanding and guiding the architecture; see Section 11.3
- Creating the right technical environment; see Section 11.4
- Creating the right non-technical environment; see Section 11.5

Each sub-section covers a different aspect of the necessary prerequisites for continuous architectural refactoring. Taken together, they offer a complete view of the enablers for successful continuous architectural refactoring.

11.3. Understanding and Guiding the Architecture

Before deciding what technical and organizational mechanisms to put in place to support continuous refactoring, the conditions under which the system operates must first be understood. Once the business and technical constraints relevant to the system have been identified, structures can then be put in place that will allow evolution within those constraints. Fitness functions will allow actual testing that the architecture is fit for purpose, and guardrails will contribute to the guidance referred to in the definition of architecture in Ford [Ford et al., 2017], keeping development teams from going astray in their system designs.

11.3.1. Constraints

Every organization operates under a range of constraints, which restrain the valid choices that can be made by a business in achieving its aims. They come in many guises, including financial, cultural, technical, resource-related, regulatory, political, and time-based. The very nature of the word "constraint" implies a limiting, constricting force which will choke productivity and creativity, and it is human nature to try to dismiss them or rail against them. However, constraints need not be negative forces; they can force the description of current reality and provide guidance as to how that reality should shape efforts. Individual constraints may be long-lived; others may be eliminated through effort; but to ignore any of them is folly.

Inevitably, some of these constraints will be manifested in software as architectural constraints. Technical constraints may mandate an infrastructural topology (e.g., "Organization A only deploys on Infrastructure as a Service (IaaS) Vendor B's offerings"), an architectural style of development (e.g., "Organization C is a model-driven development software house"), or an integration requirement (e.g., "Financial transactions are always handled by System D"). Financial and resource constraints can shape software development team members and their skill sets, as well as imposing hardware and software limitations. Time-based constraints may manifest as software release cadences, which will influence development architectural choices. Regulatory constraints can have big impacts on development practices, deployment topology, and even whether development teams are allowed to continuously deploy into production.

Constraints can also take the form of business constraints, or LOB constraints, in a large organization. These constraints can also shape the architecture, and, indeed, drive a decision between refactoring an existing solution or embarking on the development of a new solution. However, business constraints may also be managed by organizational changes; for example, using the Inverse Conway Maneuver.

When embarking upon a journey of continuous architectural refactoring, the identification and documentation of such constraints is vital. As Rozanski [Rozanski & Woods 2005] sagely notes, one of the first jobs for an architect is to *"come up with the limits and constraints within which you will work and to ratify these with your stakeholders"*.

11.3.2. Fitness Functions

A frequent complaint about the discipline of software architecture is that it is all too easy for teams to regard it as an academic, rather abstract endeavor. Even with relatively mature development teams, whose architectural descriptions accurately describe how the system will implement the most important non-functional requirements, it has been difficult to demonstrate that the system actually does so. Even worse, as the nature and importance of these requirements change over time, it is easy for the architectural descriptions to lag behind, with the effect being that a shared understanding of how the system will meet its non-functional requirements is no longer maintained. If the methods to test that the architecture is meeting its goals are unknown, then how can confidence in it ever be established? It is worth noting that the same charge can be leveled against architectural descriptions being out-of-date in the face of changing functional requirements; however, that is not a focus in this instance.

As an antidote to such problems, Ford [Ford et al., 2017] introduces the deceptively simple concept of "fitness functions". Fitness functions objectively assess whether the system is actually meeting its identified non-functional requirements; each fitness function tests a specific system characteristic.

For example, a fitness function could measure the performance of a specific API call: Does the API complete in under one second at the 90th percentile? This question is far from abstract; it is an embodiment of a non-functional requirement that is testable. If an evaluation of the fitness function fails, then this aspect of the system is failing a key non-functional requirement. This is not open to opinion or subjectivity; the results speak for themselves. To take the example further, imagine that one of the proposed architectural refactorings was to implement database replication to meet availability requirements. If this is implemented and the "API performance" fitness function subsequently failed, then it becomes known early in the development cycle that the architecture is no longer fit for purpose in this respect, and the problem can be addressed or a pivot can occur.

It follows, therefore, that fitness functions are key enablers of a goal to continuously restructure the architecture. They are measurable tests used to evaluate whether a system meets it is non-functional requirements. They allow teams to ensure that those system characteristics which need to remain constant over time actually do so. They reduce the fear of breaking something inadvertently and also increase the ability to show stakeholders this has not occurred. They represent a physical and tangible manifestation of constraints and architectural goals.

11.3.3. Guardrails

Another mechanism that organizations use to bake evolvability into their system architectures is the concept of architectural guardrails. As with their real-world roadside equivalents, software guardrails are designed to keep people from straying into dangerous territory.

In real terms, guardrails represent a lightweight governance structure. They document how an organization typically "does" things — and how, by implication, development teams are expected to "do" similar things. For example, a guardrail may document not just the specific availability requirements for a new service, but also how the organization goes about meeting such requirements. Typically, guardrails are used in combination with an external oversight team — be this an architecture board, guild, or program office. Typically, oversight teams communicate a simple message: adherence to guardrails eliminates the need to justify architectural choices — approval is automatic. However, when guardrails cannot be followed, discussion becomes necessary. Sound reasoning may lead to agreement and modification of the guardrails, though the oversight team retains the authority to require approach changes when deviation from guardrails lacks justification.

The key to their power is that they are not mandates. They do not impose absolute bans on teams taking different approaches; rather they encourage creativity and collaboration, and encourage the evolution of the governance structure itself.

11.4. Creating the Right Technical Environment

Successful continuous architectural refactoring needs the development team to be empowered to iteratively make architectural changes. There are a number of key technical enablers for this:

- Continuous delivery
- Componentization

In addition, Agile development practices are a key enabler for continuous architectural refactoring. As described in Chapter 6, there are a number of practices which are promoted by Agile working. These practices allow continuous architectural refactoring to be successfully implemented; in particular, rapid iteration and experimentation, which allow architectural evolution to be readily incorporated into ongoing development activities.

11.4.1. Continuous Delivery

For some years now, the concept of continuous delivery has been key to a solid foundation for software development. Fowler simply defines it as *"a software development discipline where you build software in such a way that the software can be released to production at any time"* [Fowler, 2013]. To do this, he says, it is necessary to continuously integrate the developed software, build it into executables, and test it via automated testing. Ideally, such testing is executed in an environment that is as close as possible to a production environment.

With a seminal work on the topic, Humble and Farley [Humble & Farley, 2010] converted many software teams to the advantages of an Agile manifestation of configuration management, automated build, and continuous deployment. Most recently, Forsgren et al. [Forsgren et al., 2018] have statistically illustrated the advantages of continuous delivery — there is now no question that its adoption will help teams deploy on-demand, get continuous actionable feedback, and achieve one of the main principles of the Agile Manifesto [Agile Manifesto]: to *"promote sustainable development"*. It is, moreover, difficult to achieve scalable continuous architectural refactoring without it.

Continuous integration and continuous delivery are important elements to support continuous architectural refactoring. Continuous integration and continuous delivery are often considered as a single concept and, in many cases, are linked by a single implementation. However, this is not a requirement, and, for flexibility, they will be discussed separately here.

Continuous integration is about the work of developers being frequently merged into a single branch. Some source control tooling makes this the default but, irrespective of the technology choice, it is possible to implement continuous integration with a combination of development practices and build processes. One of its most important elements is the integration of automated testing into the build process, so that there is confidence in the quality of the code on the main branch at all times. The key benefit in terms of architectural refactoring is the removal of "long-running" branches, which mitigate against architectural change but extend the window of potential impact of a change until all branches have merged. In practice, this can make it so cumbersome for developers to manage the impact of architectural change that it will prevent change from happening.

Continuous delivery is about being able to release at any time, which can be realized as releasing on every commit. It is important to note that in organizations with compliance, regulatory, or other mandatory checkpoints, continuous delivery may not be about a fully-automated release to production. Rather, the aim of continuous delivery should be that as each change is integrated it should be possible to release that version, and in particular that the entire team is confident that it is releasable. The key benefit in terms of architectural refactoring is in empowering the developers to make architectural changes, knowing that the combination of continuous integration and continuous delivery will guarantee that the change is compatible in terms of functionality and deployment.

It is possible, and in many cases desirable, to evolve to have a continuous integration/delivery pipeline, rather than trying to take one step to a fully-automated process. The key to this is to understand the required steps in the process, and work to automate them one at a time. It is also important to look at the larger environment and make the decision to find the right solution for the organization, even if that means that some manual checkpoints remain.

Finally, it is key here to take the advice of Humble and Farley [Humble & Farley, 2010] that "*in software, when something is painful, the way to reduce the pain is to do it more frequently, not less*". Building toward a continuous integration/delivery pipeline is hard, but it is all the more important to do it because if not, the effort to deliver it manually will be all the more limiting in the company's evolution.

11.4.1.1. Feature Toggles

Feature toggles (or feature flags) are an important mechanism in creating an environment to allow continuous architectural refactoring. They allow features to be developed and included on the main stream (see Section 11.4.1) without exposing them to end users. This gives the development team options to factor their work solely based on their needs.

In addition, as described by Kim et al. [Kim et al., 2016], the key enablers arising from the use of feature toggles are the abilities to:

- Roll back easily to the previous version of the changed behavior
- Gracefully degrade performance by allowing services/features to be selectively disabled where performance issues or constraints emerge
- Increase resilience through a Service-Oriented Architecture (SOA), where calls to services can be independently enabled/disabled

Hodgson [Hodgson, 2017] details the different categories of feature toggles: ops toggles, permission toggles, experiment toggles, and release toggles. Ops toggles are used to control the operational behavior of the system; for example, a manual implementation of the circuit breaker pattern. Permission toggles are used to control access to features that have a limited audience; for example, "premium" features that would only be enabled for (higher) paying customers. Experiment toggles are typically used to support A/B testing; for example, a dynamic switch in system behavior based on the current user. However, release toggles are of particular note to discussions on continuous architectural refactoring; such toggles allow untested or incomplete refactorings and restructurings to be released into a production environment, safe in the knowledge that such code paths will never be accessed.

11.4.2. Componentization

The structure of the architecture can play a key role in mitigating against continuous architectural refactoring. As an organization expands, or as the need for flexibility increases, a monolithic architecture, while not inherently bad, can become a key constraint. As Kim [Kim et al., 2016] observes: "*... most DevOps organizations were hobbled by tightly-coupled, monolithic architectures that — while extremely successful at helping them achieve product/market fit — put them at risk of organizational failure once they had to operate at scale ...*".

The key, therefore, is to evolve the architecture to have sufficient componentization to support an organizational evolution on an ongoing basis. The strangler pattern [Fowler, 2004] can be key in this kind of evolution by creating the space for the implementation to evolve behind an unchanging API.

This can be achieved as a staged process, as described by Shoup [Shoup, 2014], moving from a monolithic architecture to a layered architecture, and then on to microservices.

11.5. Creating the Right Non-Technical Environment

Technical mechanisms such as continuous delivery and feature toggles are powerful enablers of continuous architectural refactoring, but they are certainly not the only ones. For example, what if the buy-in of senior management is not made available to do any refactoring? (Hint: architectural refactoring gets continuously prioritized behind functional evolution.) Even with such buy-in, to paraphrase the definition of architecture in Ford [Ford et al., 2017], continuous refactoring needs to be guided and incremental. The guidance comes in the form of an architectural roadmap, a best-guess hypothesis of how the architecture needs to evolve. Finally, organizations need to balance the tensions between these forces; sometimes refactoring should occur, sometimes new functionality should be built.

Before continuing, it is worth noting that the development team structure is also a key enabler for continuous architectural refactoring, in particular the Inverse Conway Maneuver. This technique has been described separately in Chapter 8.

11.5.1. Justifying Ongoing Investment in Architectural Refactoring

A frequent frustration among software developers is the perception that their management team only values things that can be sold. To management, they believe, architectural refactoring is wasted money, occupying development teams for months at a time without a single additional thing being produced that can be sold. And for that matter, why does it take so long for them to add a feature? (Possible answer: that would be because the architecture has not been refactored in years.)

Management teams do have a business to run, and customers do not typically invest time and money for architectural refactorings, no matter how elegant they are; so without shiny new things to sell, there may be no time or money to continue to employ the development teams who want to do the refactoring.

As such, this issue has two aspects: firstly, development teams need to learn how to justify such investment; and secondly, such non-functional investment will always have to be balanced with functional requirements.

It is worth, at this point, returning to Fowler's distinction [Fowler, 2019] between code refactoring and architectural restructuring. Fowler would strongly promote the view that code refactoring requires no justification; rather it is part of a developer's "day job". This does not mean that a massive code restructuring exercise for a legacy codebase must be undertaken; on the contrary, there may be no reason whatsoever to restructure the code for a stable legacy project. However, that said, developers should refactor their code when the opportunity arises. Such activity constitutes a "Type 2" decision as documented in [Ries 2011].

Architectural refactoring (restructuring), however, often requires explicit investment because the required effort is significant. In such cases, it is incumbent on development teams and architects to "sell" the refactoring in monetary, time, or customer success terms. For example, "if we perform refactoring A, the build for Product B will be reduced by seven minutes, resulting in being able to deploy C times more frequently per day"; or, "implementing refactoring D will directly address key Customer E's escalated pain point; their annual subscription and support fee is $12 million per annum". Note, however, that claims that "refactoring F will make G% more productive" should be avoided as software productivity is notoriously difficult to measure.

11.5.2. Developing an Architectural Roadmap

An architectural roadmap needs to meet several key criteria to achieve continuous architectural refactoring:

- Vision: A target end-state is key to assessing individual changes in moving toward the target state
- Step-wise: A number of intermediate states need to be described between the "as-is" and "to-be" architectures, documenting the benefits and challenges of each state
- Flexible: The target and intermediate states may evolve as the understanding of the architecture and the constraints themselves evolve
- Open: A successful architecture is rarely defined by a committee, but the process and documentation of the architectural roadmap needs to be available to the whole team, and everyone must feel empowered to comment/question
- Breadth: The roadmap needs to be broad enough both in scope and planning horizon to meaningfully inform the team's decision-making

In order to create the space for the Agile implementation, it is also important that the roadmap remains high-level. There is tension here between the need to keep the project within its constraints, and giving the team the space and support to make Agile decisions as they are implementing the architectural roadmap. Beyond the roadmap and, in particular, the vision of a Target Architecture, guardrails are key to supporting and enabling emergent architecture, while allowing the overall architecture to remain effective and meet all of its identified requirements.

In particular, the suggested aim is to create an environment where the risks of architectural change can be removed by the supporting conditions, allowing the team the freedom to make architectural changes knowing that the process and culture will support them. To quote from Kim [Kim et al., 2013]: "*Furthermore, there is hypothesis-driven culture, requiring everyone to be a scientist, taking no assumption for granted, and doing nothing without measuring.*" The measuring of the impact of architectural change was discussed in Section 11.3.2.

11.5.3. Progressive Transformation (Experience)

Delivering continuous architectural refactoring is more than the sum of the pieces already described in this section. It also needs a pragmatic approach from the entire team; what is "good enough" at every point to allow the product to evolve (in the right direction) and keep the business moving forward. Simon [Simon et al., 2018] describes this as "liquid software", allowing the product (and its architecture) to evolve as needed, while also having an environment that ensures it continues to meet all the requirements placed on it.

This can also have a varying focus over time; sometimes the business needs to "win" and the focus shifts to business features at the expense of architectural evolution. But it is critical that the environment for architectural evolution persists, so that if and when the focus shifts back to architecture concerns, the option to continue to evolve it will remain open.

Part 3B — Architecture Deliverables

This part describes the key architecture deliverables of Agile Architecture.

Chapter 12. Product Architecture

Product architecture is the first of the three main architectures defined within the O-AA architecture development model, the other two being operations architecture and software architecture. Within an Agile development they are developed in parallel. This parallel development is important in order to incorporate the required modularity.

> "Perhaps the most important characteristic of a product's architecture is its modularity."
>
> — Karl Ulrich

Product architecture is the assignment of the functional elements of a product to its building blocks or product components [Ulrich et al., 2020]. A modular architecture exhibits the following properties:

- Product components implement one or a few functional elements in their entirety
- The interactions between components are well-defined and are generally fundamental to the primary functions of the product

The most modular architecture is one in which each functional element of the product is implemented by exactly one building block, and in which there are a few well-defined interactions between building blocks.

This document recommends using a Design Structure Matrix (DSM) to measure the degree of modularity of a system. Alan MacCormack and his co-authors show how to calculate the **propagation cost** of a system, which measures its degree of modularity [MacCormack et al., 2007].

Using DSMs, the Harvard Business School authors show that a loosely-coupled organization develops a product with a more modular design than that of a tightly-coupled organization, which is consistent with the Inverse Conway Maneuver; see Axiom 12. *Organization Mirroring Architecture*.

The opposite of a modular architecture is an integral architecture, in which the implementation of functional elements is spread across building blocks resulting in a high degree of coupling. It exhibits one or more of the properties below:

- Functional elements of the product are implemented using more than product components
- Implementation of functional elements may be distributed across multiple components
- A single component implements many functional elements
- The interactions between components are ill-defined

In an integral architecture, many functional elements may be combined into a few product components to optimize performance. However, modifications may require a significant redesign of the product.

Product architecture decisions have far-reaching implications on product variety, component standardization, product performance, manufacturability, and product development.

12.1. Defining Product Architecture

In a manufacturing context, Karl Ulrich gives a definition of product architecture [Ulrich, 1993]. Several years later, Edward Crawley gives a systems architecture definition that is quite similar [Crawley et al., 2016].

> "Product architecture is: (1) the arrangement of functional elements; (2) the mapping from functional elements to physical components; and (3) the specification of the interfaces among interacting physical components."
>
> — Karl Ulrich

The quality of customer experience, with its emotional dimension, is not part of Karl Ulrich's definition. Experience design identifies the functional elements or features that contribute to the quality of customer experience.

In a manufacturing context, product refers to goods and not services. The following describes how this definition can be interpreted in a service context.

Product features are the equivalent of functional elements. In a service context, the physical elements are mostly the physical evidences and devices used by clients, employees, and other stakeholders. Therefore, the definition needs to be extended to cover non-physical components.

Fabrice Seite and his co-authors describe a service product at three levels [Seite et al., 2010]:

- The top level is the service result; i.e., the result of a service operation visible to the customer
- The second level offers a perspective on the processes enabling the service result
- The third level of the model addresses the required resources for performing the processes that lead to the final result; three types of resources are considered: human, physical, and informational

At the second level, defining the modularity of the enabling process is a major product architecture decision. The mapping of product features to process steps is specified in alignment diagrams; see Figure 17-1.

At a higher granularity level, the theory of interdependence and modularity addresses architecture questions.

> Products, services, and even entire industries have architectures that dictate which components or steps are required to make something work and how they should fit together.

Product architecture breaks down products into components and specifies the interfaces that link components.

"Products and services have multiple constituent components, and they go through several value-added processes before reaching consumers. The place where any two components fit together is called an interface. Interfaces exist not just within products but also between stages in the value-added chain" [George & Ting, 2018].

12.2. Interdependence and Modularity

Clayton Christensen defines a product in a way that focuses on how components interact, fit, and work together [Christensen & Raynor 2013]:

> "A product's architecture determines its constituent components and sub-systems and defines how they must interact — fit and work together — in order to achieve the targeted functionality."
>
> — Clayton Christensen and Michael Raynor

According to Clayton's theory, architecture is *interdependent* at an interface if one part cannot be created independently of the other part. He claims that interdependent architectures:

- Optimize performance in terms of functionality and reliability
- Are, by definition, proprietary

In contrast, a modular architecture specifies the fit and function of all elements so completely that it does not matter who makes the components or sub-systems, as long as they meet the specifications.

This theory formulates the hypothesis that flexibility comes at the cost of performance because a modular architecture gives engineers less freedom. When the basis for competition is functionality and reliability, a modular architecture is at a disadvantage.

However, Clayton Christensen observes that, over time, an inferior product targeting an underserved market will improve to such a point that its performance will challenge established products. When that happens, any further product improvement by incumbents is likely to overshoot customer expectations. This implies that customers will no longer be willing to pay a premium price, which is disruptive for incumbents.

12.2.1. Modularity Wins

Christensen's theory was inspired by the history of the PC industry. It provides a credible explanation for the demise of the minicomputer industry and the acquisition of Digital Equipment Corporation (DEC™) by Compaq®. Initially, the performance of a PC was much lower than the performance of a minicomputer. The PC industry started by catering to the needs of new customers or underserved ones.

At some point, the performance of PCs, especially when connected to a network, was good enough to meet the needs of minicomputer clients. When this happened, customers ceased to be willing to pay a premium. Minicomputers began to "overshoot" the customer's required performance level. Other factors, such as the difference in cost of sales, contributed to the fall of the minicomputer industry.

The modular PC industry won over the minicomputer industry, which was not modular, because it offered good enough performance at a lower price.

12.2.2. Integration Wins

The Christensen Institute and Li & Fung™ Limited interpret the success of Zara™, an apparel retailer specializing in fast fashion, as being due to an interdependent architecture strategy. Zara gained competitive advantage by:

- Integrating customer demand and design
- Rethinking their operating model to produce smaller batches of apparels nearshore

Zara developed business agility by sensing fashion trends sooner and responding to them faster; see Figure 3-2. Zara is capable of designing, producing, and shipping new apparel models in a matter of weeks thanks to their integrated product architecture [Ton et al., 2010].

The Zara business model is based on a high level of integration between customer research and new apparel design. It also relies on the operational capability to rapidly produce small batches of clothes at a competitive cost, though its manufacturing plants are located in a high-wage country, and deliver these clothes to stores within a 24/48-hour window after orders have been placed.

12.2.3. Modular Goods

Many goods use a modular architecture to offer innovative benefits to customers; for example:

- The "Lifebuoy Boat" product works by incorporating separate sections for each member of a family or group in order to increase the safety factor; the sections can come apart from one another to become individual life raft buoys that float independently, which could come in handy when it comes to rescue operations or if one module is compromised; see Linkable Individual Lifeboat
- The Poiray® watch that modularizes watch straps; an innovative feature that lets the watch owner easily and instantly change the strap of the watch to match any chosen outfit
- Mosivi.com has created a portfolio of modular products; for example, a modular office shelving product built up on one single element that allows endless configurations and the possibility to easily alter an interior according to the customer's changing needs

12.2.4. Modular Services

The level of modularity of the financial services industry differs by geography and product family. In modular markets, integrated financial institutions are increasingly challenged by regulated and unregulated competitors (shadow banking).

The shadow banking system performs the financial intermediation function in the same way as the traditional banking system. The main distinguishing characteristics of the shadow banking system are looser supervision and greater fragmentation between operators at each link in the intermediation chain.

The United States (US) mortgage market has long been characterized by modular supply. Government Sponsored Enterprises (GSEs), such as Fannie Mae® and Freddie Mac®, enable a robust secondary market with a large portion of mortgage assets held by non-banks. In the first quarter of 2018, Quicken Loans®, a shadow bank, was the largest mortgage lender in the US. Wells Fargo™ and JPMorgan Chase™ were second and third. The fourth largest mortgage lender was loanDepot®, a shadow bank.

In the United Kingdom (UK) and Germany, the traditional Property and Casualty (P&C) personal life insurance business is disrupted by aggregators. In motor insurance, most UK and German direct players have outperformed their markets in both premium growth and profitability [Marcuson, 2025; Mintel & Mordor Intelligence, 2024].

Modularization can also benefit integrated firms which productize part of their value chain. Amazon exemplifies this. By unbundling its infrastructure services from its core e-commerce business, Amazon created Amazon Web Services™ (AWS™), which is now the largest player in the public cloud market.

12.3. Modularity-Integrality Trade-Off

The trade-offs that an integrated enterprise must make between integration and modularization are illustrated below.

In an Agile at scale organization, team autonomy is important because a large number of Agile teams work in parallel. Autonomy minimizes inter-team dependencies. A modular architecture reduces dependencies, but could degrade the overall system's performance.

Vente-privée.com offers a complete service to sell unsold goods from well-known brands. The value proposition for these brands is to make money from an unsold inventory without hurting the brand. It organizes, exclusively for its members, event-driven sales of products with strong brand names and big discounts (-30% to -70%).

The service to brands includes the shooting of products, the selection of photos, the original trailer, the creation of a catalog, putting it online, issuing invitations to members, sales, online payment, and delivery to the members.

The value proposition for consumers is to be able to buy brand name products at very attractive prices. Although the quality of service for the consumer was not always there, the value proposition was so strong that it did not impact the triple-digit sales growth. However, the expectations of quality of service and personalization have continued to rise under the influence of tech giants.

For example, Amazon has created the expectation of fast delivery. Although Vente-privée's business model is different to that of Amazon, it becomes difficult to ignore these new expectations. As the business model is based on building inventory upstream of the sale, it becomes necessary to develop predictive algorithms to anticipate demand and thus be able to deliver quickly.

Because of this lack of predictive analytics, the logistics system is not capable of estimating delivery times in real time. The company is also not able to put items acquired from different sales in the same basket. Vente-privée must upgrade its delivery service in a way that is well-integrated with sales. This makes it difficult to outsource a logistics system that has such specific requirements.

Vente-privée has developed a studio capable of creating high-quality videos to present brand products. It only takes a few days to produce a new video clip whereas a communication agency would take a month and cost much more. Vente-privée's studio creates its own music and has a network of models that it mobilizes to shoot scenes featuring models wearing clothes. The video studio service can be easily modularized. Vente-privée could decide to make it a product that it would sell to other enterprises, emulating Amazon's creation of AWS.

The Vente-privée example illustrates that the modularity–integrality trade-off is more subtle than Christensen's theory says. Christensen's theory does not account for modular systems that at the same time show or require high degrees of integrality. Increasing modularity does not necessarily entail decreasing integrality, and high levels of modularity are not always a sufficient condition to facilitate system reconfiguration, or architectural innovation [Miraglia, 2014].

The delivery service can be loosely-coupled with the sales service via a standard set of APIs. However, the specificity of the Vente-privée's business model directly impacts the logistics system design. This creates indirect coupling. On the other hand, the services the studio provides are similar to those provided by communication agencies. Therefore, they could be productized and sold to an outside market, though these services are part of the Vente-privée's integrated product.

This document adopts the modularity and integrality definitions proposed by Stefano Miraglia:

- Modularity is the system's property of being made up of modules; a module is a system element that presents a high, albeit not complete, independence of other elements; modularity is a relative property in dimension and degree: a system is fully modular along a given dimension when all of its elements behave independently of other elements along the same dimension
- Integrality is the system's property of being made up of elements that behave consistently as a whole; it is a relative property in dimension and degree; a system is fully integral along a given dimension when all of its elements consistently concur to determine the system behavior along that dimension

These definitions recognize that modularity and integrality must be analyzed along several dimensions. Modularity and integrality are separate and concurring properties of complex systems.

> "Dimensions of modularity reflect the different traits of independence among modules and describe component-level interrelationships. Dimensions of integrality encompass factors that affect the relationship between the component level and the system level, and describe cross-level interrelationships. The interplay between modularity and integrality is crucial to the dynamics and evolution of systems."
>
> — Stefano Miraglia

12.4. Product Platforms

Products built around modular product architectures can be more easily varied without adding tremendous complexity to the manufacturing system. For example, Swatch® produces hundreds of different watch models, but can achieve this variety at a relatively low cost by assembling the variants from different combinations of standard chunks.

Product platforms support the development of highly differentiated products that share a substantial fraction of their components. Product platforms are also referred to as innovation platforms [Cusumano et al., 2020]; their main benefits are:

- Products are highly integral and highly modular at the same time
- The platform supports rapid and effective architectural recombination

The challenge is to resolve the tension between the desire to differentiate products and the desire for these products to share a substantial fraction of their components. Different methods in different industries emerged to create and manage product platforms; for example:

- In the software industry, software product lines accelerate the creation of new products by specifying a common architecture and developing a set of common components; each product is formed by taking applicable components from the base of common components, tailoring them as necessary through preplanned variation mechanisms such as parameterization or inheritance, adding any new components that may be necessary, and assembling the collection according to the rules of a common, product line-wide architecture [Northrop & Clements, 2012]
- In the automotive industry, a vehicle platform provides a structure for major components by determining the body size as well as the size and type of engine and transmission [Cusumano & Nobeoka, 1998]

  Auto makers modularize platforms and related components to enable multi-car project strategies. Vehicle platforms incorporate critical aspects of design and manufacturing know-how.

The classical integration-oriented platform approach in software product lines should evolve from a layered and hierarchical model toward a truly Agile model. Splitting the product teams into a platform team and several product teams suffers from limitations:

- Integration and testing are done both at the platform and at the product level, which results in growing integration costs as the scope of the product line widens

- The broad scope of the platform functionality impedes flexibility and time-to-market for new features
- Software developed by a product team cannot be reused by other product teams before it is included into a new platform release, which can take time

Christian Prehofer and his co-authors recommend evolving toward a compositional product family approach [Prehofer et al., 2007]. Instead of being a fully integrated software solution, the software platform becomes a set of components, architecture guidelines, and documentation as code. Powerful digital platforms can be created by combining the compositional product family approach and the modern software architecture patterns as described in Chapter 14.

Now that software in a car costs more than the engine, and anticipating that this trend will continue with autonomous driving and electric engines [Kersten, 2018], vehicle and software platforms could converge.

Product platform decisions are architecturally important decisions that impact product performance and product development cost. It impacts positively or negatively the ability of the enterprise to innovate. It also impacts customer experience.

For example, the Toyota™ New Global Architecture (TNGA) created a powerful competitive advantage in both its product development system and its products [Morgan & Liker, 2019]. TNGA enabled a substantial boost in driving performance by creating a lower center of gravity while also allowing for more freedom in design. This illustrates the impact of platform architecture decisions on customer experience: better driving performance and increased ability to create styles that customers like.

12.5. Concluding Words

As described, the two major types of product architecture decisions are modularity-integrality trade-off and product platform decisions. These product architecture decisions affect the competitiveness of the enterprise. They combine intentional and continuous architecture. The higher the upfront investment to create the platform, the more front-loading design is required, as is the case in the automotive industry.

In such circumstances, SBCE is the way to go, rather than the iterative MVP approach. Once the platform is created, using an MVP approach is more realistic because of the reuse and flexibility the product platform provides. This reflects the parallel development of the product, operational, and software architecture.

When products are mostly made of software, it is easier to develop product platforms incrementally. As a general rule, this document recommends combining set-based innovation with Agile iterations, as described in Chapter 10.

Chapter 13. Operations Architecture

Operations architecture defines and optimizes the lean value streams and processes that deliver products and design the Target Operating Model (TOM), which is composed of:

- Client journeys, lean value streams, and processes
- The resources required to operate them

Lean value streams and processes can be operated by humans, and can be fully or partially automated. They use tangible or intangible assets, and consume resources. Examples of tangible assets include factories, data centers, or machines. Examples of intangible assets include patents, relationships with suppliers, or knowledge. Examples of resources include electricity, raw materials, or cloud services.

Operations architecture is about defining and improving or redesigning enterprise operations to better meet client needs in alignment with the enterprise strategy; see Figure 13-1. The main levers operations architecture uses are lean value stream mapping, automation, and employee development and sourcing.

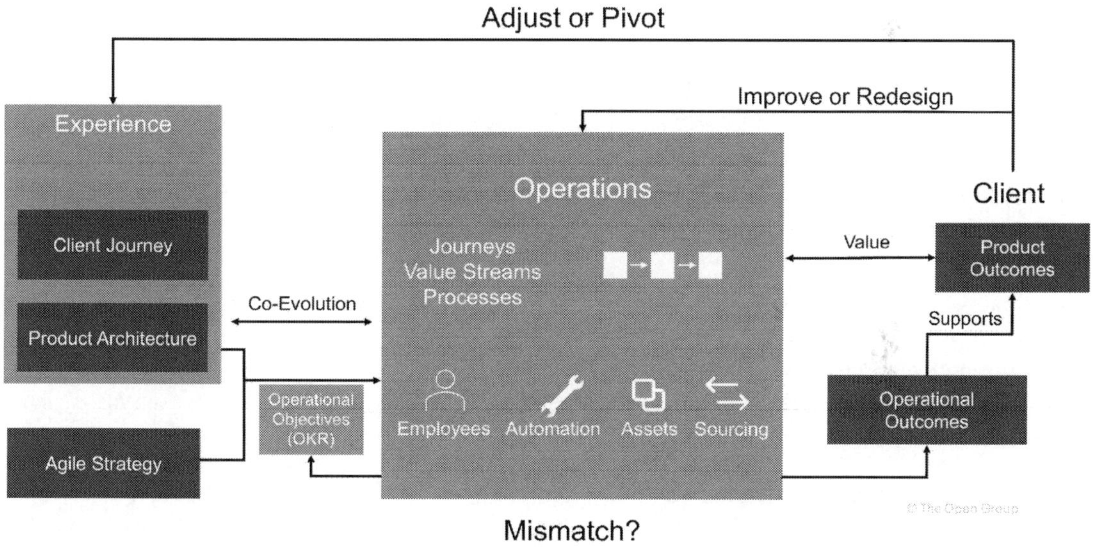

Figure 13-1: Operations Architecture

Operations management and strategy frameworks use the **capability** concept [MIT OCW, 2010] without providing a commonly agreed definition. There is confusion regarding what an operational capability is and what differentiates operational capabilities from resources or practices, because they are closely related [Wu et al., 2010].

Capabilities-based planning means different things to different people, and some aspects of its implementation have been appropriately controversial [Samaras & Willis, 2013].

13.1. Capability

The following definitions show that the term capability has several meanings:

- Capabilities are **self-contained business activities**, usually belonging to an end-to-end business process, which result in discrete outcomes [Blumberg et al., 2018]
- Business capability modeling is a technique for **representing an organization's business** independent of organizational structure, processes, people, or domains [Burton, 2014]
- An **ability** that an organization, person, or system possesses; for example, Enterprise Architecture, marketing, customer contact, or outbound telemarketing [C182]
- Capabilities are a person's **real freedoms** or opportunities to achieve functionings [Sen, 1992]
- The ability to achieve a **desired effect** under specified standards and conditions through a combination of means and ways [Samaras & Willis, 2013]
- Capability modeling treats the operating system as a **black box** and focuses on the desired and actual dimensions along which the system **does well** [Van Mieghem & Allon, 2015]

In the first three definitions, capabilities provide a representation of the enterprise. To differentiate capability modeling from other enterprise's representations, these definitions use qualifiers; for example:

- Sven Blumberg and his co-authors from McKinsey describe capabilities as **self-contained** activities, but do not explain what distinguishes a self-contained activity from a regular one
- Betsy Burton from Gartner® states this representation should be **independent of** organizational structure, processes, people, or domains
- The definition from Amartya Sen brings the idea of choice; when a person enjoys a capability, it implies they have freedom to exercise it

The definition from Constantine Samaras and Henry H. Willis relates capability to achieving a desired effect. A capability becomes a result that must be achieved, rather than a representation of the enterprise.

The definition from Jan Van Mieghem and Gad Allon adds a criterion: the operating system should be treated as a **black box**. This helps further filter out capabilities that are just activities carried out by the operating system.

This document asserts that operational capabilities should refer to the outcomes the operating system delivers; to what it does well or should do well.

The following examples illustrate the concept of operational capability:

- Delivering inexpensive food quickly from a standard menu with a well-defined quality level
- Computing an estimate of earned commissions in near real-time and issuing a payment next business day
- Quickly delivering a selection of over 10,000 new apparel styles at a reasonable cost

When capabilities are defined in this way, the focus is on the **what** and **why** questions. When capabilities remain in the problem space, it opens the range of possible solutions. When the term capability is used to mean an activity, even at an abstract or self-contained level, it raises two issues:

- Terminology becomes a source of confusion; the word **capability** meaning different things to different people
- The risk of limiting the range of possible solutions is higher

OKRs must be defined for each operational capability. The objective defines the "to-be" operational capability. Key results should measure operating system outcomes, not outputs or tasks. In applying the OKR discipline when defining operational capabilities, this document aims to:

- Remain consistent with the operations strategy definition as formulated by the Kellogg School of Management [Kellogg]
- Limit the confusion that results from using an unclear terminology

13.2. Operations Architecture Decisions

Operations architecture starts with an outward view that specifies the operational capabilities that products need. The analysis of operational capabilities is conducted for each targeted customer segment and is prioritized around cost, lead time, quality, flexibility, and agility.

Product architecture specifies what operations architecture must do particularly well: the required operational capabilities. As there is more than one way to architect operations, the solution space shall be explored by developing scenarios that combine several levers:

- Redesign or optimize the customer journeys and lean value streams that produce goods and services
- Develop an organization and culture capable of hiring and developing competent and motivated employees
- Revisit in-sourcing/out-sourcing trade-offs
- Evaluate production, logistic, distribution, and customer support units for fit
- Leverage technology, including AI, to raise the automation level
- Build "elastic" capacity to better match supply and demand

One of the major challenges of operations architecture is that trial and error is not an option when the magnitude of investments and time required to build new operational capabilities are too high. When operational decisions are difficult to reverse (Type 1), this document recommends following the method defined in Section 5.2 to test-drive the most critical decisions.

Many operations architecture decisions can be experimented and reversed if necessary (Type 2 decisions); for example:

- Lean value stream optimization can be done incrementally and does not require an “all or nothing” approach
- Setting up process competency centers and platforms facilitates the incremental automation of processes
- When a fact-based decision-making culture spreads, advanced analytics can incrementally improve the outcomes of operational decisions

Instead of applying these levers in isolation and in a piecemeal manner, this document recommends combining them to drive operational transformation guided by customer/UX outcomes.

Combining Lean redesign, advanced automation, and analytics provides a multiplier effect. This is illustrated in Figure 16-4.

Providing a great experience is challenging for insurers because they must balance the experience quality while collecting the most accurate information at a time when the customer is going through an unpleasant situation; for example, dealing with a traffic collision. Digital technology can help collect needed information without degrading experience quality.

13.3. Leveraging Digital Technology

Mobile technology combined with open APIs can reduce the burden of collecting the required information while improving its quality. The insurer can dispatch the vehicle’s location to emergency services. The driver can upload pictures of the damaged vehicles and file a claim with their smartphone.

The insurer can use advanced analytics to identify suspected fraud up front and expedite the claim handling process for the majority of claims. It can also triage the claims that require special investigation and streamline the process for others.

The manual and time-consuming tasks that are done by customer service agents such as verifying insurance coverage can be automated. This not only reduces costs, it improves customer experience by reducing the lead time required to settle claims.

By combining these levers, the insurer can at the same time dramatically improve operational efficiency and the quality of customer experience. This is an example of operations innovation that enables experience innovation. Operations and experience design are not conducted in sequence, but concurrently by a cross-functional team.

13.4. Example: AR

NOTE This fictional example is presented here for illustrative purposes only, to support the text and to enable a clearer understanding for the reader.

The two types of operations decisions are now illustrated with operations at AR, a fictitious apparel retailer.

When AR invested €100 million to open a logistics center for children's clothes to reduce transportation costs, this decision could not follow a trial and error approach.

When AR introduced the automatic replenishment of basic products (10-15% of all products) it did not require a big upfront investment. With the help of academics in operations management, AR developed an algorithm for allocating inventory at logistics centers to stores.

The decision to introduce automatic replenishment did not change the essence of the decision system; it only automated non-essential decisions to reduce the store manager's workload. This type of operational improvement can be conducted in an iterative manner using prototyping and experimentation.

The success of AR shows that operational excellence requires a great operational design and great people to carry it out. Neither can make up for the lack of the other.

The culture at AR encourages fast decision-making and autonomy, but not at the expense of operational excellence or brand consistency. Improvement ideas often come from the field. They are first tested and experimented locally.

When improvements are proven and ready for prime time, they are deployed incrementally on a global scale. For example, AR generalized the Japanese practice of having a five-minute staff meeting before opening time to discuss the day's objectives.

This practice has become known elsewhere as "the Japanese meeting". An AR executive commented, *"You'll get great ideas from the stores if you have the ability to hear them"*.

Continuous improvement is ingrained into the culture at AR, which has similarities with the Toyota way. A standard practice is a best practice at some point in time. It can be challenged and improved at any time. When the new practice is proven, it is applied with discipline and consistency across the board. As Toyota does, AR pays attention to disseminating its culture.

Regional directors, Human Resources (HR) directors, and country managers constantly visited stores to explain the culture directly to the staff and to monitor store performance.

AR illustrates how operations architecture and product architecture complement each other and must evolve concurrently.

13.5. Product Variety

Determining what should be the right level of product variety is a critical decision which requires proper interlock between product and operations strategies. In *Fast Innovation*, Michael George and his co-authors report that a formidable impediment to achieving operational excellence is the burgeoning complexity in a portfolio of offerings [George et al., 2005].

> If a company doubles the number of its offerings, the lead time to deliver those products or services will at least double, all other things being equal.

In itself, complexity is neither good nor bad; it depends on how complexity is perceived and valued by customers. Too often, complexity is driven by product owners who prioritize features rather than outcomes; see Section 16.4.4.

Higher product variety increases costs throughout the supply chain, production, distribution, and customer support.

More product variety also increases the likelihood of errors and operational problems. A European bank tried to understand the patterns that would drive demand for banking help desk support. It found a strong correlation between new product introduction and the rise in volume of help desk calls. Further investigation demonstrated that additional calls were due to either:

- Banking employees who did not know the new products enough to answer customer questions
- Defects in processes that did not handle new products well

In the retail industry, the more product variety in a category, the more inventory to be carried. The more inventory, the more working capital to fund that inventory, which hurts profitability.

Before offering too many products or variants of the same product, customer research should verify that:

- Customers are not confused
- Customers are willing to pay for this variety

In case of doubt, the opportunity to simplify the enterprise's product portfolio should be analyzed and experimented.

Chapter 14. Software Architecture

This chapter defines software architecture and covers key software architecture styles, patterns, and practices for the digital age.

14.1. Context

One of the challenges within Agile is designing and implementing solutions that provide the required software agility. It involves setting up and structuring solutions and development to enable business agility, which supports business model evolution and innovation. As outlined in product architecture (see Chapter 12) and operations architecture (see Chapter 13), the software architecture should be developed in parallel with these Architecture Building Blocks (ABBs) to achieve this objective.

14.2. What is Software Architecture?

Modern software systems are composed of multiple components that communicate and interact to deliver end-to-end solutions. Within the O-AA architecture development model, the software ABB:

- Deals with significant elements of the components (Componentization; see Section 11.4.2) of modern systems and their structure, as well as how they interact
- Has a strong focus not only on the structure of code but also on all the non-functional requirements:
  - Security; see Section 14.6.1
  - Reliability; see Section 14.6.2
  - Performance; see Section 14.6.3
  - Operability; see Section 14.6.4
  - Maintainability; see Section 14.6.5
  - Interoperability; see Section 14.6.6
- Covers the cross-cutting inner concerns of software (see Section 14.7), including selecting technology, planned evolution, and defining roadmaps by following market and community evolution

14.2.1. What is the Starting Point for Software Architecture?

The software architecture together with the operations architecture is positioned in the solution space. Inputs and starting points come from the problem space which is captured in the product architecture. The outcome of the experience design is translated into the product architecture; both are driven by value. The product architecture defines the modular components as highlighted in the Enterprise Segmentation Approach.

As such, the product architecture explores the modularity–integrality trade-off, defines how to decompose products into modular components and identifies product platforms; see Figure 9-4. This partitioning/segmentation is essential as it allows each part of the system to evolve as autonomously as possible.

14.2.2. Building Block Dependencies

Within an Agile context, organizations move away from the BDUF. Instead, software architecture is developed concurrently with the product architecture and the operations architecture; see Figure 9-2. The outcome of event storming and the domain-driven design building blocks help define the right modular structure of the software architecture, thus enabling greater software agility.

14.3. The Role and Responsibilities of the Software Architect

Software architects deal with system decomposition and their responsibilities and dependencies. They use models, such as the C4 Model [C4 Model], to describe software system architecture effectively through simple diagrams with boxes and lines.

The process and practices of the team(s) that produce software systems are also closely related to the topic of software architecture; these practices include:

- Requirements and use-case design
- Design of the software: Tactical building blocks and principles of domain-driven design
- Software-craftmanship practices
- Source code management: How the team works with version-control systems like Git™, and their branching strategy
- Testing strategy and practices: Test-driven development, behavior-driven development, property-based testing, etc.
- Release engineering (a reliable release process is the foundation of a reliable service [Beyer et al., 2016])
- Quality insurance and control
- Defining standards such as reference architectures, practices, tools, etc.
- Project management framework (Kanban, Scrum, etc.)

Besides the pure engineering role, software architects also need to have good soft and human skills in order to:

- Coach and mentor software engineers
- Help people to grow their skills
- Provide leadership through publications, blogs, conference talks
- Own the system's big picture
- Foster a culture of quality and improvement
- Be a good communicator and decision-maker

14.4. Event-Driven Architecture

As its name implies, event-driven architecture is centered around the concept of an "event"; that is, whenever something changes an event is issued to notify the interested consumers of such a change. An event is a powerful concept around which to build architecture because of the immutable and decoupling nature of events, as well as being a great way to design and build domain logic. The following sections detail the concepts and benefits of event-driven architecture, and then dive into the practical details of implementing such an architecture.

14.4.1. Concepts of Command, Query, and Event

First, before diving into the event-driven architecture style, it is necessary to define the *command*, *query*, and *event* concepts and their relations regarding time and state management:

- A command represents the intention of a system's user regarding what the system will do that will change its state
- A query asks a system for its current state as data in a specific model
- An event represents a fact about the domain from the past; for every state change the system performs it will publish an event to denote that state mutation

Figure 14-1 illustrates these time-related concepts.

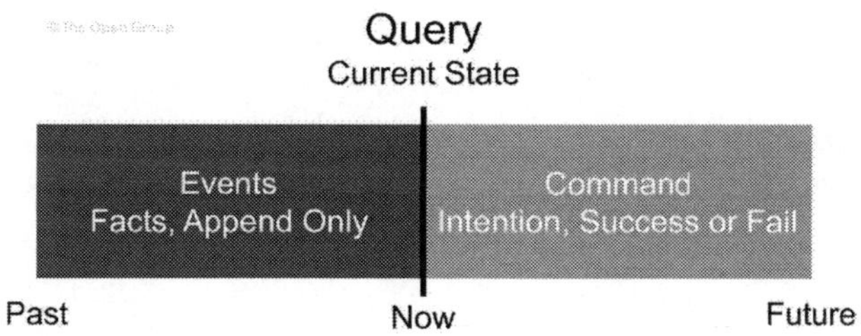

Figure 14-1: Concepts of Command, Query, and Event and their Relation to Time

14.4.1.1. Command

> A command is a request made to do something.

A command represents the intention of a system's user regarding what the system will do to change its state.

Command characteristics:

- The result of a command can be either success or failure; the result is an event
- In case of success, state change(s) must have occurred somewhere (otherwise nothing happened)
- Commands should be named with a verb, in the present tense or infinitive, and a nominal group coming from the domain (entity of aggregate type)

14.4.1.2. Query

> A query is a request asking to retrieve some data about the current state of a system.

A query asks a system for its current state as data with a specific model.

Query characteristics:

- A query never changes the state of the system (it is safe)
- Query processing is often synchronous
- The query contains fields with some value to match for, or an identifier
- A query can result in success or failure (not found), and long results can be paginated
- Queries can be named with "get" something (with identifiers as arguments) or "find" something (with values to match as arguments) describing the characteristics of the data to retrieve

14.4.1.3. Event

> Something happened that domain experts care about.
>
> — Evans 2003

An event represents a fact about the domain from the past; for every state change the system performs, it will publish an event to denote that state mutation.

Event characteristics:

- Events are primarily raised on every state transition that acknowledged the new fact as data in the system
  - Events can also represent every interaction with the system, even when there is no state transition as the interaction or the failure can itself be valuable; for example, the failure of a hotel booking command due to no-vacancies can be an opportunity to propose something else to the customer

- Events reference the command or query identifier that triggered them
- Events can be ignored, but cannot be retracted or deleted; only a new event can invalidate a previous one
- Events should be named with a past participle
- There are *internal* and *external* events:
  - *Internal* events are raised and controlled in the bounded context; see "Bounded Context" in Section 20.2
  - *External* events are from other upstream bounded contexts that are subscribed to

Events are published whenever there is an interaction with the system through a command (triggering or not a state transition; if not, the failure is also an event) or a query (no state transition, but the interaction is interesting in itself, such as for analytics purposes).

14.4.2. Benefits of Event-Driven Architecture

14.4.2.1. Better Handling of State, Concurrency, and Time

Basically, command and query represents the intention of end users regarding the system:

- A command represents the user asking the system to do something — they are **not safe** as they will mutate the state
- A query asks the current state of the system — they are **safe** as they will not mutate any data

This distinction relates to state and time management as well as expressing what the user wants the system to do and, once the state has mutated, the system will publish an event notifying the outside world that something has happened.

14.4.2.2. The Real World is Event-Driven

The world is event-driven as the present is very difficult to grasp and only the past and future can be clearly separated. The past is the only thing that can (almost) be certain and the event way of describing the result that occurred in the past, or should occur with the future system, is to use an event. It is as simple as "*this happened*". The event storming workshop format (see Chapter 19) is one of the most efficient and popular ways of grasping a domain for people involved in software design.

14.4.2.3. Loose-Coupling and Strong Autonomy

Event mechanisms loosen the coupling between the event publisher and the subscribers; the event publisher does not know its subscribers and their numbers. This focus on an event also enforces a better division of concerns and responsibility as too many events or coarse-grained events can be a design issue.

14.4.2.4. Focus on Behavior and Changeability

Commands and events force software designers to think about the system's behavior instead of placing too much focus on its structure.

Software designers and developers should focus on separating their domain logic between:

- **Contextual data**:Retrieving data for that command to execute
- **Decision logic**:Whether this command is actually able to operate given the current contextual state (that includes any data coming from external systems, such as market data as well as time)
- **State mutation logic**:Once the context data is retrieved and decisions are made, the domain logic can issue what the state mutations are — whether internal or external
- **State mutation execution**:This is where transactional mechanisms come into play, being automated for a single data source or distributed using a Saga pattern (see Section 14.4.7) and compensating transactions
- **Command execution result**: The command execution result, be it a success or a failure, is expressed as an event published for private or public consumption

This separation of different concerns leads to greater changeability of software systems.

14.4.2.5. Better Operability with Events: Stability, Scalability, Resilience, and Observability

Commands can be used to better represent the user's intention, and fit well with the deterministic domain logic that benefits from consensus algorithms, such as the Raft Consensus Algorithm [Raft], to distribute the execution of business logic on several machines for better resiliency and scalability, along with some sharding logic [Ries, 2009].

Good operability needs good observability of the running system, and this is reached by strong logging practices. Good logs are actually events in disguise; replaying a system's behavior through logs is actually following the flow of technical and domain events that exhibit what the system has done.

14.4.3. Event Sourcing

> The main idea of *event sourcing* is to store all the events that represent stimuli, asking for state change of the system, and then being able to reconstruct the system's end-state by applying the domain logic for all of these events in order.

The event store becomes the source of truth and the system's end-state is the end result of applying all these events. Event-driven architecture does not mean event sourcing.

14.4.4. Command Query Responsibility Segregation (CQRS)

> CQRS is an architecture style that advises us to use a different data model and storage for command (asking for a state change, *aka* a "write") and query (asking for the current state, *aka* a "read").

The main motivation of CQRS to use these dedicated models is to simplify and gain better performance for interactions with a system that is unbalanced (read-intensive/write-scarce or write-intensive/read-scarce interactions). If CQRS simplifies each model in itself, the synchronization and keeping all the models up-to-date also brings some complexity. CQRS can be implemented sometimes without proven requirements and can lead to some over-engineering.

14.4.5. Command, Query, and Event Metadata

Every command, query, and event should share the same metadata, essentially showing who is emitting when, where, and with what relevance. Also, each artifact should be uniquely identified. This metadata can be the following:

- Identifier: An identifier, such as a Universally Unique Identifier (UUID) or a Uniform Resource Name (URN) [IETF®, 2017]
- Type: An identifier of the type of this artifact; it should be properly namespaced to be unique among several systems
- Emitted-by: Identifier of the person or system emitting the command/query/event
- Emitted-at: A timestamp in Coordinated Universal Time (UTC) of when the command/query/event was emitted by the source
- Source: The source system that emitted the artifact (in the case of a distributed system, it can be the particular machine/virtual machine that emitted that artifact)
- Various key: For partitioning the artifact among one or several values (typically, the command issued for a particular use organization of the system, etc.)
- Reference: For event, the command or query that triggers that particular event
- Content-type: The content type of the payload
- Payload: A payload as a data structure containing everything relevant to the purpose of the artifact

The Cloud Native Computing Foundation (CNCF) issued a specification describing event data in a common way [CloudEvents].

14.4.6. System Consuming Other Systems' Events

Events that originate from a bounded context must be explicitly defined and then they can be consumed by the bounded contexts of others. The traditional domain-driven design context map and the various strategic patterns of bounded context integration are very useful tools for mapping the landscape.

It is also recommended to **translate each event** that comes from another bounded context **into a command** from the context that consumes it, to denote explicitly the intention behind the event's consumption.

14.4.7. Ensuring Global Consistency with Saga Patterns

To ensure global consistency across multiple systems mechanisms are needed to "rollback" or compensate the effect of applying a command to get the system's global state back to a consistent one (a consistent state does not mean reverting to the state that existed before applying all those commands; a consistent state is where all the sub-systems are consistent with their data).

As an example, think about the way a bank "cancels" a contentious movement in an account; the bank does not remove the contentious movement, instead it issues a new movement compensating the effect of the bad one. For instance, given a contentious debit movement of $100, the bank issues a credit movement of $100 to get back to a consistent balance even if the movements list of the account now exhibits two movements canceling each other.

As a first step, identifying the inverse of each command that will cancel the effect or "compensate" a former one is necessary. The Saga patterns describe the structure and behavior needed to attain such a consistency goal: in case of the failure of one command, the other services issue new commands that compensate the former one, and thus "rollback" the whole distributed transaction as a result. Two types of the Saga pattern exist: choreography and orchestration.

14.4.7.1. Saga Pattern: Choreography

> In the choreography Saga pattern, each service produces and listens to the events of other services and decides whether an action should be taken.

- Benefits:
  - Simple and easy to understand and build
  - All services participating are loosely-coupled as they do not have direct knowledge of each other; a good fit if the transaction has four or five steps
- Drawbacks:
  - Can quickly become confusing if extra steps are added to the transaction as it is difficult to track which services listen to which events
  - Risks adding cyclic dependency between services as they subscribe to each other's events

14.4.7.2. Saga Pattern: Orchestration

> In the orchestration Saga pattern, a "coordinator" service is responsible for centralizing the Saga pattern's decision-making and sequencing business logic.

- Benefits:
  - Avoids cyclic dependencies between services
  - Centralizes the orchestration of the distributed transaction
  - Reduces complexity for participants as they only need to execute/reply to commands
  - Easier to implement and test; rollback is easier
- Drawbacks:
  - Risk of concentrating too much logic in the orchestration
  - Increases the infrastructure complexity as there is one extra service

14.5. Hexagonal Architecture: Why? Benefits?

One of the greatest challenges of Application Architecture is to reach a good separation of concerns between the domain, application, and infrastructure logic in the code. Keeping the domain logic clean of any technologic concerns (persistence, distribution, User Interface (UI), etc.) is essential. Big maintainability and evolvability troubles occur when domain logic is scattered all over the codebase. Hexagonal architecture decouples the application, domain, and infrastructure logic of the considered system.

Hexagonal architecture, created by Alistair Cockburn [Cockburn, 2005], brings an interchangeability of adapter implementation and, therefore, a great suppleness in composing the domain with various ways of interacting with the software, as well as implementing infrastructure capabilities. Hexagonal architecture allows an effective decoupling of application, domain, and infrastructure concerns.

Hexagonal architecture is a departure from layered architecture that is considered not to be solving correctly the coupling challenge between the different "layers". The name "hexagonal architecture" was used because a hexagon is a shape that composes easily, has a great natural symmetry, and allows people drawing schema to have room to insert ports and adapters wherever they need to. There is a notable symmetry not only denoted by its shape, but also with the inbound ports and adapters on the left side and outbound on the right side.

14.5.1. Domain, Application, and Infrastructure Code

The domain code is the code dealing with the domain concepts and related behavior. The application code is the code that interacts with the external world. It makes the software concrete; applications receive requests from end users or other systems.

14.5.2. Inside and Outside, Ports and Adapters

Hexagonal architecture emphasizes that the "inside" of an application, its domain core, must be kept safe from the "outside", the application and infrastructure logic that embeds the domain into the real world. The domain part of an application is its most valuable asset. Application and infrastructure code change very rapidly given the pace of technology evolutions; just look at the changes in the front-end world in recent years.

All dependencies in the application are directed toward the center of the hexagon: the domain. The application and infrastructure logic depend on the domain.

Isolating the code of the domain from the rest of the code is crucial. To ensure the domain part is valuable and not anemic, architects need to ensure that all the domain logic is in the domain part and not scattered in the application and infrastructure code. A good enforcing practice is to automate business scenario tests to run on the domain code only, which ensures that no logic stays in other parts. Domain code should be runnable as a stand-alone library, capable of executing all the domain logic in-memory.

Ports represent the boundaries of the domain. Adapters are any implementation that adheres to the protocol exposed by a port and follows the correct behavior. Adapters can be plugged into the domain to make use of its logic.

This pattern decouples interaction from the domain code by using interfaces located in the domain part (ports) and implementations (adapters) located in the application and infrastructure parts that are wired into the domain, as shown in Figure 14-2. Hexagonal architecture makes heavy use of the interface/implementation decoupling mechanism found in many programming languages nowadays.

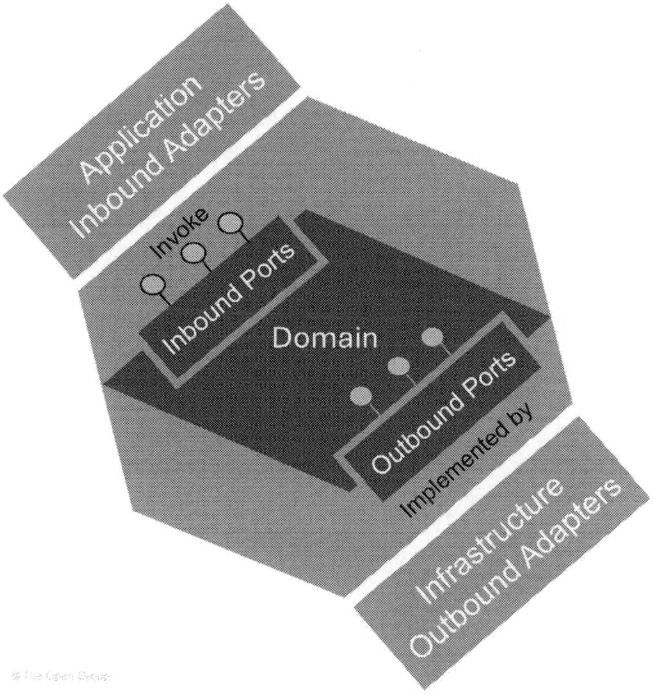

Figure 14-2: Illustration of Hexagonal Architecture with Inbound and Outbound Ports and Adapters

14.5.3. Inbound Ports and Adapters (or Primary, Driving, Left, API)

Inbound ports are entry points to the domain. These ports are "driving" the domain; they receive requests from other systems or end users and have the domain react on these stimuli. Inbound ports are located on the left side of the hexagon. Inbound ports are sometimes named as primary, left, driving, or simply API to the domain.

Inbound adapters are implementations of inbound ports that invoke the domain entry point. Common inbound adapter examples are: REST API, Graphical User Interface (GUI), or Command Line Interface (CLI). Inbound adapters are "driving" the domain.

14.5.4. Outbound Ports and Adapters (or Secondary, Driven, Right, SPI)

Outbound ports are exit points invoked from the domain. These ports are "driven" by the domain to perform infrastructure-related tasks. These ports expose contracts abstracted from the underlying infrastructure. Outbound ports are located on the right side of the hexagon. The interfaces that represent these ports are located in the domain code, their implementation being outside of it in the infrastructure code. Outbound ports are sometimes named as secondary, right, driven, or simply Service Provider Interface (SPI).

Outbound adapters are implementations of outbound ports that are invoked from within the domain. The domain exposes outbound ports as the interface of the operations it intends to invoke while being completely agnostic of their implementation; infrastructure code then implements these ports. Of course, implementation of the interface must obey the Liskov Substitution Principle (LSP) [LSP] that states that components must be interchangeable regarding not only their operations signature but also, and in particular, their behavior. Outbound adapters are "driven" by the domain. Common outbound adapter examples are: Database repository, Message-Oriented Middleware (MOM), Identity and Access Management (IAM) systems, and other external systems upon which the domain depends.

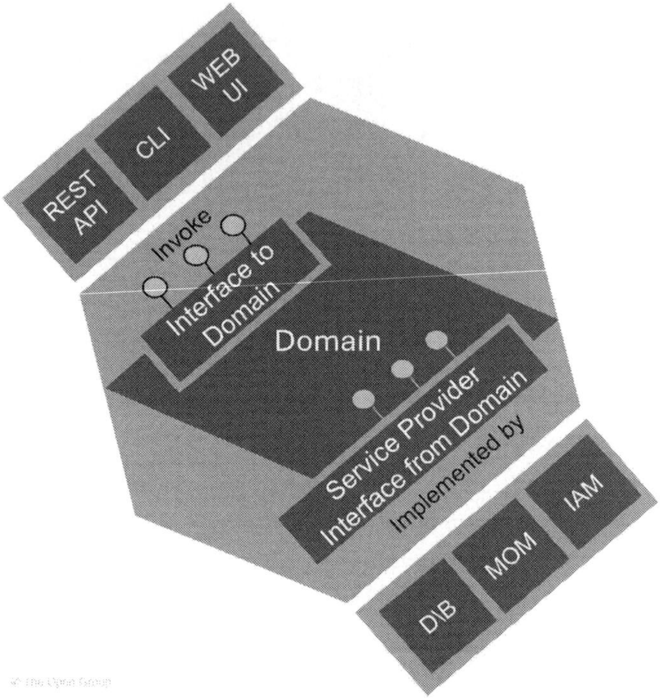

Figure 14-3: Hexagonal Architecture with Example Adapters

14.6. Non-Functional Software Requirements

Software architects must assess the priority of every non-functional requirement of the system they are building. Given that it is impossible to reach the maximum for every quality attribute, and that cost and delay add themselves to the equation, trade-offs must be made given the system context and the priorities given. By the way, a name with no negation would be better, so *Operational Requirements* could be instead of non-functional requirements, but people are used to them.

The following sections give an overview of software quality attributes that must be dealt with by software architects.

14.6.1. Security

Major security topics are:

- Global architecture view and governance of IAM
- Proper and unique identification of persons and systems accessing software systems
- Standard authentication modes
- Authorization: what permissions on what resources for who, and what workflow services?
- Audit logs of access
- Monitoring abilities (metrics and alarms)
- Data security and privacy (including logs produced by the software itself)
- Security incident management
- System and communication protection
- Integrity and confidentiality of data at rest and in transit with encryption, signature, and key management
- Vulnerability and patch management (breach testing)

Software security needs a plan and a budget defined by business, security teams, and IT teams.

14.6.2. Reliability

> Software reliability is defined as the probability of failure-free software operation for a specified period of time in a specified environment [ANSI/IEEE].

Reliability is decomposed into three quality attributes: maturity, recoverability, and fault tolerance.

14.6.2.1. Maturity (*aka* Stability)

> Maturity is about decreasing the failure rate and downtime of software systems.

Maturity relates to the mitigation of negative side effects that change can introduce (especially with high velocity development). Maturity can be measured with mean time between failures, test coverage, and availability of integration and deployment pipelines.

Practices that improve maturity are:

- Standardized development cycle
- Thorough tests (unit, integration, end-to-end)
- Fully automated continuous integration (test, packaging, build, release)

- Continuous deployment pipeline (with staging, canary, production phase)
- Progressive rollout of new version (deploy, release, post-release) in relation to feature toggling
- Dependencies (known with fallback in case of failure)
- Routing and discovery
- Deprecation and decommissioning

14.6.2.2. Recoverability

> Recoverability is about minimizing the duration to get the system back up after a failure or incident, and reducing the impact upon users.

Recoverability can be measured with mean time of failure detection and alert, mean time to mitigate, mean time to resolve, recovery point and recovery time, and data backup coverage.

Practices that improve recoverability are:

- Good failure detection
- Reversion mechanisms (ability to roll back to previous version of code and data with backup)
- Process for handling incidents and outages
  - Levels and impact of failures
  - Clearly defined mitigation strategies
  - Five stages of incident response (assess, coordinate, mitigate, resolve, follow-up)

14.6.2.3. Fault Tolerance

> Fault tolerance is the property of a system to continue operating properly in the event of the failure (or one or more faults) within some of its components.

Fault tolerance can be measured with failure rate and proportion of degraded features after failure.

Practices that improve fault tolerance are:

- Avoiding single points of failure (redundancy)
- Proper fault isolation (circuit breaker, bulkheads, etc.)
- Identifying failure scenarios on all layers: hardware, network, dependency, internal

- Resiliency testing:
    - Unit, integration, end-to-end tests
    - Regular/automated load testing
    - Chaos testing (including degraded network conditions)
- Implementing the “stability” patterns [Nygard, 2018]

14.6.3. Performance

14.6.3.1. Scalability

> Scalability is the ability of the system to cope with increased load, related to how the processing of tasks is divided and conquered.

Scalability can be measured with Requests per Second (RPS), latency percentiles, Queries per Second (QPS), and business metrics (*x* per second, percentiles).

Practices that improve scalability are:

- Effective load testing
- Quantitive growth scales are well known (RPS, QPS)
- Qualitative growth scales are well known (e.g., business metrics growth scale related to the system)
- Capacity planning is automated and performed on a scheduled basis
- Scalability of dependencies is known and managed
- Traffic:
    - Patterns are understood (burst, etc.)
    - Can be re-routed in case of failures

14.6.3.2. Performance

> Performance is described by throughput (the number of requests processed per second) and latency (the duration it takes to serve a request).

Bare performance is different to performance with an increased load; system performance and efficiency change when load is increased, and a system with poor performance during unitary usage has fewer chances to get a better performance with multiple concurrent usages. Performance is usually measured by: RPS, latency percentiles, QPS, business metrics (*x* per second, percentiles).

Practices that improve performance are:

- Effective load testing
- Bottlenecks of resources and requirements have been identified (profiling)
- Handling and processing tasks in a performant manner (favor statelessness, non-blocking Input/Output (IO))
- Handling and storing data in a scalable and performant way (best database for a use case?)

14.6.3.3. Efficiency

> Efficiency measures the quantity of resources used by the application to process its tasks.

Efficiency can be measured with RPS, QPS, and business metrics (maximum *x* per second, percentiles).

Practices to improve efficiency are:

- Effective load testing
- Use hardware resources efficiently
  - Dedicated or shared hardware?
  - Resource abstraction or allocation technology?
- Resource awareness
  - Resource requirements are known (Central Processing Unit (CPU), Random Access Memory (RAM), etc.)
  - How much traffic one instance can handle (CPU/RAM required?)
  - Resource bottlenecks?

14.6.4. Operability

> A system with good operability is one that minimizes the time and effort needed in order to make and keep it running. Similarly, it makes the diagnosis and anticipation of errors straightforward, as well as easing unplanned intervention.

14.6.4.1. Observability

> Observability is a property of a system that exposes high-level observation metrics of its health and inner workings, state, and context.

Observations are event logs, metrics, traces (end-to-end flow in case of distributed system), and errors with context. Practices to improve observability are:

- Collecting logs, metrics, and traces effectively for each layer: Host, infrastructure, platform, application
  - Scalable and cost-effective centralized logging solution?
  - Does logging accurately reflect the state of the system at any given time?
- Dashboard with key metrics and easy to interpret (how is the system working?)
- Effective alerting: Appropriate thresholds, actionable, with entries in an on-call runbook
- Building a culture of engineering based on facts and feedback

14.6.4.2. Documentation

> A system needs to provide good documentation and be well-understood to be production-ready.

Practices to improve the understanding of systems are:

- Comprehensive and useful documentation, updated regularly (distinguish "How-to" and "Why" documentation, living documentation whenever possible)
- Documentation contains:
  - Descriptions of the system
  - Architecture diagrams
  - On-call information, runbook (updated after postmortem)
  - Endpoints, request flow, dependencies
  - Frequently Asked Questions (FAQs)
- Architecture is reviewed and audited frequently (with shared checklist)
- Developers understand production-readiness standards

14.6.4.3. Deployability

> Deployability measures the ease of deploying a new version of software in a target environment.

Some practices to improve deployability are:

- Environments parity (development, staging, production, etc.)
- Build and deployment pipeline with different stages: build, packaging, testing, deployment, releasing in canary environment (small percentage of production traffic), slow rollout to full production
- Versioned configuration, separated from code
- Proper versioning scheme, semantics, and behavior with each release
- Treat dependency as attached resources
- Fast startup time and graceful shutdown
- Zero-downtime mechanisms

14.6.5. Maintainability

> Maintainability represents the capacity of software to be modified. Modifications include fix, improve, or any adaptation needed due to software environment or requirements changes.

Maintainability designates the amount of effort needed to modify the software. A lot of practices exist to improve maintainability; some widely accepted practices are:

- Software-craftmanship approach to software development:
  - Activities that improve developers' skills: kata, pair programming, mob programming
  - Define software quality criteria:
    - Meet user needs through clearly defined use cases
    - Develop with controlled costs and deadlines
    - Intrinsic qualities of the project: modularity, stability, scalability, readability
  - Build and maintain teams of passionate, involved, pragmatic, humble, and legitimate developers
  - Promote communication and pairing practices in order to maintain the team's homogeneity in its practices and values
  - Let the developers choose their tools as far as possible and within the constraints
  - Encourage an environment conducive to design practices (domain-driven design), testing (behavior-driven development and test-driven development), and frequent code refactoring

  - Set up moments of exchange on techniques and practices so that each employee (business, technical, manager) can learn from the knowledge of the other
  - Rely on the community to benefit from its innovations (conferences, meetups, etc.)
- Domain-driven design
- Test-driven development
- eXtreme programming practices (still valuable):
  - Coding practices: Simplicity, refactor mercilessly, develop coding standards, develop a common vocabulary
  - Developer practices: Integrate continuously, practice pair programming, test-driven development, collect code ownership
  - Business practices: Sustainable pace, add customers to the team, planning game, release regularly

Maintainability can be refined further into quality attributes, as detailed in the next sections.

14.6.5.1. Testability

> Testability refers to the ability of software to have its behavior validated against some accepted criteria.

Elements promoting testability are:

- Stateless design and distinction between mutable and immutable data; the functional programming approach greatly increases testability
- Test datasets that do not vary between execution
- Easy substitution of component implementation behind the interface — usually the greater the coupling and mutable state inside the software, the lower the testability, so a good separation of concerns, low coupling, and high cohesion promotes good testability

14.6.5.2. Coupling, Modularity, and Stability

> Coupling is a property indicating the level of dependencies between components of a system; it is a global property obtained from the calculation of incoming and outgoing dependencies for each component.
>
> Modularity expresses the topology of the architecture with the number of components dependent on a particular component.
>
> Stability refers to the ability of a software product to avoid unintended effects as a result of software modification.

14.6.6. Interoperability

Interoperability refers to the ability of software systems to exchange data and use common protocols to do so. The elements that promote good interoperability are to be classified according to:

- **Semantic interoperability**,which deals with the meaning of information (i.e., words) exchanged between entities

  It is directly related to the domain model; entities agree on the meaning of the data they exchange. Semantic interoperability characterizes the ability to agree on:

  - The context of the exchange that defines the meaning of words (e.g., a person is seen as a patient in a health application and as a citizen in a public administration application)
  - The process of the exchange: what are the actors, events, and activities related to the exchange?
  - The meaning and structure of the information exchanged needs some kind of agreement, often through documentation

    There are some initiatives on the web for structuring common data [Schema.org] and various industries have their own data exchange standards.

- **Syntactic and technical interoperability**, which conveys information defined at the semantic level and formatted at the syntactic level

  It deals with technical norms and standards for:

  - Navigation and restitution technologies
  - Technologies for data exchanges between systems (e.g., REST API over HTTP)
  - The basic technologies necessary for exchanges (infrastructure, including network protocols)

Software interoperability is contextual to its environment and is promoted through easy connection with other middleware services that allow quick and easy integration. Some communication protocols like REST API over HTTP are now ubiquitous and provide good openness, but context should drive particular technology usage. Asynchronous communication can also be considered but is more tied to a particular technology stack (e.g., Kafka®, etc.). When dealing with legacy middleware, integration or a bridge can be provided (e.g., Cross File Transfer (CFT), MQSeries®, etc.). The implementation of security and “meta” mechanisms in data that transits through middleware (who, where, when, what) is also an important concern.

14.7. Software Cross-Cutting Concerns

Software architects need to address several cross-cutting concerns in their decisions while building software:

- Programming language choices: Platform more than languages (Common Language Runtime (CLR), Java® Virtual Machine, JavaScript™ engine, etc.); in choosing the best tool for the job, consider the language ecosystem and available skills
- Testing strategy: A test strategy provides a rational deduction from organizational, high-level objectives of quality to actual test activities to meet those objectives, and a modern testing approach and techniques are crucial to balance the speed of delivery with actual quality

  Tests are the safety net of modern software practices like continuous integration/delivery and, beyond the fundamental test-driven development approach, testing techniques have been greatly increased and enhanced recently (generative and property-based testing, resiliency testing, etc.).
- Persistence of data: Particularly the consistency aspect of data, and the storage model (document, relational, graph, etc.)
- Session handling
- Business rules
- UI with unidirectional architecture
- Parallelism and concurrency
- Load balancing and fault tolerance
- Error handling
- Configuration
- Stability patterns
- Monitoring and troubleshooting: logging, metrics, alerting
- Release, packaging, and deployment mechanisms
- Versioning
- Documentation (living documentation)
- Batch processing: May affect multiple parts of a system at once, which requires a consistent approach for scheduling, reliability, performance, and data handling to keep the whole architecture stable and predictable
- Reporting
- Legacy migration or integration strategy

Chapter 15. Software Management of Computing Resources

Digital means that a signal of interest is being represented by a sequence or array of numbers. Analog means that a signal is represented by the value of some continuously variable quantity. This variable can be the voltage or current in an electrical circuit [Steiglitz, 2019].

The shift from analog to digital makes it possible to control hardware with software. IT infrastructure is becoming fully digital. Compute and storage resources are digital and have been virtualized for quite a while. Add network infrastructure virtualization to the mix and an unlimited number of possibilities for system administrators is created.

Digital technologies enable the decoupling of infrastructure from the underlying hardware, turning it into data and code. When infrastructure is becoming code, software practices can replace the old way of working; for example, DevOps, which merges source control systems, test-driven development, and continuous integration with infrastructure management.

The software engineering discipline is spreading into domains where the combination of software and hardware creates new and powerful capabilities; for example, autonomous vehicles and connected objects.

This chapter will briefly introduce Infrastructure as Code and illustrate the power of software engineering for managing hardware using the DevOps (see Section 15.2) and SRE (see Section 15.3) examples.

15.1. Infrastructure as Code

Infrastructure as Code is the process of managing and provisioning computer data centers through machine-readable definition files, rather than through physical hardware configuration or interactive configuration tools.

The machine-readable definition files provide a descriptive model describing an abstract model of the hardware and infrastructure resources that are needed. This descriptive model is using the same versioning as DevOps teams use for source code. Infrastructure as Code tools transform this descriptive model using dynamic infrastructure platforms to create the actual configuration files required by the hardware and infrastructure components.

A dynamic infrastructure platform is the system that provides computing resources in a way that can be programmatically allocated and managed.

Most common dynamic infrastructure platforms are public clouds (e.g., AWS or Microsoft® Azure®) or private clouds that provide server, storage, and networking resources.

Infrastructure can also be managed dynamically using virtualization systems or even bare metal with tools such as Cobbler [Cobbler] or Foreman [Foreman].

15.2. DevOps Example

DevOps is a way of running systems requiring developers and operators to participate together in the entire system lifecycle, from design through development and production support. Operators use the same techniques as developers for their systems work (test, automation, etc.).

The DevOps approach drives better organizational performance by relying on an organization's ability to efficiently deliver and operate software systems to achieve their goals.

15.2.1. DevOps Objectives: Organizational and Software Delivery Performance

Organizational performance measures the ability of an organization to achieve commercial and non-commercial goals such as: profitability, productivity, market share, number of customers, operation efficiency, customer satisfaction, quantity and quality of products or services delivered, etc.

The outcomes of better performance are met when capabilities (see Section 15.2.4) are implemented and principles (see Section 15.2.3) followed; those capabilities relying on behavior and practices (see Section 15.2.5) from development and operations teams using tools (see Section 15.2.6) to do so.

15.2.2. Four Key Metrics

A key takeaway of the DORA State of DevOps report [DORA, 2019] is the four key metrics that support and measure the software delivery performance of an organization:

- **Lead time of changes**: The time it takes to go from code committed to code, successfully running in production
- **Deployment frequency**: The number of deployments to production per unit of time, aggregated by teams, departments, and the whole organization
- **Mean time to restore**: The time to restore service, or Mean Time to Recover (MTTR) metric, calculates the average time it takes to restore service
- **Change failure rate**: The change failure rate is a measure of how often deployment failures occur in production that require immediate remedy (in particular, rollbacks)

These four metrics provide a high-level systems view of software delivery and performance, and predict an organization's ability to achieve its goals. They can be summarized in terms of throughput (deployment and lead time) and stability (MTTR and change fail). A fifth useful metric is the **availability of systems** (a count-based availability is also more meaningful than a time-based one.

15.2.3. DevOps Principles

The DevOps approach is based on some fundamental principles that are listed below; some principles come from the Agile Manifesto [Agile Manifesto] but some are specific to operations; for example, automation and repeatability:

- **Continuous delivery of value**: Deliver working software that delivers value to end users frequently with the shortest lead time possible; working software in the hands of the user is the primary measure of progress
- **Collaboration**: Business people, operators, and developers must work together daily — face-to-face conversation is the most efficient and effective method of conveying information to and within a development team
- **Feedback and testing**: Feedback is crucial for every activity in the Agile and DevOps chain; without that feedback loop developers and operators cannot have any confidence that their actions have the expected result, and a good testing strategy supports that feedback loop, with tests taking place early and frequently to enable continuous integration
- **Culture and people**: Build projects around motivated individuals, giving them the environment and support they need, and trusting them to get the job done; the best architectures, requirements, and designs emerge from self-organizing teams
- **Continuous improvement**: At regular intervals, the team reflects on how to become more effective, then tunes and adjusts its behavior accordingly
- **Design and simplicity**: Attention to technical excellence and good design enhances agility; simplicity is essential, reducing toil and maximizing the amount of work not done are crucial (toil is the kind of work tied to running a production service that tends to be manual, repetitive, automatable, tactical, devoid of enduring value, and that scales linearly as a service grows)
- **Automation**: Assigning tasks to the machine to avoid human intervention cuts down on repetitious work in order to minimize mistakes and save time and energy for the human operator

  The gain from automation, apart from saving time, is consistency, scalability, faster action and repair, and robustness; automated actions provide a "platform" (something that can be extended and applied broadly).

  The drawbacks of automation are that the effects of an action can be very broad; once an error is introduced the consequences can be enormous (does it strike a chord?) — that is why some stability patterns, like a governor, are useful in such cases.

  Automation means "code" and, like developers that implement best practices to manage their code, operations engineers should do the same with their automated tasks: design it (what are the problems/solutions?), build it, test it, and deploy it.

  A good test coverage and testing habits within the team are mandatory for automation to deliver its results; testing provides a safety net and confidence that changes can be deployed without breaking anything.

- **Self-service**: Enables consumers of services to use services independently as the IT team has done what was needed beforehand to ensure there are minimal interruptions and delays in service delivery, thus achieving a state of continuous delivery
- **Shift left**: An approach in which testing is performed earlier in the lifecycle (moved left on the project timeline) so that the team focuses on quality and works on problem prevention instead of detection as testing begins and decisions are validated early in development and delivery

  Shift-left testing helps to prevent waste on uncovered requirements, architecture, and design defects due to late testing.

- **Repeatability**: DevOps is all about creating a repeatable and reliable process for delivering software, where every step in the delivery pipeline should be deterministic and repeatable: provisioning environment, building artifacts, deploying those particular facts, etc.

15.2.4. Capabilities

The capabilities leading to better software delivery performance are:

- Continuous delivery
- Architecture
- Lean Product Development and management
- Improved organizational culture

15.2.5. Behavior and Practices

DevOps promotes a set of good practices:

- **Infrastructure as Code**: Infrastructure is code and should be developed and managed as such (see the automation and repeatability principles [Section 15.2.3]), particularly the testing part to ensure the operations code is reliable and safe; testing the “automated tasks” means checking that some acceptance criteria are met
- **Test automation** of application code as well as operations code
- **Application and infrastructure monitoring**
- **Automated dashboards**
- **Automated release and deployment**
- **Continuous “everything”**: Integration, testing, delivery, and deployment
  - **Continuous integration**: The process of integrating new code written by developers with a mainline or “master” branch frequently throughout the day, in contrast to having developers working on independent feature branches for weeks or months at a time and merging their code back to the master branch only when it is completely finished
  - **Continuous delivery**: A set of general software engineering principles that allow for frequent releases of new software through the use of automated testing and continuous integration;

closely related, continuous delivery is often thought of as taking continuous integration one step further, that beyond simply making sure new changes can be integrated without causing regressions to automated tests, continuous delivery means that these changes can be deployed

  - **Continuous deployment**: The process of deploying changes to production by defining tests and validations to minimize risk; while continuous delivery makes sure that new changes can be deployed, continuous deployment means that they get deployed into production
  - **Continuous improvement**: Retrospective and postmortem activities performed by the operations team following every incident or outage

15.2.6. DevOps Tools

Categories of tools that support a DevOps approach:

- Analytics
- Application performance management
- Cloud infrastructure
- Collaboration
- Containers and orchestration solution
- Continuous integration/deployment
- Provisioning and change management
- Configuration and deployment
- Information Technology Service Management (ITSM)
- Logging
- Monitoring
- Project and issue tracking
- Source control management
- Functional and non-functional testing tools

15.3. Site Reliability Engineering (SRE)

> SRE is what you get when you treat operations as if it is a software problem.

SRE is a job role and a set of practices from production engineering and operations at Google and now largely adopted by the industry. An SRE team is responsible for the availability, latency, performance, efficiency, change management, monitoring, emergency response, and capacity planning of their services.

For details about SRE, refer to:

- *Site Reliability Engineering: How Google Runs Production Systems* [Beyer et al., 2016]
- *The Site Reliability Workbook: Practical Ways to Implement SRE* [Beyer et al., 2018]
- *Building Secure and Reliable Systems, Best Practices for Designing, Implementing, and Maintaining Systems* [Adkins et al., 2020]

15.3.1. SRE Principles

- Operations is a software problem
- Managed by Service-Level Objectives (SLOs) and Service-Level Indicators (SLIs)
- Managing risk with an error budget; a happy medium between velocity and unreliability
- Work to minimize toil (manual, repetitive, automatable, reactive, grows at least as fast as its source)
- Automation
- Shared ownership with developers
- Use the same tooling as software engineers

15.3.2. SRE Practices

15.3.2.1. On-Call in Parallel with Project Work

On-call engineers take care of their assigned operations by managing outages and performing changes on production systems within minutes. As soon as a page is received, the on-call engineer is expected to triage the problem and work toward its resolution, possibly involving other team members and escalating as needed. Project work should be at least 50% of SRE time, and of the remainder no more than 25% has to be spent on-call; the rest being operational, non-project work.

Why is this practice important? A balanced on-call activity alongside engineering work allows scaling production activities, maintaining high reliability despite the increasing complexity and volume of systems to manage.

15.3.2.2. Incident and Emergency Response

Everything fails, all the time. A proper response to failure and emergency, with a clear line of command and roles, a working record of actions, etc., takes preparation and frequent, hands-on training. Key activities are needed to reduce mean time to recovery and reduce stress while working on problems:

- Formulating an incident management strategy in advance
- Structuring this plan to scale smoothly
- Regularly putting the plan to use

15.3.2.3. Postmortem, "Near Miss" Culture

Completing a postmortem ensures that any incident is documented, all contributing root causes are well understood, and effective preventive actions are put in place to reduce the likelihood and/or impact of recurrence. Even "near misses" should contribute to improvement. A key factor of success is to commit to a blameless culture and spread the values of these postmortems by sharing them.

15.3.2.4. Managing Load

Managing load is important to ensure good performance and reliability, and services should produce reasonable but suboptimal results if overloaded. Every request on the system has to be correctly balanced both between data centers and also inside the data center to distribute work to the individual servers that process the user request. Avoiding overload is a goal of load balancing policies, but eventually some part of any system will become overloaded. The graceful handling of overload conditions is fundamental to running a reliable serving system, ensuring no data center receives more traffic than it has the capacity to process. The rules are:

- Redirect when possible
- Serve degraded results when necessary
- Handle resource errors transparently

15.3.2.5. Non-Abstract Large System Design (NALSD)

NALSD describes the ability to assess, design, and evaluate large systems. Practically, NALSD combines the elements of capacity planning, component isolation, and graceful system degradation crucial to highly available production systems. Because systems change over time, it is important that an SRE is able to analyze and evaluate the key aspects of the system design.

Non-abstract means turning whiteboard design into concrete estimates of resources at multiple steps in the process.

15.3.2.6. Configuration Design and Best Practices

Configurations are parameters that allow someone to modify system behavior without redeploying code. Configuring systems is a common SRE task. Systems have three key components: code, data the system manipulates, and system configuration.

A good configuration interface allows quick, confident, and testable configuration changes. Reliability is highly dependent on good configuration practices as one bad configuration can wipe out entire systems.

15.3.2.7. Canarying Releases

Release engineering describes all the processes and artifacts related to getting code from a source repository into a running production system. Canarying releases are the partial and time-limited deployment of a change in a service and its evaluation. The evaluation helps to decide whether or not to proceed with the rollout. The part of the system that receives the change is "the canary", and the remainder of the system is "the control". The logic underpinning this approach is that usually the canary deployment is performed on a much smaller subset of production, or affects a much smaller subset of the user base than the control portion.

15.3.2.8. Data Processing Pipelines

Data processing is an important topic nowadays given the growing datasets, intensive data transformations, and requirement for fast, reliable, and inexpensive results. Data quality errors become business-critical issues whenever they are introduced in the resulting data.

A pipeline can involve multiple stages; each stage being a separate process with dependencies on other stages. Best practices identified by SRE include:

- Defining and measuring SLOs for pipeline
- Planning for dependency failure
- Creating and maintaining pipeline documentation
- Reducing hotspots and workload
- Implementing autoscaling and resource planning
- Adhering to access control and security policies
- Planning escalation paths

15.3.2.9. Configuration Specifics

The task of configuring and running applications in production requires insight into how those systems are put together and how they work. When things go wrong, the on-call engineer needs to know exactly where the configurations are and how to change them. The mundane task of managing configurations replicated across a system leads to replication toil; a toil particularly frequent with distributed systems. Configuring production systems with confidence needs the application of best practices to manage complexity and operational load. Configuration mechanisms require:

- Good tooling (linters, debuggers, formatters, etc.)
- Hermetic configurations (configuration languages must generate the same configuration data regardless of where or when they execute)
- Separation of configuration and data (configurations should, after evaluation, drive several data items downstream, providing clear separation of evaluation and side effects)

15.3.3. Cloud-Native Infrastructure

There has been a profound mutation at work for several years: hardware is now controlled by software through APIs, and hardware now comes in interconnected pools that can grow and shrink dynamically.

The following five characteristics are the foundation of a paradigm change for running software:

- **On-demand self-service**: Consumers can provision computing resources as needed; automatically, and without any human interaction required
- **Broad network access**: Capabilities are widely available and can be accessed through heterogeneous platforms (e.g., mobile phones, tablets, laptops, and workstations)
- **Resource pooling**: Provider resources are pooled in a multi-tenant model, with physical and virtual resources dynamically assigned and reassigned on-demand; the customer generally has no direct control over the exact location of provided resources, but may specify location at a higher level of abstraction (e.g., country, state, or data center)
- **Rapid elasticity**: Capabilities can be elastically provisioned and released to rapidly scale outward or inward commensurate with demand; consumer capabilities available for provisioning appear to be unlimited and can be appropriated in any quantity at any time
- **Measured service**: Cloud systems automatically control and optimize resource use by leveraging a metering capability at some level of abstraction appropriate to the type of service (e.g., storage, processing, bandwidth, and active user accounts); resource usage can be monitored, controlled, and reported for transparency

Part 4: The Ways of Supporting

This part outlines the ways of supporting architecture activities within an Agile enterprise. It examines the techniques and methods — including experience design, journey mapping, value stream mapping, event storming, domain-driven design, and data and AI approaches — that can be used to support Agile Architecture development.

Chapter 16. Experience Design

Experience design alternates divergent and convergent thinking in both the problem space and the solution space. As illustrated in Figure 16-1, "Customer Research" is in the "Problem Space" and "Product Discovery" is in the "Solution Space".

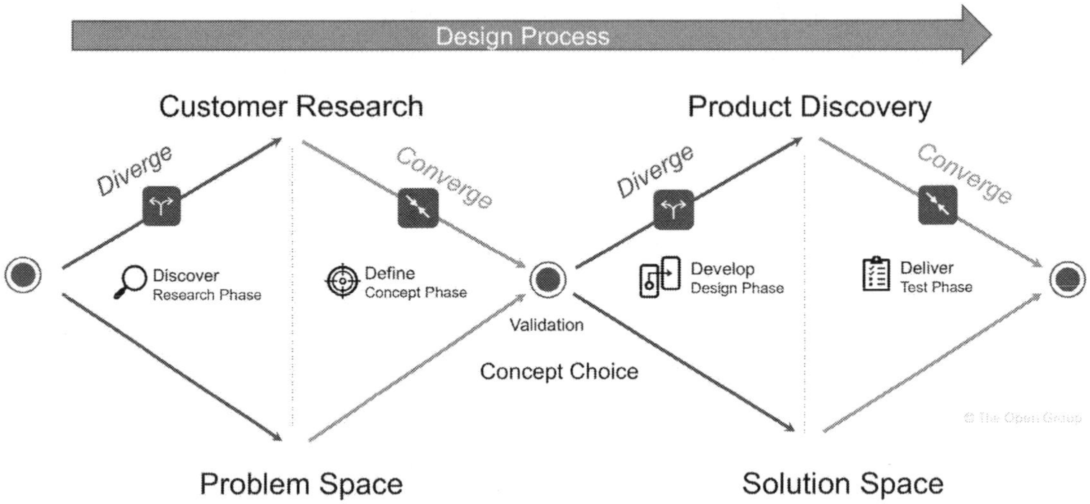

Figure 16-1: Design Thinking Logic

The purpose of customer research is to target the right customers and identify unserved needs. It requires an anticipation of the future, the identification of relevant trends, and an understanding of what is likely to change or to remain the same. Relevant trends are those the enterprise can leverage to solve customer problems in new and better ways.

Customer research aims at discovering a market which consists of all the existing and potential customers that share a particular need or set of related needs [Olsen, 2015]. It is the home of all the customer needs to which the product is desired to deliver. The word "needs" should be interpreted broadly as it includes jobs-to-be-done, pain points, desires, or emotions.

In contrast, product discovery is in the solution space: *"Any product that you actually build exists in solution space, as do any product designs that you create — such as mockups, wireframes, or prototypes"* [Olsen, 2015]. It is driven by outside-in thinking. The product is defined through the lens of the customer.

In his seminal *Marketing Myopa* paper, Theodore Levitt writes: *"The organization must learn to think of itself not as producing goods or services but as buying customers, as doing the things that will make people want to do business with it"* [Levitt, 1960].

The focus shifts from products to problems customers want to solve: *"People don't want to buy a quarter-inch drill. They want a quarter-inch hole!"*. Customer research is about discovering the *"quarter-inch holes"* that customers are looking for. Clayton Christensen coined the term "job-to-be-done" to designate them.

"Job" is shorthand for what an individual really seeks to accomplish in a given circumstance. The circumstances are more important than customer characteristics, product attributes, new technologies, or trends [Christensen et al., 2016].

16.1. Experience Design Approach

This approach drives experience design from an outside-in thinking stance. It iterates design thinking cycles, as described in Figure 16-2.

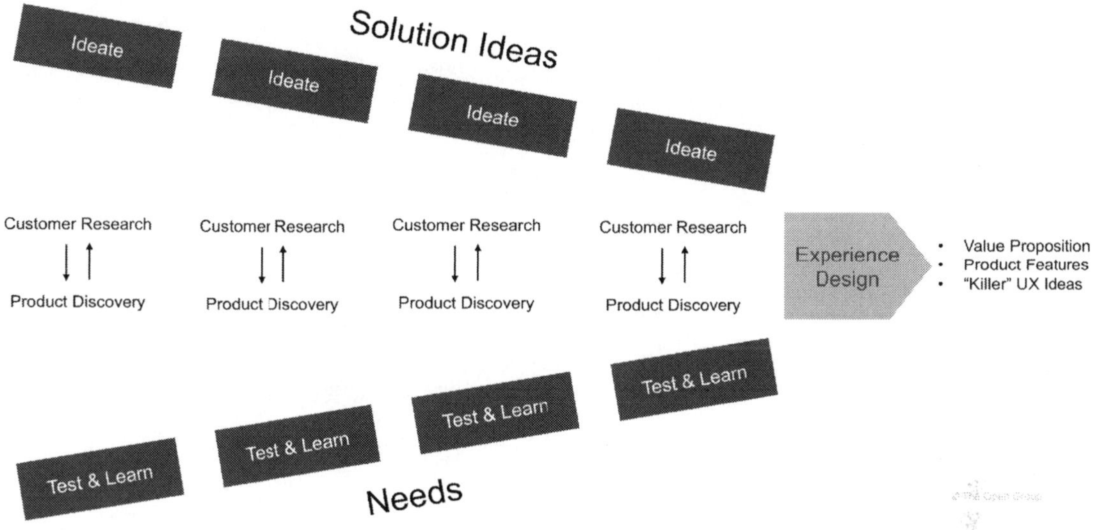

Figure 16-2: Experience Design Approach

Each iteration tests the hypotheses formulated in ideation using prototypes. As progress occurs in the product development lifecycle, new hypothesis testing practices are used.

For example, companies like Netflix® and Facebook® have pioneered techniques like "canary deployments" and "A/B testing". Two different features are tried out simultaneously, and the business results are measured. For example, are customers more likely to click on a green button or a yellow one? Testing such questions in the era of packaged software would have required lab-based usability engineering approaches, which risked being invalid because of their small sample size. Testing against larger numbers is possible now that software is increasingly delivered as a service [C196].

16.2. What is a Product?

Products are at the crossroad of strategy and marketing, design science, operations, and engineering. Understanding products requires the borrowing of practices and vocabularies from these disciplines. They jointly contribute to discover, architect, and develop products.

The term "product" is widely used in the Agile community. Though numerous articles and books discuss the shift from project to product, at the time of writing, few, if any, give a definition of product. This document believes the Agile and Enterprise Architecture communities need a shared understanding of what product means.

Theodore Levitt states that a truly marketing-minded firm tries to create value-satisfying goods and services that consumers will want to buy [Levitt, 1960]. This implies that product includes both goods and services. In his book *Innovation in Marketing* [Levitt, 1962], Theodore Levitt answers the question, what is a product?

He observes that designing a better and less expensive piano would have less impact on sales than providing a simpler and more enjoyable beginner's piano method. He concludes that the product being sold needs to be expanded. It must be defined much more broadly to include non-core elements that contribute to a user's satisfaction. It can be concluded that product refers to both goods and services.

Following Theodore Levitt's path, Marty Cagan provides a holistic definition of product [Cagan, 2018]:

> "A product includes the functionality — the features. But it also includes the technology that enables this functionality. It also includes the user experience design that presents this functionality. And it includes how we monetize this functionality. It includes how we attract and acquire users and customers. And it can also include offline experiences as well that are essential to delivering the product's value."
>
> — Marty Cagan

When using the terms product and service, ambiguity often remains:

- For some, product means a good as opposed to a service
- Sandra Vandermerwe and Juan Rada coined the term *"servitization of business"* to refer to market packages or "bundles" of customer-focused combinations of goods, services, support, self-service, and knowledge [Vandermerwe & Rada, 1988]
- Mohanbir Sawhney describes how high-end professional services firms can embed products in their service offerings [Sawhney, 2016]; product here refers to the standardization and industrialization of portions of the service value chain

To avoid terminology and meaning ambiguity, the definition of product can be found in Section 2.40.

> **NOTE**
>
> Products are bundles of services and/or goods. Products have features through which customers and users interact:
>
> - A product feature can be a service feature or a goods feature
> - A feature is a *"handle"* through which customers or users experience products

Products deliver outcomes which are defined by the customer/UX and depend on circumstances. In the piano example, the outcomes could be:

- Enjoying good music, and sometimes not so good music
- Feeling proud of a child's musical performance
- Aesthetic pleasure from a piano decorating the living room

16.2.1. Intangible Goods

The tangibility criteria is sometimes used to distinguish services from goods. While services are obviously intangible, goods can be both tangible and intangible. In the case of software, a High Court case in 2016 held that software was indeed goods, although it was intangible [Rezai, 2016].

When buying a word processor package from a software vendor, a client makes the software available to some users (including themself) to act upon this software. They use the various software features (spelling features, formatting features, printing features, etc.) to achieve the outcome of a text document. When printing, user satisfaction comes from experiencing both the printing process and the quality of the printed document.

The reasoning is not different when the word processor is an online word processor. Users still act upon the online word processor to get their printed documents. However new software-enabled services have been added to the word processor product: automated upgrade, cloud backup, etc.

The case of online banking applications is different. They are software resources used by banks to deliver web-exposed account management services. Such applications are part of the account management service provision; they are not goods. Another example is "Infrastructure as a Service (IaaS)". The main outcome of IaaS is computing resources (similar to rented computers). They are goods as there is a need to act upon these resources to install and run software on servers. Of course, IaaS products go beyond server goods as they also embed online services, such as the dynamic provisioning of resources.

Consequently, the distinctive characteristic between goods and services is that goods are *acted upon* to deliver outcomes while services are *delegated acts* that deliver outcomes. The distinctive characteristic is not tangibility.

16.3. Customer Research

Customer research combines traditional market research with customer/UX research.

16.3.1. Market Research

Market researchmarket research identifies customer segments and analyzes customer needs and behavior. It explores current and potential customers to identify unmet customer needs and/or opportunities for business growth.

Market research can focus on simple demographics of an existing or potential customer group, defined by age, gender, geography, or income level. Customer research also seeks to understand customer behavior and motivation.

The goal is to understand who is — or will be — using a product as well as the reasons behind their doing so and how they go about using it (including the contextual areas of "where" and "when").

Customer research may be conducted via a variety of quantitative and qualitative methods, such as interviews, surveys, focus groups, and ethnographic field studies. It also commonly involves doing desk research of online reviews, forums, and social media to explore what customers are saying about a product.

Examples of customer research outcomes are:

- Brand awareness analysis
- Markets segmentation
- Customer behavior modeling
- Pricing strategies assessment

16.3.2. Jobs-To-Be-Done

The "job-to-be-done" framework was created by Harvard professor Clayton Christensen, in part as a reaction against conventional techniques that: *"frame customers by attributes — using age ranges, race, marital status, and other categories that ultimately create products and entire categories too focused on what companies want to sell, rather than on what customers actually need"* [Christensen et al., 2016].

Jobs-to-be-done analysis complements classical market research techniques by shifting the focus from the customer to what the customer aspires to achieve in some context.

"Some products are better defined by the job they do than the customers they serve" [Traynor, 2016]. This is in contrast to many kinds of business and requirements analysis that focus on identifying different user personas (e.g., 45-55 married woman with children in the house). The job-to-be-done framework advocates that *"the job, not the customer, is the fundamental unit of analysis"* and that customers *"hire"* products to do a certain job [Christensen, et al., 2016].

To apply the job-to-be-done approach, Des Traynor suggests filling in the blanks in the following:

People hire your product to do the job of *every* when *The other applicants for this job are , , and* , but your product will always get the job because of__.

Understanding the alternatives that people have is key. It is possible that the job can be fulfilled in multiple ways. For example, people may want certain software to be run. This job can be undertaken through owning a computer (e.g., having a data center). It can also be managed by hiring someone else's computer (e.g., using a cloud provider). Not being attentive and creative in thinking about the diverse ways jobs can be done risks disruption [C196].

16.4. Combining Product Discovery with Customer Research

> "A lot of times, people don't know what they want until you show it to them."
>
> — Attributed to Steve Jobs

Product discovery is about defining products from an outside-in viewpoint. Experience mapping helps to articulate the product's value proposition and discover its features, outcomes, and benefits. It combines customer research and product discovery.

16.4.1. Experience Mapping

Experience shall be considered holistically as the sum of all interactions between a customer or user and the enterprise. Experience maps are made of all the stories which, together, describe the end-to-end customer or UX. Each customer/user map is defined by:

- A persona which represents the character subject of the story
- A final outcome that results from the story
- A chain of events, starting from an initial state of affairs to a conclusion (final outcome)
- External participants who interact with the persona

In the insurance claim story below, the initial event is a car accident. The persona is *Diana*, the policy owner and driver. *John* is a participant with whom Diana had an accident. The final desired outcome is a repaired car. The events represented in Figure 16-3 are:

- "Proof of Insurance (POI) Exchanged" between Diana and John
- "First Notice of Loss (FNOL)" registered by Diana to the insurance company
- "Loss Assessed": Set of interactions to determine the amount of loss or damages covered by the insurance policy
- "Car Repaired": Set of interactions resulting in the car being repaired
- "Claim Settled": Final event resulting in issuing a payment to the benefit of the car repair shop

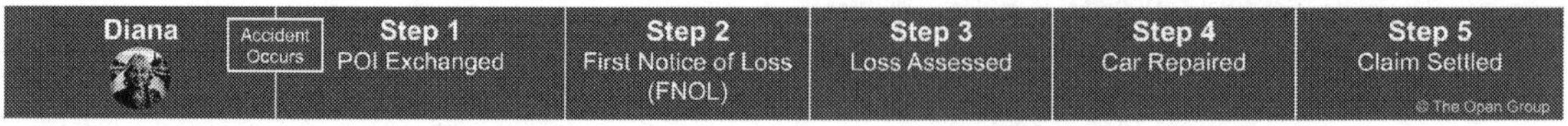

Figure 16-3: Claim Experience Events

As much as possible, each event should be connected to an intermediate outcome that is necessary to reach the final outcome. All intermediate steps should be left out for clarity. Too often, detailed steps tend to pollute the problem space with solution concerns. For instance, the fulfillment/repair event could be described as such: *Diana selects a repair appointment with a nearby repair shop; Diana's car is picked up at her office for repair*. Actually, the hidden product features are: *car repair shop selection (outcome: a car repair shop close to Diana's home)* and *repair service organization (outcome: repaired car)*. There are different ways to achieve these outcomes, ranging from an automated selection of the provider to bringing the repaired car to Diana's parking lot.

Each experience map is made of a set of touchpoints through which the persona interacts with the enterprise or with external parties; see Figure 16-4. Each touchpoint gives an opportunity to wrap product features that can provide valuable experience to users and make them more engaged and satisfied. The aspects of experience below shall be analyzed at each touchpoint:

- Understanding the job-to-be-done
- Products involved (goods or services)
- Product features used
- Pains and gains felt by customers at the touchpoint
- Improvement opportunities based on customer insights

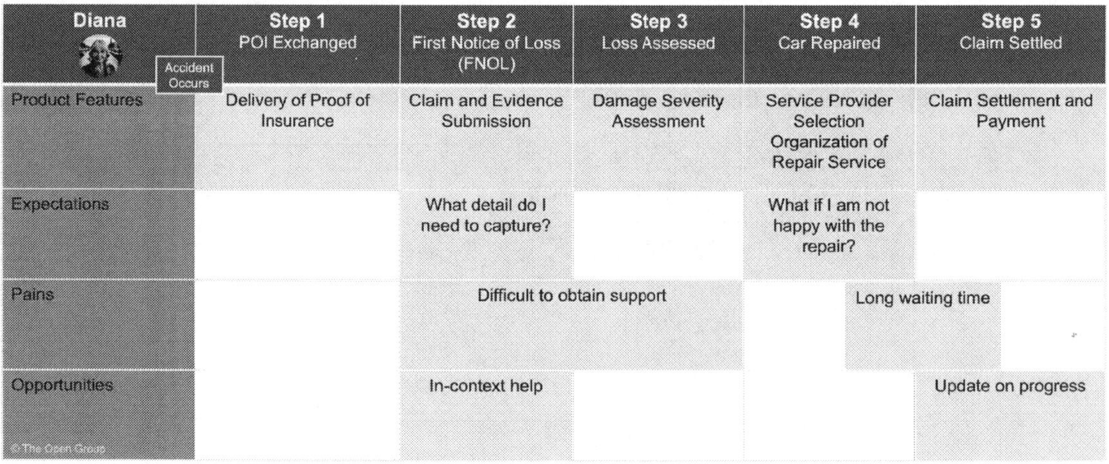

Figure 16-4: Claim Experience Map

A single event often involves several touchpoints. For instance, fulfillment and repair in the claim journey involves *car repair provider selection (outcome: a provider close to Diana's home)* and *repair service organization (outcome: repaired car)*. Pain points or gains can be identified for each of the product features involved at a touchpoint. For instance, a long waiting time is only felt for the repair product feature but not for the service provider selection.

16.4.2. Goods Features

"Goods" includes all man and machine-made objects (artifacts), whether tangible or intangible, that are offered to clients. Goods expose features through which users interact. For instance, a word processor application provides editing and printing features; refrigerators provide storage and freezing features.

The experience or value of goods comes from clients directly acting upon features. Food is properly preserved (outcome) if it is stored at the right place (acted upon) in a fridge: eggs and butter in the door, vegetables in the vegetable tray, etc. People willing to have room temperature butter (job-to-be-done) may store it in the warmest part of the fridge.

The shared experience between providers and consumers is mediated by the functional form of goods (temperature) and the physical manifestations (various trays in the fridge) upon which clients act.

16.4.3. Service Features

"Service" is work done by one person or group that benefits another. A service involves at least two parties. One applies competence (a provider) and the other experiences an outcome (a consumer). For example, a taxi ride is a service used by a person to travel (outcome) and is delivered by a taxi driver (provider).

Clients *delegate some acts* to the provider to get the desired outcomes. Banks provide consumer credit, which allows clients to defer payments. A mechanic fixes a car to provide the outcome of a repaired car. Barbers provide a haircut service, applying their competence to perform acts clients would otherwise have to perform for themselves.

Service featuresservice features are the functionalities of a service. For example, beyond the basic car wash, a car cleaning service could also propose wheel cleaning or rust protection.

Service provisionservice provision may include the mediation of some artifacts, such as an ATM machine used to retrieve cash. However, such artifacts are not goods *per se* but instruments used to provision the service.

16.4.4. Feature Outcomes and Benefits

A feature should not be confused with a service benefit. For example, for a few more dollars car washing companies offer to spray a solution on the vehicle's exterior that washes off in short order. Given its lack of durability, this feature does not protect the car from rusting.

A better rust protection feature would include opening up body panels, door panels, getting under the hood and into trunk areas, and finally accessing the boxed areas of the vehicle frame or unibody construction. This improved feature delivers a lasting benefit but costs between $100 to $250 per vehicle.

A benefit is an outcome that a client or a user values. For example, spraying a solution on the vehicle exterior could deliver peace of mind (first benefit) to clients who do not know better. On the other hand, delivering true rust protection (second benefit) is valued by knowledgeable clients. Two equivalent product features (two types of rust protection) deliver results valued differently depending on the client's knowledge. For example, spraying a solution on the vehicle will not deliver the peace-of-mind benefit to knowledgeable clients.

16.4.5. Digital Products: Connected Goods and Fingertip Services

Digital technologies have provided the ability to embed software in objects. They range from traditional ATM machines, connected wearables, connected cars, to healthcare devices.

When goods become connected, a direct experience can be established between providers and consumers beyond the mediation of users acting upon goods. Goods become agents through which consumers and providers can interact. Through sensors, connected goods provide a wealth of information to providers, with an increased ability to reach customers at various touchpoints. When service provision includes connected resources, these new mediating agents can enrich service delivery by offering self-care features. Services come closer to their consumers; they become fingertip services, bringing product features to sight: smart cars can learn about their passengers to provide tailored entertainment experiences, smart locks can open based on face recognition, smart lighting can adjust brightness and color hue based on both the weather outside and the user's mood.

16.4.6. Quality Properties: The "ilities" of Products

Product features and their outcomes are not completely defined until measurable properties are specified. Altogether, they help define the purpose of products. Purposes shall not be confused with objectives or goals. For instance, the purpose of a chair (its main feature) is sitting. Chairs have other features such as the ability to be carried by a single person. Providing better sitting and/or easier lifting is setting improvement objectives. They do not change the purpose of the chair product.

The various quantitative and qualitative properties of product features are often named -ilities after the suffix most of the words share (availability, maintainability, scalability, etc.). The term "non-functional requirements" is also used, but it is vague and belongs to traditional requirement-driven approaches.

A quality property is a measurable, testable, and experienceable property that indicates how well a product feature and/or its outcome satisfies customers in a specific usage context.

Wikipedia® records a plethora of quality properties [Wikipedia] and academia has defined multiple taxonomies over the years, including a couple of ISO Standards such as ISO/IEC 9126 [ISO/IEC 9126-1] and ISO/IEC 25002 [ISO/IEC 25002]. While many of these taxonomies are related to software quality properties, many of them apply to any product. Among all quality properties, Don Norman [Norman, 2013] identifies three main kinds that matter for product experience:

- Discoverability: The product must be self-explanatory — the user should be able to discover what actions are possible and how to perform them
- Understandability: Users must be able to understand how the product is supposed to be used, and what all the features mean
- Usability: How easy and pleasant product features are to use

There are many other quality properties, and each discipline has a different perspective: products have to be reliable, attractive, safe, etc. All of the quality properties may look crucial, but some tend to have a negative influence on others. For instance, maximizing maintainability may lead to a sacrifice in efficiency; increased reliability may have a negative effect on performance or usability. A study from Professor De Weck at the MIT [De Weck et al., 2016] reveals a highly-connected network of quality properties.

16.5. Example: Ride-Hailing Company

NOTE	This fictional example is presented here for illustrative purposes only, to support the text and to enable a clearer understanding for the reader.

Ride-Hailing Company provides the features below:

- **Geolocation**: Live tracking, positioning, map display, routing
- **Ride management**: Instant ride request, scheduled ride request, rider/driver matching process, driver notification of request, acceptance, rider notification, driver rating by rider/rider rating by driver
- **Pricing**: Price estimation, surge pricing of ride request, fixed price, fare splitting, wait time fees, tips management
- **Cashless payment**: Card registration, in-app card payment, receipt
- **Driver administration**: Driver registration, driver profiling, status, payment and transaction history, ride history, vehicle management, earning report
- **Rider administration**: Rider registration, rider profile, payment and receipt history, ride history, SOS, promotion and loyalty program
- **Generic features**: Notification, Internationalization (i18n), multiple currency, SMS verification, authentication

This list of features does not say much about the outcomes that riders and drivers experience. The major outcome for riders is to get a ride with minimum waiting time at a reasonable price. The major outcome for drivers is to maximize revenue while minimizing idle time. The relationships that link features to outcomes are indirect and require an understanding of the system as a whole.

The business model of Ride-Hailing Company is based on a two-sided market platform. One side of the market caters to riders who need transportation. The other side of the market caters to drivers who need to earn money.

The value to each of its participants grows the more people use the service [Parker et al., 2016]. Ride-Hailing Company's network effect is captured in Figure 16-5.

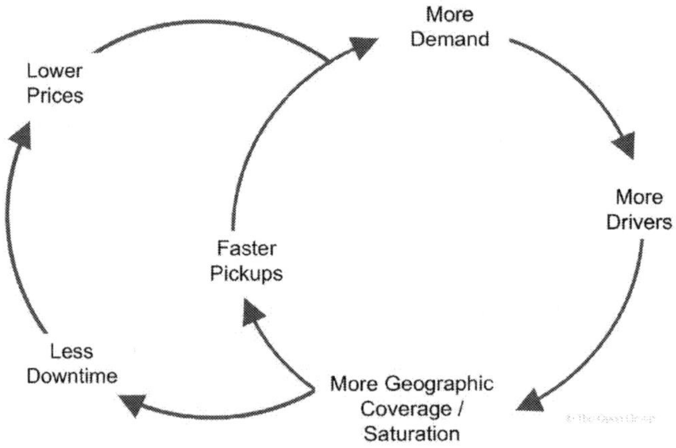

Figure 16-5: Ride-Hailing Company Network Effect

Ride-Hailing Company has to balance rider demand with driver capacity, and needs to motivate drivers so enough of them show up at pickup time, otherwise riders have to wait too long.

The interest of the drivers is not aligned with that of the rider. The more drivers, the less waiting time for riders but the more idle time for drivers.

Behavioral science has shown how drivers can be subtly influenced to act against their own interests through the employment of social scientists and data scientists who experiment *"with video game techniques, graphics, and non-cash rewards of little value that can prod drivers into working longer and harder — and sometimes at hours and locations that are less lucrative for them"* [Scheiber, 2017].

This example epitomizes the complex relations that can link features to outcomes. Just adding new features or managing a feature backlog does not guarantee success. Instead of prioritizing features, a competent product manager should prioritize outcomes. This implies shifting from a product owner role toward a product manager role, as described in Section 4.4.1.

Last but not least, the experience delivered by features can be enhanced by "killer" UX ideas; for example, see Figure 16-6. However, what used to be a killer UX is no longer differentiating. For example, several online services now include an equivalent UX to track delivery. Enjoying a lasting competitive advantage requires much more than adding features and flashy UIs.

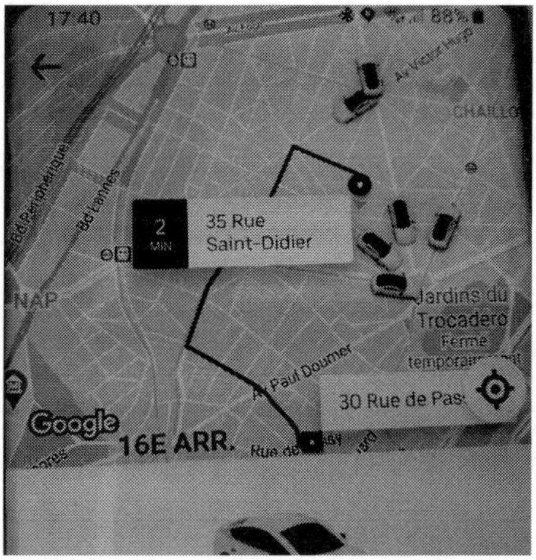

Figure 16-6: UX Example

Chapter 17. Journey Mapping

This document uses the term “journey map” to refer to an **alignment diagram**, which is any map, diagram, or visualization that reveals both sides of value creation in a single overview [Kalbach, 2016]. Alignment diagrams have two parts: a description of an experience and a description of an enterprise product, with the interaction between the two. Journey maps and service blueprints are alignment diagrams.

Some touchpoints, such as a newsletter or an advertisement, do not allow users to interact. Interactions can be automated; for example, interacting with a chatbot in a self-care situation. Human-to-human interactions can be “in person” or conducted remotely using collaboration technology.

Figure 17-1 is an example of an alignment diagram which represents both sides of value creation.

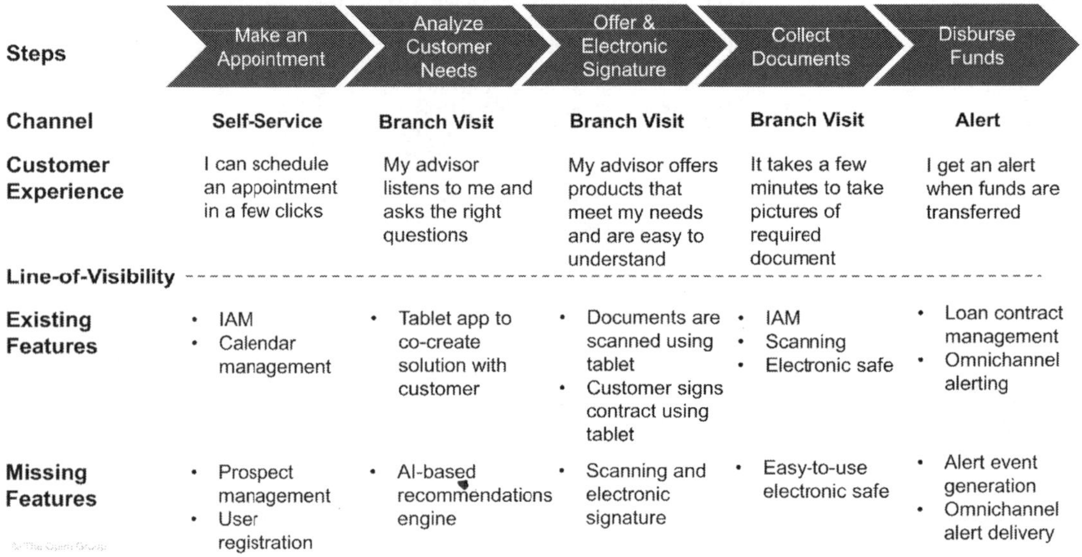

Figure 17-1: Service Blueprint

Each step:

- Specifies the channel(s) that support(s) the interaction
- Describes the actual or desired customer experience
- Presents the needed features or functionalities

If the existing operations or software are not good enough to support the targeted experience quality, it is necessary to settle for a lesser quality unless the supporting operations or software are improved.

The “Missing Features” line identifies the new functionalities that must be developed to deliver the expected customer experience.

Not all interactions are equal. Some interactions, referred to as "moments of truth", matter more than others.

17.1. Moments of Truth

McKinsey defines moments of truth as:

> Those few interactions (for instance, a lost credit card, a canceled flight, a damaged piece of clothing, or investment advice) when customers invest a high amount of emotional energy in the outcome [Beaujean et al., 2006].

How well or how poorly the enterprise handles moments of truth has a decisive impact on the quality of the customer experience. Moments of truth test the quality of operations because:

- They require that at the same time employees respect service standards and show initiative to resolve a client's problems, even though they may be unexpected
- Lessons learned solving unexpected problems should be incorporated into service standards to help prevent similar problems from happening in the first place
- Defects in existing processes and software are a frequent cause of poor customer experience

This document recommends using moments of truth to prioritize operational improvements [Patton, 2014].

> Focusing on specific target outcomes is the secret to prioritizing development work.

The goal should be to maximize outcomes while minimizing costs by minimizing new features development. The focus on moments of truth gives the opportunity for cross-functional teams to develop their level of understanding of what really matters and to explore the space of solutions to discover the best way to deliver an outstanding experience.

This is illustrated by the example of a housing rental enterprise. The first moment of truth for new prospects is to be rapidly informed when available properties that meet their needs become available.

What does it mean to be informed rapidly? Is it to receive a choice of properties immediately? The next business day? How can the enterprise ensure the choice of property meets client needs? Answering these questions requires a deep understanding of client expectations and also the ability to determine which operating model improvements are required.

Generating a short list of available houses or apartments that meet needs most of the time is critical to the moment of truth. If clients rapidly receive a list containing mostly properties that do not match their needs, they will be rapidly disappointed. In order to prevent this, the enterprise needs a very large inventory. This may require the enterprise to develop new sources of rental properties that it can add to its inventory.

In addition to the large inventory requirement, new features are needed:

- The enterprise needs access to an inventory of available housing for rent
- That inventory must be updated in real time
- Smart search algorithms that select properties on criteria such as the number of rooms or the distance to public transportation

17.2. The Human Side

Mistakes and errors are inevitable, but dissatisfied customers are not. Paradoxically, when a service defect such as a late delivery or a lost parcel is fixed, frustrated customers can become more loyal than they would if no problem had occurred.

The difficulty is to grant employees the freedom and the responsibility not to follow "standard operating procedures" when solving urgent or important customer problems. The enterprise needs to:

- Give meaning and clarity of purpose to front-line employees
- Influence the mindset of employees so they develop their emotional intelligence
- Adjust the reward system to reinforce the right behavior
- Design the work system so it has enough slack for employees to take the time to solve customer problems

Addressing the human side cannot be done locally to improve a specific customer journey. It requires a broader transformation approach, such as the one described in Chapter 6.

17.3. The Role of Automation

Digital technologies, in particular AI, dramatically expand the scope of what can be automated. Does this mean the automation potential should be pushed to its limits? Not necessarily; for example:

- Automation increases the need for maintenance, which requires skilled workers
- The impact of automating one task is felt beyond that one task
- When automation is visible to the client it can change customer experience
- New risks can emerge when automation fails; for example, when operators have lost essential skills

Automating requires a careful assessment of benefits and drawbacks. Instead of automating in a big bang manner, the Agile enterprise will conduct experiments and automate using an incremental approach when possible.

Automation failures come in two forms: misses and false alarms. For example, the system has failed to detect a harmful situation, or the system acted when it should not have.

A failure to detect can harm the customer; for example, a fraudulent payment not being prevented by an automated fraud detection algorithm. On the other hand, if the fraud detection algorithm disables a credit card when the client is abroad late at night and during a weekend, it becomes a service failure in the case of a false-positive.

Computers and humans have distinct abilities. Therefore, augmenting the human with the power of automation and AI could be a legitimate goal if the man-computer symbiosis is achieved.

When automation is used as an augmentative tool, it leaves decisions to humans. Now that deep learning scores better than humans in the accomplishment of many tasks, should the switch to fully-automated decisioning be made? What happens when an unforeseen event occurs that the machine is not capable of handling?

A Few Concluding Words

Journey mapping is a great tool to help align experience mapping with the operating system that is supposed to deliver it. When the mismatch between experience and TOM cannot be solved locally, it is necessary to look at the operating system as a whole. Improving the human side and automating will often require a holistic approach.

Chapter 18. Lean Value Stream Mapping

The lean value stream is one of the most popular Lean concepts. The term "Lean" was coined in 1988 by John Krafcik in an article that compared the Toyota Production System with North American and European automotive plants: *Triumph of the Lean Production System* [Krafcik, 1988]. Despite the similarity in name, these should not be confused to the Business Architecture value streams; see the *TOGAF Series Guide: Value Streams* [G178].

John Krafcik observed that *"plants operating with a "Lean" production policy are able to manufacture a wide range of models, yet maintain high levels of quality and productivity"*. Lean relies on a true grassroots involvement with all aspects of the operation at the workforce level.

Lean is often defined as a system that delivers the most value from a customer perspective, while consuming the fewest resources. Although true, this is a reductionist view of Lean.

Steven Spear and Kent Bowen believe observers of the Toyota Production System confuse the tools and practices they see with the system itself [Spear & Bowen, 1999]. Toyota creates a community of *scientists* at all levels of the organization. It uses *"a rigorous problem-solving process that requires a detailed assessment of the current state of affairs and a plan for improvement that is, in effect, an experimental test of the proposed changes"*.

18.1. From Process to Value Stream

James Martin observes that *"a value stream is often referred to as a process"* [Martin, 1995]. Unfortunately, the word process is used in many ways by different professionals; for example, systems analysts would call accounts receivable a process. *"Accounts receivable is not a value stream; it is not an end-to-end stream of activities designed to satisfy a customer."*

This section describes the evolution of the process and value stream concepts. It will describe them in detail.

18.1.1. Visualizing Processes

In 1921, Frank and Lillian Gilbreth made a presentation at the annual meeting of the American Society of Mechanical Engineers. This was entitled *Process Charts: First Steps in Finding the One Best Way to Do Work* [Gilbreth & Gilbreth, 1921]. The Gilbreths introduced their notation to visualize processes in order to improve them.

The main objective is to help people in the organization discover the one best way to do work. Noting that every detail of the process can be affected by other details, they argue that it is necessary to visually represent the process as a whole before changing parts of it.

They point out that a local change that does not take into consideration all upstream and downstream operations could pose operational problems during implementation.

It is interesting to note that three concepts still relevant today were formalized so early:

- The process represents a whole; not just the sum of its constituent parts
- The visual representation of the process makes it easier to communicate and build consensus on how it works
- The standardization of symbols contributes to the dissemination of best practices; the standard having been published in 1947 by the American Society of Mechanical Engineers

The Gilbreths formalized a three-step process improvement method [Gilbreth & Gilbreth, 1921]:

- Discover and classify best practices
- Deduce laws (or rules)
- Apply them to standardize practices

To justify their method, the Gilbreths refer to the calamitous losses that result from wastage due to useless movements and gestures. They observe that work-related fatigue is one of the greatest wastes.

18.1.2. Value-Driven

Deming, Juran, and Ishikawa [Ishikawa, 1985], three key thinkers in total quality, argue that knowing what customers want is essential to providing quality products or services. Explicitly identifying and measuring customer requirements is the starting point of a quality approach. Ishikawa points out that collecting and analyzing customer requirements is a lever in developing cross-functional cooperation.

Customer requirements help focus on those parts of the process that have the greatest impact on customer satisfaction. The quality of products and services depends mainly on the quality of the processes used to design and produce them. Management must therefore train and coach employees in the evaluation, analysis, and improvement of processes.

In a book published in 1991, James Harrington [Harrington, 1991] defines the efficiency of the process as its ability to meet customer requirements. For the author, there is no product or service without process and, reciprocally, there is no process without product or service. Customer requirements are a necessary input, but are not sufficient. James Harrington's definition of value has three shortcomings:

- It is independent of costs incurred
- It does not include all stakeholders
- It reduces value to meeting requirements

This document promotes (see Section 8.2.3) a value-driven approach that borrows from several disciplines, including VE. It is aligned with Lean Enterprise, which defines value as [Murman et al., 2002]:

> "How various stakeholders find particular worth, utility, benefit, or reward in exchange for their respective contributions to the enterprise."

Value stream mapping is driven by a definition of value that includes all stakeholders.

18.1.3. Value Stream Mapping

Toyota uses a visual representation of production processes: Material and Information Flow Diagrams (MIFDs), the "ancestor" of value stream mapping.

In 1995, James Martin defined a value stream as *"the end-to-end set of activities that delivers particular results for a given customer (external or internal)"* [Martin, 1995].

In their book, *Lean Thinking* [Womack & Jones, 1996], Jim Womack and Dan Jones use the term "value stream". Value stream mapping as a term became popular when Mike Rother and John Shook published *Learning to See* [Rother & Shook, 2003]. The term value stream mapping has since been borrowed by other disciplines, including Agile, DevOps, and Enterprise Architecture. The focus on applying value stream mapping as a tool without understanding the whole Lean system at best does not create value; at worst, it creates waste.

> "Value stream mapping is not a solution to a problem, but a tool to help us see."
>
> — Liker & Ross, 2017

Value stream mapping is illustrated using a client on-boarding example; see Figure 18-1.

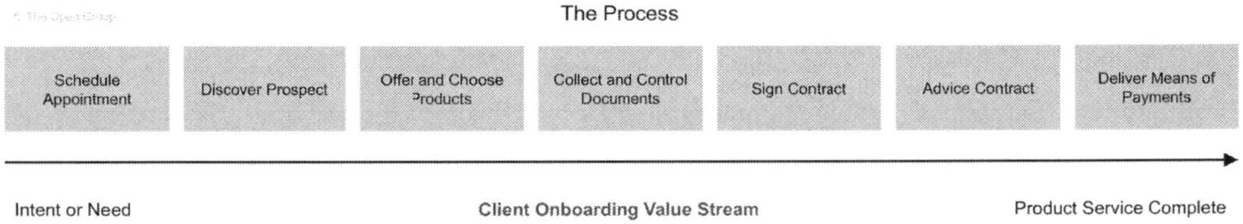

Figure 18-1: Client On-Boarding Value Stream

The value stream is end-to-end, starting from the need for banking services to the delivery of the means of payment.

18.1.4. Granularity Level

One of the first value stream architecture decisions is to determine at which level of granularity client on-boarding should be mapped.

Mapping a generic value stream that works for all on-boarding cases would impose the most complex design onto simple cases, resulting in:

- Waste, because some activities are not required to handle simple cases
- Poor customer and employee experience due to wasted time

Who has not been frustrated when a service representative argues that the system or procedure itself prevented them from solving a problem?

On the other hand, mapping a specialized value stream for each client segment, product, or channel is likely to result in many almost identical value stream maps.

An example of classical granularity analysis is illustrated in Figure 18-2.

© The Open Group	Step 1	Step 2	Step 3	Step 4	Step 5	Step 6	Step 7	Step 8	Step 9
Product A		X	X		X	X		X	X
Product B		X	X		X	X			X
Product C		X	X		X	X		X	X
Product D	X	X		X	X				X
Product E	X	X		X	X				X
Product F		X	X			X	X		X
Product G		X	X			X	X	X	X
Product H		X	X			X	X	X	X

Figure 18-2: Product Step Matrix

Products which have comparable production steps and use similar equipment are regrouped into product families:

- Product Family 1 regroups products A, B, and C
- Product Family 2 regroups products D and E
- Product Family 3 regroups products F, G, and H

A value stream map is created for each product family.

In a digital world, it is important to include additional factors to determine the appropriate granularity level of value stream maps. Table 18-1 illustrates the granularity analysis that helped define the client on-boarding value streams.

Table 18-1: Value Stream Granularity Analysis

Criteria	Simple On-Boarding	Medium Complexity On-Boarding	Complex On-Boarding
Number and Roles of Stakeholders	Single account holder	Joint account	Trustee or agent
Country of Residence	France	European Union	Other
Age and Legal Capacity	Capable adult	Underage	Protected adult
Housing Type	Tenant or owner	Hotel, student residence	In transit
Revenue Type	Salary or retirement pension	Commercial or independent income	Other
Needs	Checking account, credit card, consumer credit	Mortgage loan, simple investment	Investment advice

The scope of the first value stream covers simple client on-boarding. The second value stream addresses medium complex on-boarding situations. The third value stream addresses cases that require more expertise; for example, to set up an account for a protected adult or a foreign diplomat.

18.2. Approach Overview and Key Concepts

Value stream mapping is about applying the scientific method to improve the whole. The value stream improvement steps are:

- Make the value stream visible (learning to see)
- Thoroughly understand current conditions, which includes talking to stakeholders and observing what is happening in the field (*"Going to the Gemba"*)
- Define "next target" conditions
- Plan implementation
- Implement next target conditions
- Check if the solution works as anticipated
- Decide what to do next

Value stream mapping starts with the whole value stream to initiate an improvement cycle at that level. This helps to identify inter-process dependencies. Equivalent improvement cycles can then be applied to each of the processes that compose the value stream; see Figure 18-3. In summary, value stream mapping iterates Plan, Do, Check, and Act (PDCA) cycles, and improvement cycles can be conducted concurrently on different parts of the value stream.

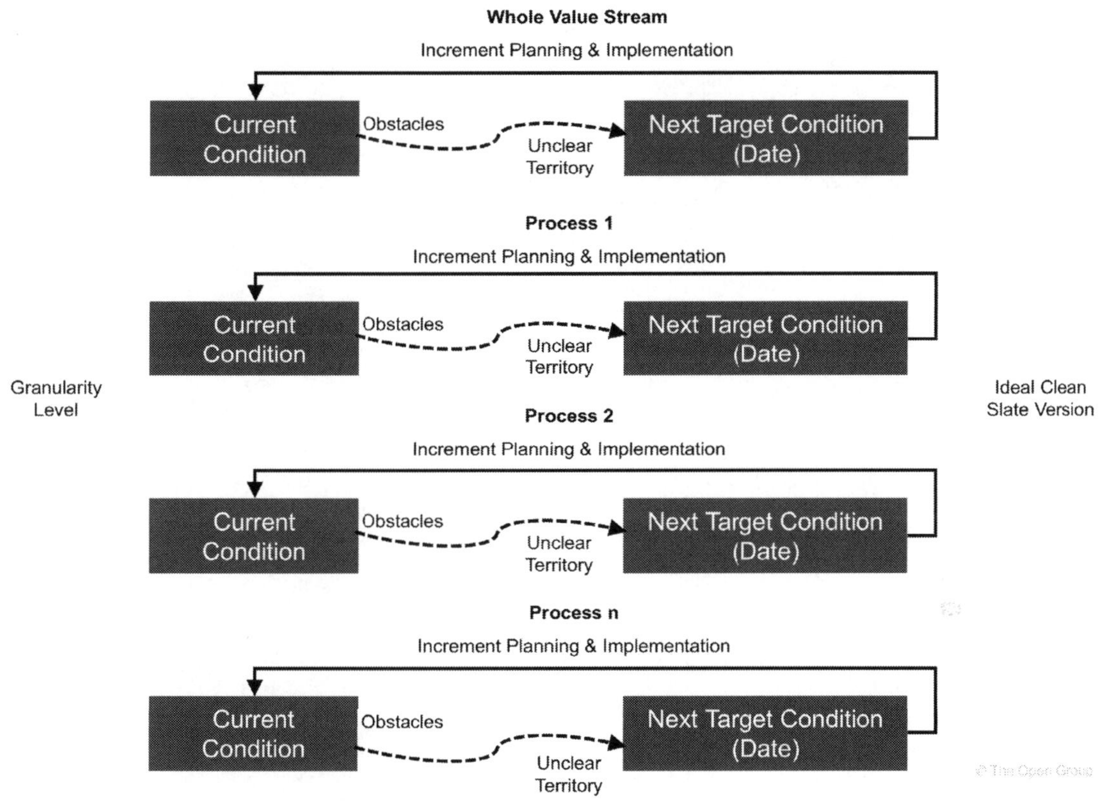

Figure 18-3: Value Stream Mapping

Improvement cycles follow PDCA:

- **Plan**: What it is intended to do
- **Do**: The actual implementation
- **Check**: Whether or not the implemented solution works
- **Act**: The question of *what to do next*

Figure 18-4 illustrates this.

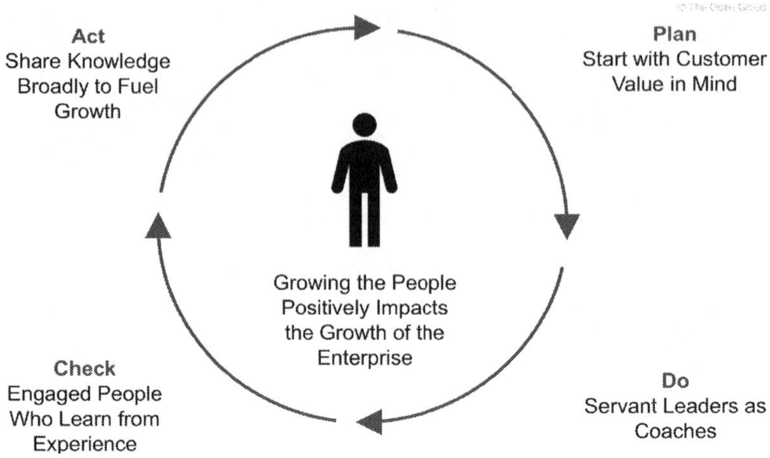

Figure 18-4: PDCA Cycle

The following section describes the current conditions of client on-boarding.

18.2.1. Current Conditions

Understanding current conditions is about collecting facts. It can be done through research techniques such as client and employee interviews, direct observation, "mystery customers", or workshops, to name a few.

The cross-functional improvement team has learned:

- It takes too long to make an appointment
- Some appointments are postponed due to the lack of availability of client advisors
- Too many supporting documents are required, and sometimes intrusive data requests further degrade client experience
- Too many flyers and tools make product selection complex
- Manual controls often result in back-and-forth communication with clients and the back office
- The process is too slow; the lead time sometimes exceeds seven days
- Client advisors spend too much time performing administrative tasks

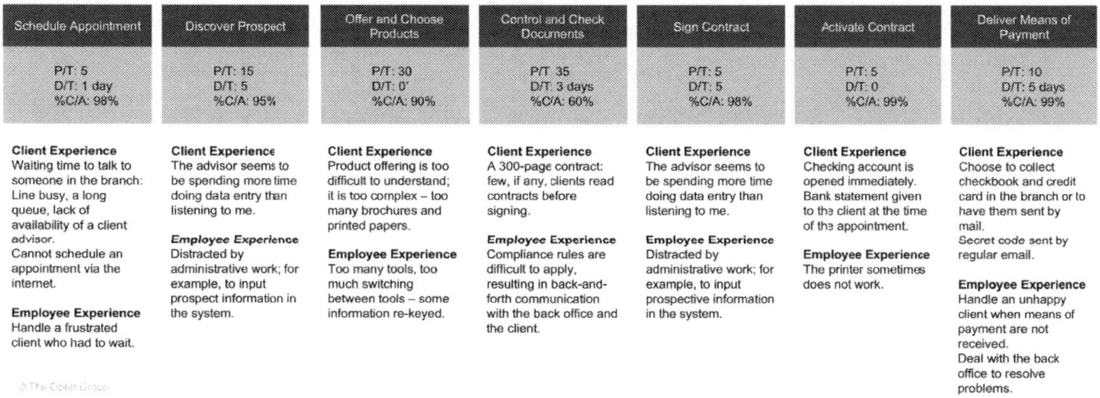

Figure 18-5: Current Conditions

Value stream measures are displayed in Figure 18-5:

- Process Time (P/T) is the time spent performing the work of the process
- Delay Time (D/T) is the time spent waiting during a process or between processes
- Percentage Complete & Accurate (%C/A) measures quality

The diagram shows that the total P/T is 105 minutes. P/T during the customer meeting is 90 minutes, the sum of time from "Discover Prospect" to "Activate Contract". Lead Time (L/T) is the sum of P/T plus D/T from the client intent to the delivery of the means of payment. L/T can reach nine days. This is mostly due to:

- D/T and rework time due to missing or incorrect supporting documents
- D/T to print the credit card and send it to the branch or the client

Other measures can be collected; for example:

- Changeover (C/O) time to switch from producing one product type to another; especially useful in a manufacturing environment
- Value-Added (VA) time, which is P/T that produces value for which customers are willing to pay

The equation VA < P/T < L/T is usually verified.

18.2.2. Ideal "Clean-Slate" Vision

Capable adults represent 69% of all new client on-boarding. 60% of these are capable and resident adults who need a checking account and a credit card. 26% of them are looking for a mortgage loan. The ideal "clean-slate" vision focuses first on creating a streamlined and enjoyable on-boarding experience for the simple on-boarding value stream.

The ambition is to:

- Open an account and get a credit card without an appointment
- Reduce the administrative time required to 10 minutes
- Provide the minimum set of products that is needed during a first appointment
- Enable an omnichannel model
- Create a set of applications and apps that are highly usable for both clients and advisors
- Offer full digital contracting and signature
- Dramatically raise the automation level, especially to verify the authenticity of identity documents as well as supporting documents
- Instant issuance and activation of credit cards

The ideal scenario is described below:

1. I come to the branch without an appointment to open a checking account and get a credit card. While I am waiting for the advisor, I discover the bank's range of products
2. The advisor welcomes me and checks the time I have available. The advisor spends five minutes actively listening and asks some essential questions to understand my needs
3. Using a tablet, the advisor takes a picture of my identity card plus my proof of address
4. The system uses optical character recognition to pre-fill an electronic form that I verify and complete as needed
5. In the background, the authenticity of my documents is verified
6. I sign my contract using the advisor's tablet
7. I immediately receive a text message with a link to install the bank's app
8. My credit card is printed and activated
9. I receive a secret code on my smartphone
10. I can use the branch's ATM to deposit cash
11. Before I leave, the advisor books a second appointment to continue to discuss my needs
12. If I am missing a document, I can take a picture of it at home, which activates my account
13. I can choose to return to the branch to get my credit card or get it sent home
14. I can access my bank statement and other banking services using my banking app or a browser

18.2.3. Waste

Waste is anything other than the minimum amount of resources that add value to a product, including the information customers need. Waste is also referred to as “Muda”. Waste can be classified as Type 1 or Type 2 Muda:

- **Type 1 Muda**: Activities which create no value but are currently necessary to maintain operations; for example, to meet regulatory requirements
- **Type 2 Muda**: Create no value for any stakeholders, including customers, employees, or regulatory bodies

VA time can be measured. It is P/T that produces value. The efficiency of a value stream or process is calculated by dividing the VA time by the L/T.

```
Efficiency = VA time / L/T
```

Taiichi Ohno and Norman Bodek [Ohno & Bodek, 1988] have identified seven types of waste:

- **Overproduction** is producing too much, too early, or just in case; overproduction gets in the way of a smooth flow of goods and services, and causes excessive L/T
- **Waiting** is the enemy of smooth flow, as waiting directly impacts L/T; a short L/T can be a source of competitive advantage, while a long L/T causes customer frustration
- **Unnecessary motion** results from poor workplace arrangement and ergonomics
- **Transportation** is movement that does not create value; for example, sharing important data and files via email rather than hosting data in some shared repository
- **Over processing** is adding more value to a product than customers require
- **Inventory** is storing products or work products that are needed for future use or not needed at all
- **Defects** which cost money both immediately and later

Other waste typologies have been developed; for example, Allen Ward and Durward Sobek identify three primary categories of knowledge waste [Ward & Sobek, 2014]:

- **Scatter** is about actions that make knowledge ineffective by disrupting its flow and affecting the subtle interactions required for teamwork; for example, adding more developers to a team usually slows things down because increasing team size increases the number of interactions within the team
- **Hand-off** occurs whenever knowledge, responsibility, action, and feedback are separated, causing defects and demotivating team members who cannot relate to their work in a meaningful way
- **Wishful thinking** is making decisions without data or operating blindly; for example, testing to specifications, leaving products vulnerable to problems too infrequent for the specifications to catch

A word of caution — do not go out and look for waste guided only by some waste taxonomy; doing so would be wasteful. Instead, be guided by value as defined by the client and keep in mind the purpose of the system. Identify what specifically prevents the value stream from reaching its ideal state. Waste typologies are just an aid to identify symptoms that are likely to reveal deeper problems.

> Muda or waste is a symptom, not a cause.

Muda points to underlying problems at the value stream level or at the process level. Analyzing what causes waste helps identify countermeasures that have the potential to improve the overall system performance. Value stream mapping is misused when it becomes a cost-cutting tool (attacking symptoms), rather than solving the underlying problems that cause waste.

This can be illustrated with the *"collect and control documents"* process. The main problems are:

- Only 60% of new client files meet compliance requirements because of missing or incorrect supporting documents (defect waste)
- The bank must organize a systematic control of client files in the back office (inspection waste)
- Advisors request clients to provide missing documents (rework waste)
- Advisors scan missing documents (rework waste)

Discovering why so many client files are not meeting compliance requirements is a prerequisite to improving the value stream. Figure 18-6 lists a set of first-level causes.

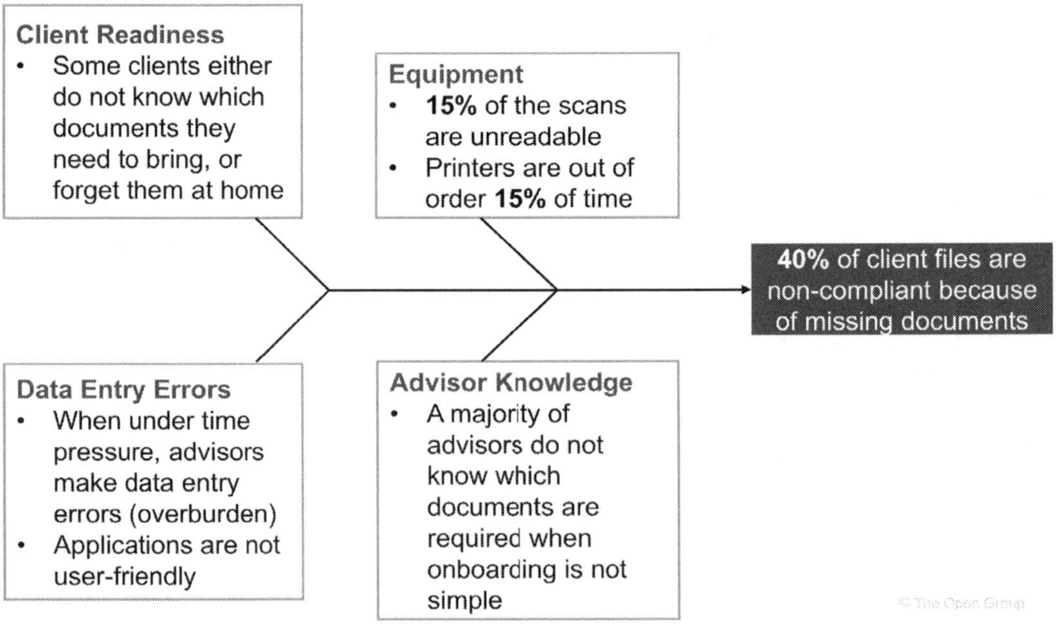

Figure 18-6: Fishbone Diagram, Example of Waste

The "five whys" technique can be used to analyze the root causes of problems; for example:

- Discover why 15% of scans are unreadable: Is this due to a hardware or a software problem, or a scanner handling problem — perhaps due to bad ergonomics, etc.
- Analyze when and why advisors experience time pressure: Is the time for the next appointment coming up, or is the advisor busy with administrative tasks while the client asks questions, etc.

Two usual generic causes of waste (Muda) are unevenness or variability ("Mura") and overburden ("Muri").

18.2.4. Mura and Muri

Unevenness causes people or machines to be either overburdened at times of peak activity or underutilized in times of low activity. This can be illustrated using on-boarding appointments.

The ideal "clean-slate" vision states: *"Open an account and get a credit card without an appointment"*. This is possible if an advisor has enough time to meet the prospect soon after they arrive.

The available work time per day in a branch depends on the number of advisors available that day and the percentage of their time that can be allocated to on-boarding appointments.

Using the hypothesis that a branch has three advisors who can allocate five hours of their time to on-boarding appointments, the total available work time is 15 hours or 900 minutes a day.

If 10 clients show up that day, the target rate for "producing" on-boarding meetings is 900 divided by 10, which is equal to 90 minutes. This is the **takt time**, which measures how often the branch should produce on-boarding appointments.

> Takt time = available work time per shift / customer demand rate per shift

The takt time measures how often one part or product should be produced, based on the rate of demand, to meet customer requirements. In this example, it measures how often customer on-boarding meetings should be held. Takt time is a reference number that provides a sense of the rate at which a process should be producing.

If the hypothesis is used that the new P/T for handling an appointment is reduced to 60 minutes, everything being equal, the branch is in overcapacity to meet customer demand: The branch can conduct on-boarding meetings every 60 minutes while customer demand only requires it to conduct meetings every 90 minutes.

If a new hypothesis is used, that 20 clients a day request to meet an advisor, the new takt time to meet customer demand would be:

> Takt time = 900/20, which is equal to 45 minutes

In this hypothesis, the branch does not have enough capacity to meet customer demand. In order to meet demand, advisors would have to reduce the on-boarding duration from 60 minutes to 45 minutes. This would obviously overburden advisors who would make more mistakes and deliver a poor customer experience.

In a service context, customer demand often varies intraday. If the hypothesis is made that 10 clients show up during lunch time, the three advisors could not satisfy demand. Therefore, in a service context, computing takt time may not be sufficient to manage demand variation (Mura) and avoid overburden (Muri).

18.3. Future State Mapping

A future state map provides a set of challenges and target conditions. A target condition is a work pattern that is hypothesized to advance progress toward desired goals [Liker 2017]: *"A good understanding of the current condition relative to the challenge will help us identify whether this target condition, or some others, makes sense to test"*.

Remember, Table 18-1 helped to identify three specialized client on-boarding value streams. The following section illustrates how to develop a future state map using the simple on-boarding value stream example.

18.3.1. Schedule an Appointment

The first challenge is to sort prospects so that only capable resident adults who own or rent their housing go through the simple on-boarding value stream. The intention is to rapidly streamline the simple value stream because it is a "low hanging fruit" that can improve the experience of the biggest customer segment. From a marketing perspective, the more prospects that the branch can on-board on the spot, the better. When an appointment is handled later, the bank may lose a customer to competition.

The second challenge is to have enough capacity to meet demand. Because there is not much flexibility in adding new advisors to a branch on the spot, the team is considering two countermeasures:

- Get the branch manager do some on-boarding interviews at peak time
- When no advisor is available to meet a prospect within 10 minutes of their arrival, propose an appointment within the next 24 hours

Section 18.3.4 develops an approach that could help the bank to find new ways of solving the problem. This is illustrated with the second improvement increment.

18.3.2. Discover, Offer, and Choose Products

The on-boarding interview starts with 15 minutes of "quality time" that provides an opportunity to listen to the prospect and understand their most pressing needs. This value stream caters to clients who are likely to have straightforward needs. The advisor asks simple questions to discover which credit card best meets the prospect's needs. This simplification reduces the "offer and choose products" P/T from 30 minutes to 10 minutes.

18.3.3. Collect and Control Documents

Because the market segment served by this value stream is composed of capable adults who are residents and own or rent their housing, the list of required documents is simple enough to be remembered by advisors. Most scan quality issues are due to improper manipulation. Therefore, an information campaign can dramatically reduce scan defects.

The bank can also use Software as a Service (SaaS) services to verify in real time the authenticity of identification and supporting documents. The combination of these countermeasures can help reduce the P/T from 35 minutes to 15 minutes. Because the right documents are requested and their authenticity verified on the spot, rework is almost eliminated.

In this improvement increment, advisors will not get tablets because it would take too much time to implement and the upfront investment would be difficult to justify.

18.3.4. Capacity Management

Capacity management matches capacity and demand. The first step is to determine demand patterns and assess the causes of demand variations, as Figure 18-7 illustrates. It represents the call distribution of the bank's call center. Call distribution often needs to be analyzed at a lower level of granularity, such as by type of call. For example, credit card calls are likely to have a different distribution pattern than retail brokerage calls.

The call distribution pattern may vary during the week; for example, people who got their credit card declined during the weekend are likely to call the bank on Monday morning. The call distribution pattern may be impacted by market events; for example, a severe decline of indices is likely to increase the number of brokerage calls.

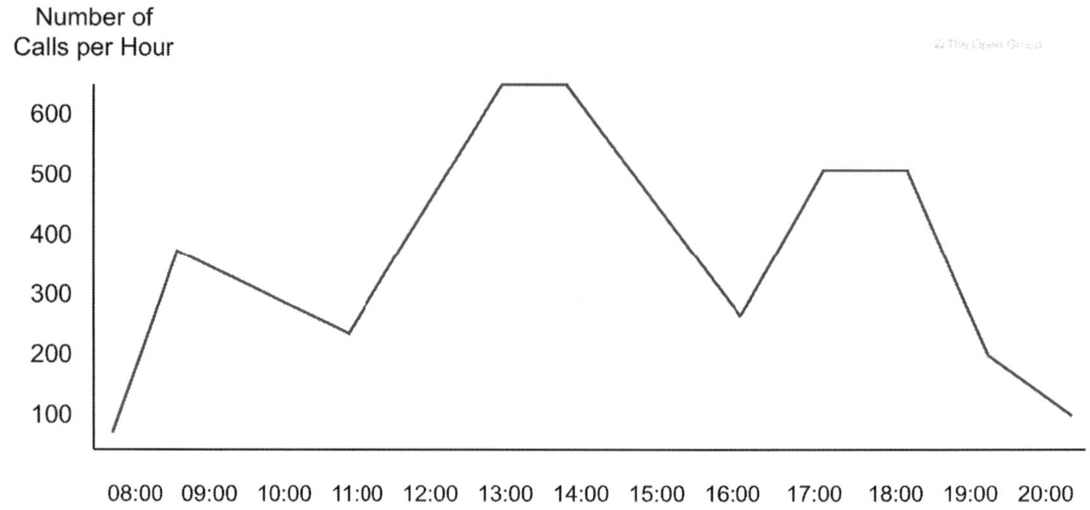

Figure 18-7: Demand Patterns

The second step is to identify, experiment, and implement countermeasures that influence demand and/or capacity.

Influencing Demand

Examples of countermeasures that lower demand:

- Communicate busy times in real time; for example, inform employees when the enterprise's restaurant suffers from an attendance peak, or inform clients how long the waiting time is likely to be
- Offer incentives to customers for usage during non-peak times
- Charge full price — no discount

Examples of countermeasures that increase demand:

- Offer discounts or price reductions; for example, two beers for the price of one between 5pm and 7pm
- Modify the offering to target new market segments
- Offer free shipping when products are ordered in the middle of the afternoon

Managing Capacity

The first countermeasure is to organize the employee work schedule to match demand. However, there are limits due to labor laws and employee well-being.

Examples of countermeasures the enterprise can take are:

- Cross-train employees so they can take on workload at peak times
- Request employees work overtime
- Increase customer participation with self-care
- Automate

When capacity matches demand, it improves the quality of customer experience. It removes any defects caused by overburden and improves employee experience. It prevents paying for underutilized resources and people.

The following section illustrates how additional countermeasures could further improve the value stream.

18.3.5. Increase On-Boarding Capacity

Unified communication tools such as Slack™, Skype®, or Microsoft Teams® allow remote working. With this technology, when all advisors in a branch are busy, an advisor located in another branch can take care of a "walk in" prospect remotely. The mutualization of resources across several branches helps absorb activity peaks.

Implementing this target condition requires the bank to:

- Assess client perception through focus groups and experimentation
- Change the layout of branches to create video conference-ready offices
- Adopt flex office practices
- Upgrade the network capacity to support video streaming
- Rethink the operating model by organizing teams by market segment
- Evolve roles and responsibilities; for example, redefine the branch manager role

The feasibility study of this new target condition is conducted by cross-functional teams composed of representatives of the sales, marketing, HR, IT, or real estate functions. Implementation is incremental. It starts with a few pilot studies conducted in different regions. The rollout is progressive and leverages a central change management team.

This new way of working can support new use cases; for example, leveraging the scarce resources that provide investment advice or instruct complex mortgage loans. The next step is to support a true omnichannel model with clients and employees interacting over the Internet. This creates new cybersecurity challenges that the bank will have to address.

18.3.6. Printing Credit Cards in Branches

Giving new clients their credit card at the end of the on-boarding appointment would be a differentiating capability. Two scenarios are explored:

- Credit card printers are installed in branches
- “Anonymous” preprinted credit cards are activated at the end of the on-boarding appointment

The credit card printer solution requires a major investment in hardware and system integration work. The micro process shown in Figure 18-8 models the tasks to be implemented. If the required APIs exist, or are easy to implement, integration work is simpler. It will also make running an experiment easier. The bank will conduct a few pilot studies before deciding whether or not to commit to funding the investment.

The bank must also factor-in the logistics implication of putting a printer in each branch. Printer maintenance and consumable renewals have a cost and must be organized.

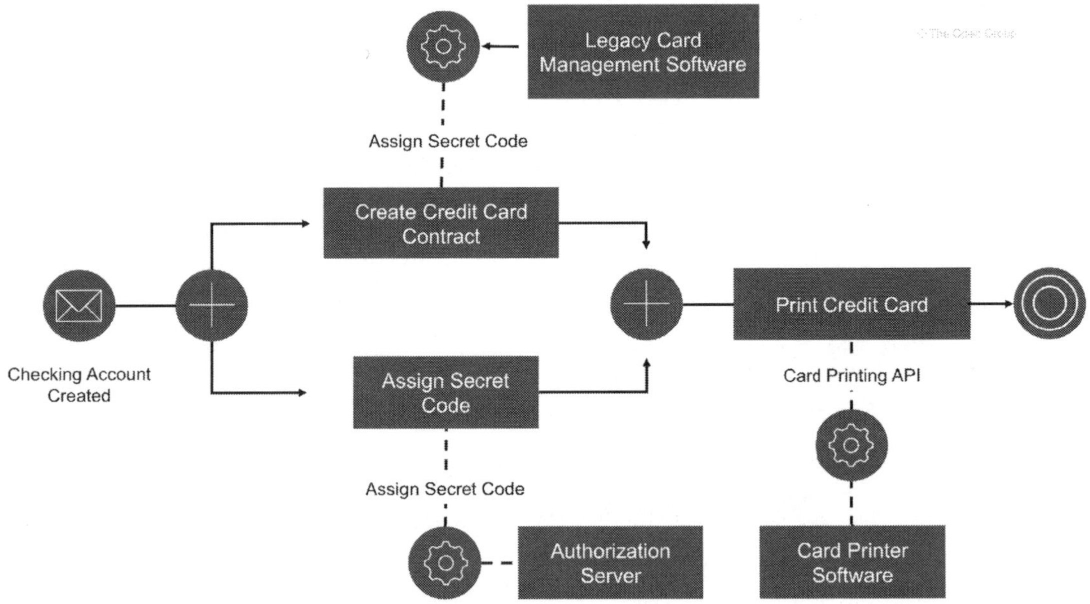

Figure 18-8: Deliver Means of Payment: New Target Condition

The alternative “low tech” solution is to provide a set of preprinted credit cards to branches. These cards would not have the client name printed on them. This would give clients access to a simple and standard means of payment. They would receive their final credit card later.

This next target condition reduces the “deliver means of payment” P/T from 10 minutes to 5 minutes. The big gain is the dramatic reduction of D/T from 5 days to 0 minutes.

18.4. Key Points to Take Away

Value stream mapping can be used to improve product development value streams and production value streams. Product development includes designing the value stream that delivers the product.

The value stream mapping tool mostly helps to identify challenges, target conditions, countermeasures, and ideas for experimentation. Value stream mapping provides guidelines to stimulate thinking; it does not provide standard solutions to be applied mechanically.

18.4.1. Benefits

- The real power of value stream mapping is in developing targets that can be achieved step-by-step
- Horizontal communication between the teams that contribute to the value stream helps participants understand the perspective of others
- Focus on the customer perspective helps to align teams around a common purpose
- Team members understand how the activities for which they are responsible impact customers positively or negatively

18.4.2. Organizational Implications

Different organizational models can support effective value stream management. Organizational models need to balance product focus with functional expertise. When the functional dimension weakens, knowledge management and career development suffer.

The value stream manager role, which is comparable to the classical process owner role, can be implemented with minimum impact on the existing organization.

At the other end of the spectrum, the Toyota chief engineer model defines a role that combines entrepreneurship with good system architecture skills. A chief engineer should be capable of:

- Defining a clear and compelling product vision
- Inspiring excellent engineers
- Designing the architecture of the product and its value stream
- Learning enough knowledge from all disciplines to facilitate the resolution of cross-disciplinary problems

In the middle of the spectrum, Agile teams are mostly stream-aligned and cross-functional. They regroup the roles and skills needed to develop products. They are led by product owners.

Chapter 19. Event Storming

> "People exploring a domain with collaborative brainstorming techniques focusing on domain events."
>
> — Jeremie Grodziski

Event storming has become very popular in the domain-driven design community to help discover a domain. This section presents the event storming workshop format, what it is, and its benefits. The event storming workshop format [Event Storming] was created by Alberto Brandolini [Brandolini, 2019].

19.1. Summary: Why? How? Who?

The goal of an event storming workshop is to **explore a domain** with several people collaboratively.

To do so, people will be placing **domain events** on sticky notes on a wall along a **timeline** with an unlimited modeling surface.

The workshop puts together three kinds of people: **people with questions, people with answers**, and a **facilitator**.

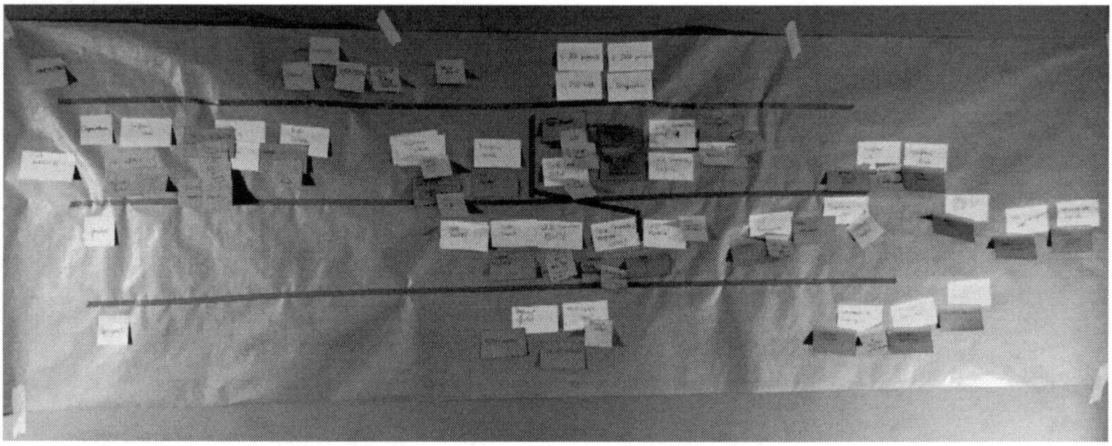

Figure 19-1: Event Storming Modeling Surface Example

19.2. Domain Event

> "Something that happened in the past that the domain experts care about."
>
> — Eric Evans

The orange color sticky note is the convention for the event.

The event is named with a past participle because of its simple semantic and notation. For example, order placed, order paid, order executed, product sent, etc.

Events are used because they are easy to grasp and relevant for domain experts.

19.3. Event Storming Principles

Event storming workshops focus on domain events structured along a timeline.

The goal of the event storming workshop is to maximize the learning of all the participants. By the end of the workshop, the participants should have gained a shared knowledge of the domain subject of the workshop.

The physical setup is important: The surface of the wall represents an unlimited modeling surface, and everyone should stand up to increase engagement in the workshop. There must be a continuous effort of every participant to maximize the engagement. The collaborative approach involves people with questions, people with answers, and a facilitator.

Markers and sticky notes should be available in different colors and in sufficient quantity.

There should be no limitation of the scope under investigation, and the model should be continuously refined through low-fidelity incremental notation.

19.4. Types of Event Storming Session

Event storming can have different goals, but mainly these two common ones are distinguished:

- **Big-picture event storming**
  - Embrace the whole complexity
  - Maximize learning
- **Design-level event storming**
  - Assumption: People have a shared understanding of the underlying domain
  - Focus: Implementing software features that are solving a specific problem

19.5. Event Storming Notation and Concepts

The concepts used during an event storming session, apart from the event concept, are voluntarily set by the participants whenever they feel they need one. However, the facilitator can suggest the following “usual” concepts:

- **Command** (usually with a blue sticky note)
  - Represents an intention sent to a system for making something
  - Result is either success or failure
  - Named with a verb and a nominal group
- **Aggregate or entity** (usually with a yellow sticky note)
  - Cluster of domain objects, treated as a single unit
  - One of its objects is the root, ensuring the integrity of the whole aggregate by enforcing its invariant policy and transactional boundaries
- **Reaction** (usually with a purple sticky note)
  - Cluster of domain objects, treated as a single unit
  - One of its objects is the root, ensuring the integrity of the whole aggregate by enforcing its invariant policy and transactional boundaries
- **Hotspot** (usually with a red sticky note)
  - Issue or something important that the organization must care about
- **Policy or rule**
  - The flow of events and reactions together
- **Persona**
  - Person triggering a command
- **Read model/query**
  - Request asking for data in a specific model

19.6. Benefits

- Opportunities to learn and facilitate a structured conversation about the domain; this workshop is the best and most efficient way for all participants to have shared knowledge of a domain
- Uncover assumptions about how people think the system works; allows participants to identify misunderstandings and missing concepts
- Shared understanding of the problem and potential solutions
- Highly visual, tactile representation of business concepts and how they relate
- Allows participants to quickly try out multiple domain models to see where concepts work and where they break down
- Focus on concrete examples, not abstract ideas

19.7. Event Storming Workshop Facilitation Techniques

- Facilitator hangs the first sticky note
- Ask questions
    - Where does the money come from?
    - What are the targets, and how will it be clear they have been reached?
    - Is there something missing; why is there a gap?
    - For whom is this event important — end user, stakeholder, etc.?
- Visualize alternatives
    - It is too early to decide; let divergence happen
- Reverse narrative
    - Start from the end — what needs to happen beforehand so that this event can happen too?
- Interrupt long discussions
    - Visualize every opinion and ask every party if they feel their opinion is accurately represented
- Timebox
    - Use the Pomodoro Technique®; after each 25-minute Pomodoro, ask what is going well and what is not — move on even if the model is incomplete
- Constantly move sticky notes to create room for hotspots
- Hang red sticky notes when it is felt there is an issue
- At the end, take a photo
    - Throw the model away and start again with different people

Chapter 20. Domain-Driven Design: Strategic Patterns

This chapter introduces the domain-driven design strategic patterns.

The term "domain-driven design" was coined by Eric Evans in his book *Domain-Driven Design: Tackling Complexity in the Heart of Software* [Evans, 2003].

Domain-driven design offers strategic building blocks for analyzing and structuring the **problem space** and the **solution space**.

20.1. Problem Space

The problem space holds what the enterprise does — its business capabilities — to keep it running and able to operate. A business capability is a specific function or ability that the enterprise possesses in order to achieve its goals.

The problem space describes several things:

- The **usages** of the customers and employees of the enterprise
- The **words** used by the people and their **meanings** — the domain language — the language used by people as it is, so it can be messy and organic
- The **requirements and constraints** of the business
- The **people** who operate the business

20.1.1. Domains and Sub-Domains

The problem space holds the **domain** within which the enterprise operates and represents the world as it is perceived; it describes the *Business Architecture*.

The ***domain*** is the set of concepts that, through **use cases**, allows people in the enterprise to **solve problems**.

Sub-Domains

A domain can be decomposed into sub-domains, which typically reflects some organizational structure. Sub-domain boundaries are determined in part by communication structures within an organization. The sub-domains are stable; they change only for strategic reasons and are independent of software.

Example of an E-Commerce System

An e-commerce system consists of a product catalog, an inventory system, a purchasing system, and an accounting system, etc. They are sub-systems, in that the system as a whole is partitioned into them. The system is partitioned in this specific way because the resulting sub-systems form cohesive units of functionality.

How to Identify Sub-Domains

Domain knowledge is key to decomposing a domain into sub-domains that have a high level of internal cohesion and minimum dependencies with other sub-domains. Conducting an event storming workshop is a great way to accelerate the acquisition of domain knowledge and explore domain decomposition scenarios.

Distillation

The enterprise operates with several sub-domains. Depending on its business, some are *generic* (such as accounting or HR), some are *support*, and some are *core*, meaning the current strategy directly relies on the core domains to attain its goals. Not all parts of a large system will be well-designed.

> The **core domain** is the domain that directly contributes to the current enterprise strategy.

20.2. Solution Space

The business capabilities are almost the same for different enterprises involved in the same business, but their implementations — the solution space — will differ. While sub-domains delimit the applicability of domains, bounded contexts delimit the applicability of domain models. As such, the bounded context is within the solution space.

Bounded context is the solution as it is designed. It describes the software architecture and is used to manage the complexity, and is, therefore, linked to the business.

Bounded context means different models of the same thing (e.g., books, customers, etc.) and is represented by models and software that implement those models. This is where patterns and heuristics are found.

Domain Model and Ubiquitous Language

> "A language structured around the domain model and used by all team members to connect all the activities of the team with the software." [Evans, 2003]
>
> — Eric Evans, Domain-Driven Design: Tackling Complexity in the Heart of Software

The ubiquitous language is a deliberate language designed to be unambiguous and on which all stakeholders agree. This language is found in every artifact manipulated by the stakeholders (UI, database, source code, documents, etc.). The concepts conveyed by the domain model are the primary means of communication; these words should be used in speech and in every written artifact. If an idea cannot be expressed using these concepts, the designers should iterate once again and extend the model, and they should look for and remove ambiguities and inconsistencies. The domain model is the backbone of the ubiquitous language.

Bounded Context

> "An operational definition of where a particular model is well-defined and applicable. Typically a sub-system, or the work owned by a particular team." [Evans, 2003]
>
> — Eric Evans, Domain-Driven Design: Tackling Complexity in the Heart of Software

A bounded context delimits the applicability of a particular model so that team members have a clear and shared understanding of what has to be consistent and how it relates to other contexts. Bounded contexts are not modules.

Bounded contexts separate concerns and decrease complexity. A bounded context is the boundary for the meaning of a model. A bounded context creates autonomy, thus allowing a dedicated team for each. Bounded contexts simplify the architecture by separating concerns.

How to Identify a Bounded Context

Conflicts of naming suggest different contexts because they indicate that the model mixes different ubiquitous languages.

20.3. Context Map

A context map describes the flow of models between contexts and provides an overview of the systems landscape. A context map helps to identify governance issues between applications and teams. It helps to see how teams communicate, and their "power" relationships. With a context map, a clear view of where and how bad models propagate through IS landscapes is obtained.

It is possible to use the metaphor of a flowing river to describe the relations between two bounded contexts: if those upstream pollute the river, those downstream will be impacted — not the opposite. And so, a relationship between two bounded contexts is one in which the actions of the upstream group affect the downstream group, but the actions of the downstream group do not affect the upstream group. It is not about the data flow's direction, but about the model's flow.

Context map patterns are categorized in three ways:

- **Upstream patterns**: Open Host Service and Event Publisher; see Figure 20-1
- **Midway patterns**: Shared Kernel, Published Language, Separate Ways, Partnership; see Figure 20-2
- **Downstream patterns**: Customer/Supplier, Conformist, Anti-Corruption Layer; see Figure 20-3

20.3.1. Upstream Patterns

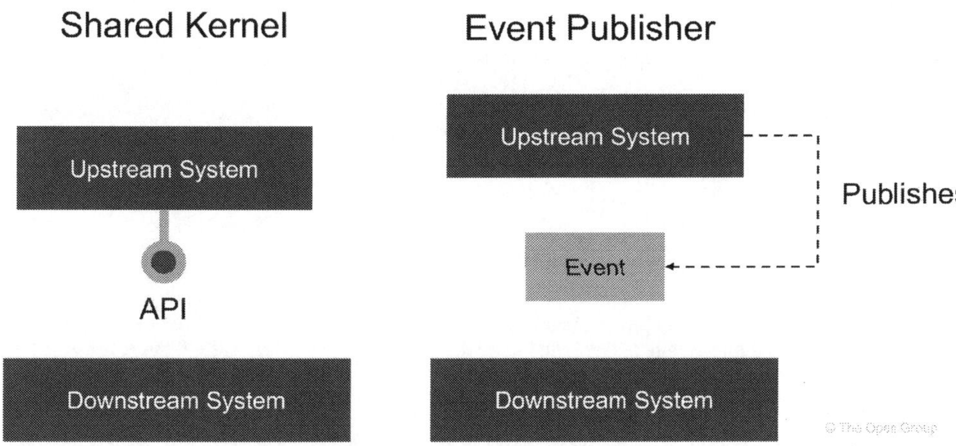

Figure 20-1: Domain-Driven Design Context Map Upstream Patterns

- Open Host Service

> "Define a protocol that gives access to your sub-system as a set of services. Open the protocol so that all who need to integrate with you can use it. Enhance and expand the protocol to handle new integration requirements, except when a single team has idiosyncratic needs. Then, use a one-off translator to augment the protocol for that special case so that the shared protocol can stay simple and coherent." [Vernon, 2013]
>
> — Vaughn Vernon, Implementing Domain-Driven Design

- Event Publisher

  Domain events are something that happens in the domain and that is important to domain experts. An upstream context publishes all its domain events through a messaging system (preferably an asynchronous one), and downstream contexts can subscribe to the events that are relevant for them and conform or transform those events in their models (following an Access Control List (ACL)) and react accordingly.

20.3.2. Midway Patterns

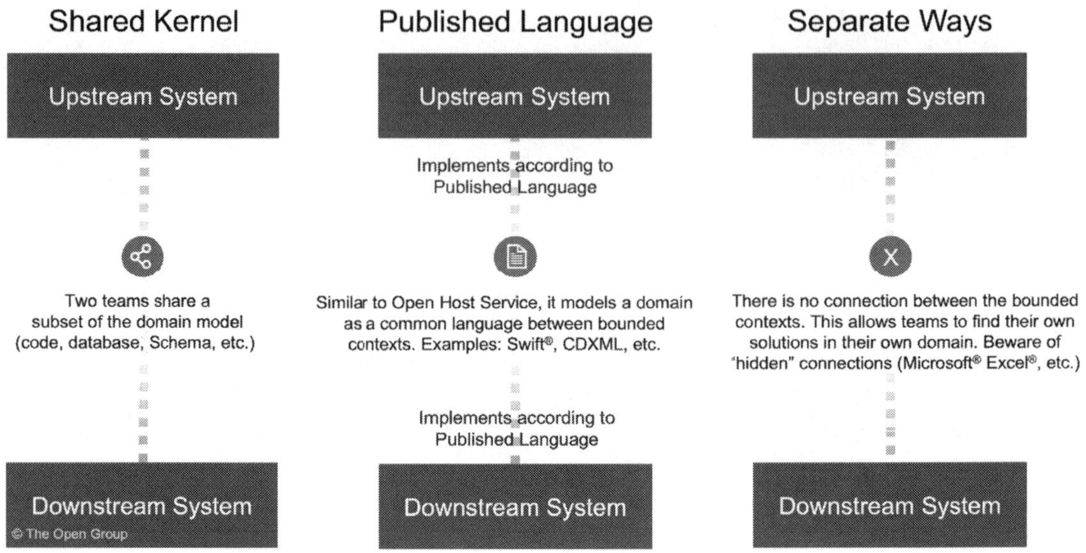

Figure 20-2: Midway Patterns

- Shared Kernel

> "Designate some subset of the domain model that the two teams agree to share. Of course this includes, along with this subset of the model, the subset of code or of the database design associated with that part of the model. This explicitly shared stuff has special status, and shouldn't be changed without consultation with the other team." [Evans, 2003]
>
> — Eric Evans, Domain-Driven Design: Tackling Complexity in the Heart of Software

- Published Language

> "The translation between the models of two bounded contexts requires a common language. Use a well-documented shared language that can express the necessary domain information as a common medium of communication, translating as necessary into and out of that language. Published Language is often combined with Open Host Service." [Evans, 2003]
>
> — Eric Evans, Domain-Driven Design: Tackling Complexity in the Heart of Software

- Separate Ways

> "If two sets of functionality have no significant relationship, they can be completely cut loose from each other. Integration is always expensive, and sometimes the benefit is small. Declare a bounded context to have no connection to the others at all, enabling developers to find simple, specialized solutions within this small scope." [Vernon, 2013]
>
> — Vaughn Vernon, Implementing Domain-Driven Design

- Partnership

> "Where development failure in either of two contexts would result in delivery failure for both, forge a partnership between the teams in charge of the two contexts. Institute a process for coordinated planning of development and joint management of integration. The teams must cooperate on the evolution of their interfaces to accommodate the development needs of both systems. Interdependent features should be scheduled so that they are completed for the same release." [Vernon, 2013]
>
> — Vaughn Vernon, Implementing Domain-Driven Design

20.3.3. Downstream Patterns

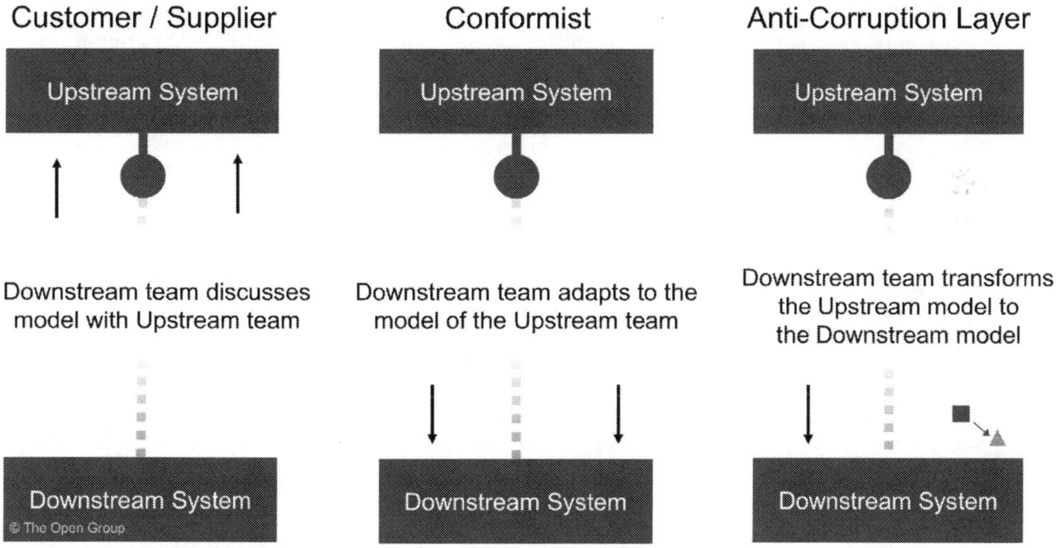

Figure 20-3: Downstream Patterns

- Customer/Supplier

> "When two teams are in an upstream-downstream relationship, where the upstream team may succeed interdependently of the fate of the downstream team, the needs of the downstream team come to be addressed in a variety of ways with a wide range of consequences. Downstream priorities factor into upstream planning. Negotiate and budget tasks for downstream requirements so that everyone understands the commitment and schedule." [Vernon, 2013]
>
> — Vaughn Vernon, Implementing Domain-Driven Design

> "The freewheeling development of the upstream team can be cramped if the downstream team has veto power over changes, or if procedures for requesting changes are too cumbersome. The upstream team may even be inhibited and worried about breaking the downstream system. Meanwhile, the downstream team can be helpless, at the mercy of upstream priorities." [Evans, 2003]
>
> — Eric Evans, Domain-Driven Design: Tackling Complexity in the Heart of Software

- Conformist

> "When two development teams have an upstream/downstream relationship in which the upstream has no motivation to provide for the downstream team's needs, the downstream team is helpless. Altruism may motivate upstream developers to make promises, but they are unlikely to be fulfilled. Belief in those good intentions leads the downstream team to make plans based on features that will never be available. The downstream project will be delayed until the team ultimately learns to live with what it is given. An interface tailored to the needs of the downstream team is not on the cards." [Evans, 2003]
>
> — Eric Evans, Domain-Driven Design: Tackling Complexity in the Heart of Software

> "The downstream team eliminates the complexity of translation between bounded contexts by slavishly adhering to the model of the upstream team." [Vernon, 2013]
>
> — Vaughn Vernon, Implementing Domain-Driven Design

- Anti-Corruption Layer

> "Translation layers can be simple, even elegant, when bridging well-designed bounded contexts with cooperative teams. But when control or communication is not adequate to pull off a shared kernel, partner, or customer-supplier relationship, translation becomes more complex. The translation layer takes on a more defensive tone. As a downstream client, create an isolating layer to provide your system with functionality of the upstream system in terms of your own domain model. This layer talks to the other system through its existing interface, requiring little or no modification to the other system. Internally, the layer translates in one or both directions as necessary between the two models." [Vernon, 2013]
>
> — Vaughn Vernon, Implementing Domain-Driven Design

20.3.4. Mapping the Context Map Patterns

As shown in Figure 20-4, the context map patterns can be organized along two axes: “Control” and “Communication”.

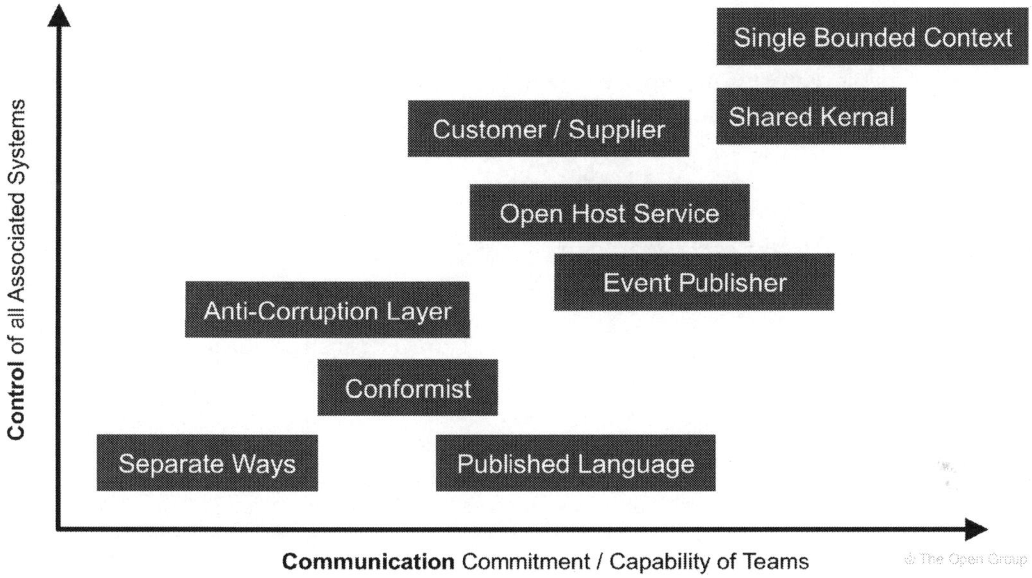

Figure 20-4: Mapping Context Map Patterns

The “Separate Ways” corresponds to bounded contexts that have no connection to others. The “Single Bounded Context” is indicative of a domain that is not modularized. The patterns in between correspond to different ways of handling upstream/downstream relations [Evans, 2003]:

- “Published Language” uses a well-documented and shared language that can express the necessary domain information as a common medium of communication, translating as required
- “Conformist” eliminates the complexity of translation between bounded contexts by slavishly adhering to the model of the upstream team
- “Anti-Corruption Layer” creates an isolating layer to provide clients with functionality in terms of their own domain model; the layer talks to the other system through its existing interface, requiring little or no modification to the other system
- “Open Host Service” defines a protocol that gives access to the sub-system as a set of services
- “Event Publisher” communicates with other bounded contexts through domain events that can be consumed by other bounded contexts
- “Customer/Supplier” establishes a clear customer/supplier relationship between the two teams
- “Shared Kernel” designates some subset of the domain model that the two teams agree to share

Chapter 21. Data Information and AI

The rapidly dropping cost of memory and storage combined with the rise in popularity of big data has motivated enterprises to collect an increasing amount of data. Some enterprises collected vast amounts of data without a clear purpose. That data is stored in data lakes as data scientists try to work out what to do with it.

In 2016, for example, Capital One® reported gathering over 450GB per day in raw data, which drove costs up. As much as 80% of gathered data is meaningless or unused, and key data is sometimes missing [Paulchell, 2016].

In a batch architecture, time to insight is too long. It can take several days just to get the right data in the right place, process it, and generate actionable insights:

- Application generates data that is captured into operational data storage
- Data is moved daily to a data platform that runs an Extract, Transform, Load (ETL) to clean, transform, and enrich data
- Once processed, data is loaded into data warehouses, data marts, or Online Analytical Processing (OLAP) cubes
- Analytics tools programmed with languages, such as R®, SAS® software, or Python®, are used in conjunction with visualization tools
- Reporting tools such as R, SAS software, SQL, or Tableau® are used to analyze data and find insights
- Actions based on insights are implemented

The batch model is prevalent even after the big data revolution. Traditional Business Intelligence (BI) technology is still used by many enterprises to manage financial, risk, or commercial data. Migrating from legacy tools and technologies is difficult and often requires the rewriting of legacy code. For example, a large bank that uses Teradata™ to run risk models had to re-implement them because the algorithms were dependent on the DBMS data schema.

21.1. Data Streaming Architectures

The shift to an architecture capable of handling large amounts of data coming at high speed, processed continuously, and acted upon in real time makes it possible to access data when and where it is needed. Technologies such as Apache Spark™ or Flink® enable the shift toward real-time data streaming. Analyzing the evolution of the technology landscape is beyond the scope of this document; it evolves so rapidly.

The requirements of well-architected streaming solutions are:

- To scale up and down gracefully
- To auto heal, in case major spikes break the system
- Throttling, to protect downstream systems that could not handle the spike
- Fault tolerance, to improve resilience
- Modularity of the solutions building blocks, to facilitate reuse and evolution
- Monitoring friendliness, to facilitate business and IT operations

21.2. Coupling Data Streaming with AI

Enterprises create innovative services by coupling real-time data streaming with AI; for example, the Capital One Auto Navigator® app [Groenfeldt, 2018].

The new service idea started with a survey of 1,000 nationally representative US adults to learn how they approach the car shopping process.

> The survey found that buying a car causes anxiety for many adults: 63% are not sure they got a great deal the last time they bought a car, and 95% would consider not buying a car the same day they went to look at it at a dealership. *"When it comes to big life decisions, half of people report researching and buying a car (50%) is more time-consuming than deciding where to go to college (43%) and choosing a baby name (22%)"*, the survey found.

Customers can use their smartphone to recognize a car, even in motion, which caught their attention. AI is used to classify the car and help find similar ones that are selling in nearby markets. The user can save the information to prepare for a visit to a dealership.

Once customers have identified cars they like, the app Auto Navigator [Auto Navigator] lets them personalize financing to simulate payments specific to the car they want. Pre-qualification has no impact on their credit score. When they are ready to purchase the car they have all the information needed, spend less time at the dealership, and get a better deal.

> "I was very impressed with how easy my buying experience was. I had my financing ahead of time and was able to make my time at the dealership so much faster."
>
> — Testimony from the Capital One Site

Now that the power of combining great customer research with fast data and AI technology to develop innovative products has been described, the Data Architecture impacts can be analyzed.

Most fundamental data management principles and best practices remain valid even though some need to be updated to account for business and technology evolution. The emergence of new data engineering patterns requires a fundamental shift in the way data systems are architected.

21.3. Data Model and Reality

The correspondence between things inside the IS and things in the real world still matters. Table 21-1 shows:

- The correspondence between data and the real world
- Data quality criteria are mostly technology-neutral, though implementation is likely to leverage technology

Table 21-1: Audit Control Objectives

Objective	Control
All transactions are recorded	Procedures should be in place to avoid the omission of operations in the account books.
Each transaction is:	
Real	Do not record fictitious transactions and do not record the same transaction twice.
Properly valued	Verify that the amounts posted are correct.
Accounted for in the correct period	Verify that the business rules that determine in which period a transaction should be posted are applied.
Correctly allocated	Verify that transactions are aggregated into the right accounts.

Data is only a model of reality; it is not reality. Depending on the context, the same territory (reality) can be represented using different maps (models).

21.4. The Monolithic Data Model

> When files get integrated into a database serving multiple applications, that ambiguity-resolving mechanism is lost.
>
> — William Kent, Data and Reality: A Timeless Perspective on Perceiving and Managing Information in Our Imprecise World

To illustrate his point, the author uses the example of the concept of a “part”. In a warehouse context, each part has a part number and occurs in various quantities at various warehouses. In a quality control context, part means one physical object; each part being subjected to certain tests, and the test data maintained in a database separately for each part.

Figure 21-1 represents the database that would serve the inventory management and quality control applications. In addition, a data model has been created to represent the part concept in each context.

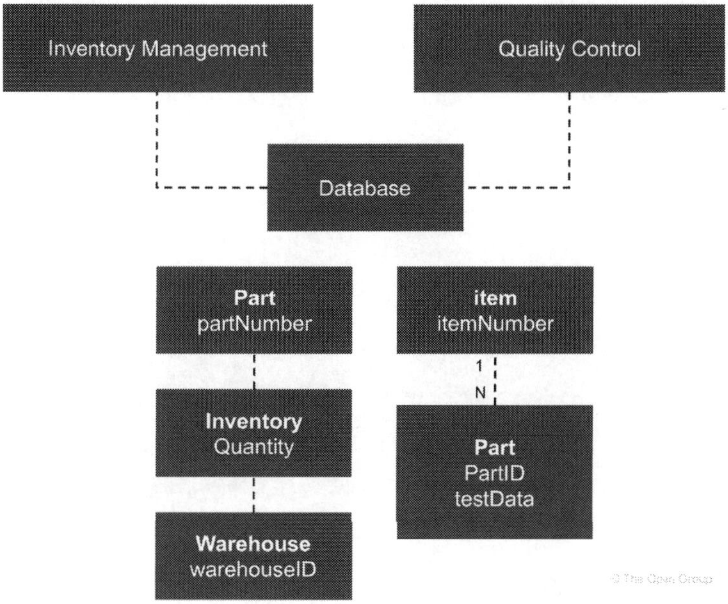

Figure 21-1: Part Modeling

The word “part” has a specific meaning in each context. In designing a shared database, the model would be unified at the expense of the vocabulary used in one of the contexts. As “Part” and “Item” mean the same thing, there are two options:

1. Rename “Item” “Part” in the “Quality Control” context and find another name for “Part” in this context
2. Rename “Part” “Item” in the “Inventory Management” context and find another name for “Item” in this context

The shared database would start using a language of its own, which could lead to communication problems and errors.

> Total unification of the domain model for a large system will not be feasible or cost-effective.
>
> — Eric Evan, Domain-Driven Design

The example of Figure 21-2 illustrates the total data unification that is common in financial systems. This type of “monster” project often fails because it is impractical to fold all source system data models into one generic data model.

This approach would create a number of problems; for example:

- Specifying translation rules between domain-specific data models and the common data model is difficult because the cognitive load is too high for data modelers
- It is unrealistic to replicate source system business rules into the data monolith; for example, lease

accounting rules require an estimate of when a leased car is likely to be returned

- When a defect occurs, it is difficult to backtrack to the root causes
- Back-and-forth data structure translation is costly and error-prone
- When new products or new regulations are introduced, mastering all the resulting side effects on the monolithic Data Architecture is challenging

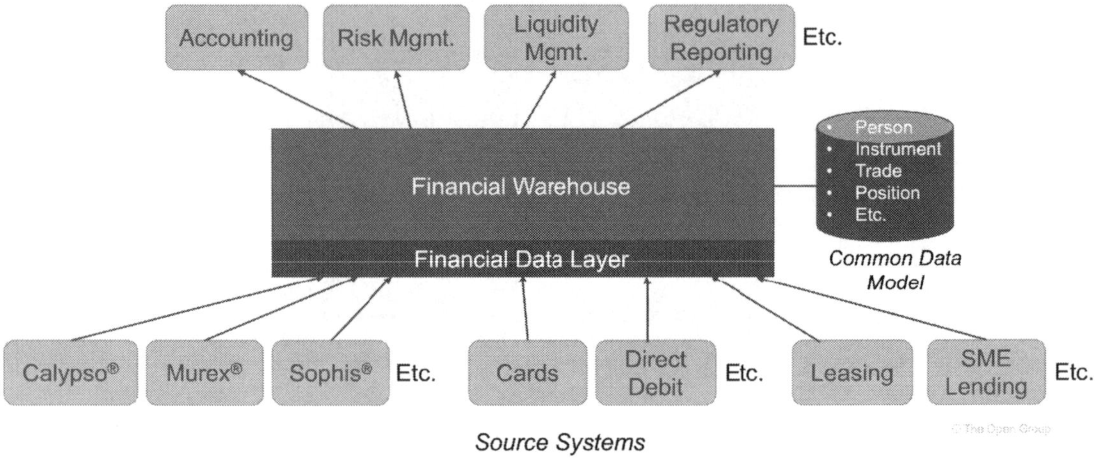

Figure 21-2: Monolithic Data Architecture

21.5. Moving Away from Monolithic Data Architectures

In a post on Martin Fowler's blog, Zhamak Dehghani shows how the learnings of the past decade in building distributed architectures at scale can be adapted and applied to the domain of data, and introduces a new enterprise Data Architecture that she calls "data mesh" [Dehghani 2019].

Zhamak argues that instead of flowing the data from domains into a centrally-owned data lake or platform, domains need to host and serve their domain datasets in an easily consumable way. This requires a shift in thinking from a push and ingest, traditionally through ETLs and more recently through event streams, to a serve and pull model across all domains.

The monolithic Data Architecture is replaced by a modular one, and composed of:

- Bounded contexts aligned with data source domains, such as fixed-income trading or consumer lending
- Bounded contexts aligned with consumption domains, such as accounting or liquidity

Business facts are represented by domain events that capture what happened in reality.

A product-thinking mindset can help provide a better experience to data consumers. For example, source domains can provide easily consumable historical snapshots of the source domain datasets, aggregated over a time interval that closely reflects the interval of change for their domain.

21.6. Machine Learning (ML) Pipelines

There is a lot of data manipulation and transformation in ML systems. ML pipelines industrialize data manipulation and transformation. They are composed of data processing components that run in a certain order. Data components usually run asynchronously. Each component pulls in a large amount of data, processes it, and puts results in other data stores.

Each data component is fairly self-contained and communicates with other data components via data stores. If a component breaks down, downstream components can often continue to run normally by using the last output from the broken component. This makes the architecture quite robust unless a broken component goes unnoticed for some time. This is why proper monitoring is required to avoid data going stale.

TensorFlow™ Extended (TFX) is an end-to-end platform for deploying production ML pipelines. Figure 21-3, which is copied from the TFX User Guide [TFX User Guide], gives an example of an ML pipeline.

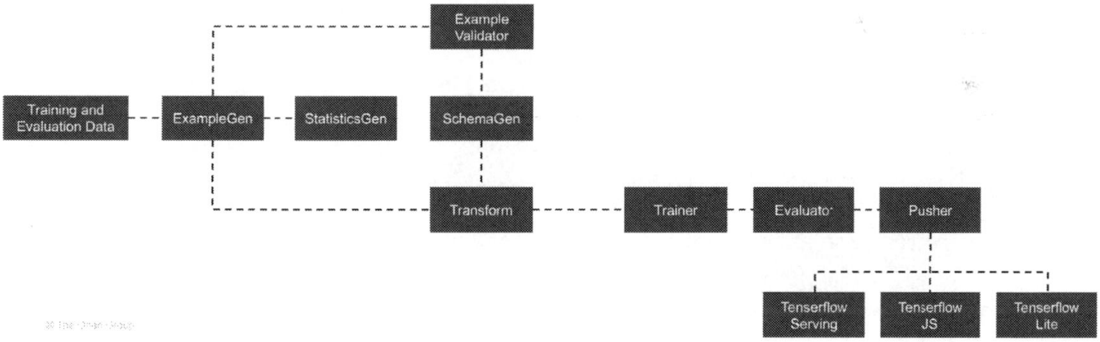

Figure 21-3: TensorFlow Pipeline

It includes a set of data components:

- **ExampleGen** is the initial input component of a pipeline that ingests and optionally splits the input dataset
- **StatisticsGen** calculates statistics for the dataset

- **SchemaGen** examines the statistics and creates a data schema
- **ExampleValidator** looks for anomalies and missing values in the dataset
- **Transform** performs feature engineering on the dataset
- **Trainer** trains the model
- **Evaluator** performs deep analysis of the training results and helps to validate exported models, ensuring that they are "good enough" to be pushed to production
- **Pusher** deploys the model on a serving infrastructure

TFX provides several Python packages that are the libraries used to create pipeline components.

21.7. Deep Learning for Mobile

Mobile devices(mobile devices are now capable of leveraging the ever-increasing power of AI to learn user behavior and preferences, enhance photographs, carry out full-fledged conversations, and more [Kent, 2012].

Leveraging AI on mobile devices can improve UX [Singh & Bhadani, 2020]:

- **Personalization** adapts the device and the app to a user's habits and their unique profile instead of generic profile-oriented applications
- **Virtual assistants** are able to interpret human speech using Natural Language Understanding (NLU), and generally respond via synthesized voices
- **Facial recognition** identifies or verifies a face or understands a facial expression from digital images and videos
- **AI-powered cameras** recognize, understand, and enhance scenes and photographs
- **Predictive text** help users compose texts and send emails much faster than before

The most popular apps now use AI to enhance UX.

21.8. A Few Concluding Words

The shift toward real-time data streaming and modular Data Architecture changes the way enterprise data systems are designed and developed. When combined with AI, it is possible to create innovative products that deliver superior customer experience, such as the one illustrated by Section 21.2.

Appendix A: Axioms for the Practice of Agile Architecture

This document includes a set of axioms which are guidelines or restrictions that Agile Architects are recommended to follow. Adherence to these axioms will help to guide the Digital and Agile Transformation of the enterprise.

The axioms are named, and then each is presented as a brief statement with expositional and narrative discussion.

In *Think like Amazon*, John Rossman [Rossman, 2019] claims that "*digital is about two things: speed and agility — externally to your customers and market and internally within your organization*".

John Rossman states that speed is "*about moving in one direction very efficiently, very precisely. Operational excellence at scale is the business equivalent to speed*".

Several of the axioms have been conceived to support speed and agility. All the axioms support the digital and Agile enterprise.

Axiom 1. *Customer Experience Focus*

Customer experience focus is a way of doing business that meets the expectations of customers. By analyzing the interactions between the enterprise and its customers, Agile Architecture shall enable the delivery of a pleasant and differentiated customer experience.

In today's digital world, the quality of customer experience is becoming a critical success factor. Consumers and Business-to-Business (B2B) customers have expectations that are shaped by Internet giants. For example, a prime delivery service that includes free shipping, preset ordering options (preset address, preset credit card), and return options with prepaid or printed return labels is becoming the new norm of the retail industry.

Axiom 2. *Outside-In Thinking*

A very large car manufacturer recently looked at cars from the perspective of "*how it is used by a customer rather than how it is created or delivered*". Does this mean these companies no longer produce cars? Absolutely not. It illustrates the shift from an inside-out stance toward an outside-in stance that could lead to reinventing the automotive industry.

Just asking clients what they need is not enough to create a differentiated customer experience. Discovering the hidden or untold customer needs is the key to success. Agile Architecture shall use marketing and design methods to discover how customers are likely to use products and services. Job-to-be-done analysis, customer journey mapping, and design thinking are examples of methods used by Agile enterprises. Design thinking, which is a human-centered approach, incorporates human cognition and emotion as key aspects of the value definition.

Axiom 3. *Rapid Feedback Loops*

Research seeks to understand the needs and desires, both explicit and latent, of target customers and users. Prototyping helps to experiment with research assumptions before a product or service is released. It can be done at any stage and helps to architect better solutions. Agile Architecture shall seek rapid feedback loops to verify customer and user assumptions. Rapid feedback loops are short, iterative cycles that enable to quickly validate assumptions about customer and user needs.

Don Norman [Norman, 2013] states that *"feedback is critical to managing expectations, and good design provides this. Feedback — knowledge of results — is how expectations are resolved and is critical to learning and the development of skilled behavior"*.

Axiom 4. *Touchpoint Orchestration*

Agile Architecture shall enable a holistic orchestration of every single touchpoint of an enterprise and its ecosystem: "*The boundaries between external and internal touchpoints are blurring and will continue to do so*" [Wind & Hays, 2015].

Clients and users are empowered to take control of their relationship with the enterprise and its media. Touchpoint orchestration delivers relevant utility or enjoyment at the right time, place, and social or physical context to the right people.

Axiom 5. *Value Stream Alignment*

Agile Architecture shall identify the enterprise value streams. Value shall be specified from the standpoint of the customer. A value stream shall be identified for each product or service family — from concept to launch and from order to delivery [Rother & Shook, 2003].

Identifying common steps across several value streams is a key input to operating model design.

Axiom 6. *Autonomous Cross-Functional Teams*

Agile Architecture shall segment the organization into autonomous cross-functional teams. Team autonomy is a prerequisite to speed. Why? If teams spend too much time managing dependencies, it increases lead time.

The way teams are structured has a major influence on productivity, employee satisfaction, and agility. William Pasmore [Pasmore et al., 2019] reports the discoveries of Eric Trist and his colleague who have analyzed why the introduction of new technology succeeds or fails. They reveal that the way work and how teams are organized is the explaining factor: "*Teams of multi-skilled workers formed spontaneously and took on responsibility for the entire cycle of mining operations ... These teams were capable of self-direction, reducing the dependence on supervisors to provide constant direction to individual workers. Problems were solved by the team as they were encountered, resulting in operations running more smoothly and safely.*"

Axiom 7. *Authority, Responsibility, and Accountability Distribution*

Experience quality and operational excellence require effective coordination and cooperation between autonomous teams. Agile Architecture shall balance freedom with responsibility and accountability. Why? Accountability and responsibility improve predictability, which is a prerequisite to:

- Meeting the customer promise
- Industrializing operations

Agile Architecture shall distribute authority, responsibility, and accountability at each layer of the organization: "*It is essential to understand how authority, responsibility, and accountability are designed and broadcast within a socio-technical system and how these concepts can be managed during an engineering process of these systems*" [Berdjag et al., 2019].

Axiom 8. *Loosely-Coupled Systems*

High-performing teams are more likely to have loosely-coupled architectures than medium and low-performing teams [DevOps, 2015; 2017]. When dependencies are minimized, teams can develop, test, and deploy new functions and features without depending on other teams for additional work, resources, or approvals, and with less back-and-forth communication [Forsgren, 2018].

Agile Architecture shall create new modular systems or decompose monolithic legacy ones into loosely-coupled sub-systems and components. Modularity matters because:

- It shortens development time as separate teams can work on each module with little need for communication
- It increases product flexibility as changes to one module have little impact on other modules [Parnas, 1972]

Axiom 9. *Modular Data Platform*

The centralized and monolithic data platform is an anti-pattern [Dehghani, 2019]. Agile Architecture shall create modular data platforms using domain decomposition logic: "*Instead of flowing the data from domains into a centrally-owned data lake or platform, domains need to host and serve their domain datasets in an easily consumable way*".

Source domain datasets represent closely the raw data at the point of creation, and are not fitted or modeled for a particular consumer. Data consumers can always go back to the business facts and create new aggregations or projections. They use data platform self-service capabilities to retrieve the data they need, formatted the way they want.

Axiom 10. *Simple Common Operating Principles*

Agile Architecture shall use a set of simple mechanisms that all elements and connections will use. For example, in the software domain all components or services will expose functionality using standard APIs, and all inter-services communication will use these APIs.

Axiom 11. *Partitioning Over Layering*

The layered architecture pattern tends to lend itself toward monolithic applications, even if presentation and business layers are split into separate deployable units [Richards, 2015]. On the business side, functional organizational units such as marketing, finance, or operations are equivalent to layers. Layering tends to create silos, which reduces agility and scalability.

To counter these drawbacks, Agile Architecture shall partition the enterprise and its systems. Partitioning shall be market-driven at the business level, capability-driven at the operating model level, and domain-driven at the software level.

Axiom 12. *Organization Mirroring Architecture*

Agile Architecture shall structure Agile teams in a way that maps the system's intentional architecture.

Conway's law states: "*Any organization that designs a system (defined broadly) will produce a design whose structure is a copy of the organization's communication structure.*" The Inverse Conway Maneuver is about shaping the enterprise's organization in a way that mirrors its intentional product and software architectures.

The interested reader can find a description of the Inverse Conway Maneuver in *Team Topologies: Organizing Business and Technology Teams for Fast Flow* [Skelton & Pais, 2019], Chapter §1: "The Problem with Org Charts".

Axiom 13. *Organizational Leveling*

Organizations shall be described at different granularity levels:

- Group level: Economic entities formed of a set of companies or public agencies, which are either controlled by the same entity or the controlling entity itself
- Entity level: An enterprise, a business unit of an enterprise, a governmental body, or state agency
- Team of teams: Large organizational units that capture at scale the traits of agility normally limited to small teams [McChrystal et al., 2015]
- Agile teams, the size of which do not exceed 10 to 12 members

Axiom 14. *Bias for Change*

Agile Architecture shall welcome changing requirements, even late in development. The architecture model is a living artifact that evolves and is continuously refined as requirements evolve and the organization learns.

Though BDUF is an Agile anti-pattern, does it mean architecture should solely be a product from emergence? As James Coplien and Gertrud Bjørnvig argue [Coplien & Bjørnvig, 2010], some intentional architecture saves waste and accelerates the decision process.

Agile Architecture shall seek a balance between intentional and emerging. Intentional architecture provides value if it is done differently. Intentional architecture represents a set of assumptions that must be verified. It should not slow down the integration of new requirements.

Axiom 15. *Project to Product Shift*

A true Agile team does not deliver a project but a product. Product-centricity shall drive the Agile organization: *"Moving from project-oriented management to product-oriented management is critical for connecting software delivery to the business"* [Kersten 2018]. The product-based focus helps to create stable Agile teams that have an end-to-end perspective and are staffed with stable resources.

In an Agile context, product-centricity refers to the shift from temporary organizational structures (projects) to permanent ones. A product-centric organization is composed of cross-functional Agile teams which are responsible for developing products and operating them. The DevOps principle *"you build it, you run it"* is core to product-centricity.

Axiom 16. *Secure by Design*

Agile Architecture shall create an environment that helps developers to build security into their design and codebase from the start. The Agile enterprise will shift from DevOps to DevSecOps, where security is embedded at every stage of the software delivery lifecycle.

Appendix B: Acronyms

ABB

Architecture Building Block

ACL

Access Control List

ADR

Architecture Decision Record

AI

Artificial Intelligence

API

Application Program Interface

ATM

Automated Teller Machine

AWS

Amazon Web Services

B2B

Business-to-Business

BBVA

Banco Bilbao Vizcaya Argentaria

BDUF

Big Design Up Front

BI

Business Intelligence

CAS

Complex Adaptive System

CD

Continuous Delivery

CDXML

ChemDraw® eXtensible Markup Language

CEO

Chief Executive Officer

CFO

Chief Finance Officer

CFT

Cross File Transfer

CGS

CUSIP Global Services

CI

Continuous Integration

CIB

Corporate & Investment Banking

CLI

Command Line Interface

CLR

Common Language Runtime

CMM

Capability Maturity Model

CMMI

Capability Maturity Model Integration

CNCF

Cloud Native Computing Foundation

CPU

Central Processing Unit

CQRS

Command Query Responsibility Segregation

CUSIP

Committee on Uniform Security Identification Procedures

DBMS

Database Management System

DEC

Digital Equipment Corporation

DOA

Design and Operations Authority

DSM

Design Structure Matrix

ETL

Extract, Transform, Load

FAQ

Frequently Asked Question

FNOL

First Notice of Loss

GSE

Government Sponsored Enterprise

GoF

Gang of Four

GUI

Graphical User Interface

HTTP

HyperText Transfer Protocol

HR

Human Resources

i18n

Internationalization

IaaS

Infrastructure as a Service

IAM

Identity and Access Management

IO

Input/Output

IoT

Internet of Things

IS

Information System

ITSM

Information Technology Service Management

JVM

Java Virtual Machine

KPI

Key Performance Indicator

LEI

Lean Enterprise Institute

LOB

Line of Business

LPPD

Lean Product and Process Development

LSP

Liskov Substitution Principle

M&A

Mergers & Acquisitions

MBWA

Management by Walking Around

MIFD

Material and Information Flow Diagram

ML

Machine Learning

MOM

Message-Oriented Middleware

MTTR

Mean Time to Recover

MVP
: Minimum Viable Product

NALSD
: Non-Abstract Large System Design

NLU
: Natural Language Understanding

NoSQL
: Not only Structured Query Language

OKR
: Objectives and Key Results

OLAP
: Online Analytical Processing

P&C
: Property and Casualty

P&L
: Profit and Loss

PDCA
: Plan, Do, Check, and Act

PMO
: Project Management Officer

POI
: Proof of Insurance

QPS
: Queries per Second

RAM
: Random Access Memory

REST
: Representational State Transfer

RPS
: Requests per Second

RWA
: Risk-Weighted Asset

SaaS
: Software as a Service

SBCE
: Set-Based Concurrent Engineering

SEI
: Software Engineering Institute

SLI
: Service-Level Indicator

SLO
: Service-Level Objective

SMS
: Short Message Service

SOA
: Service-Oriented Architecture

SPI
: Service Provider Interface

SQL
: Structured Query Language

SRE
: Site Reliability Engineering

TFX
: TensorFlow Extended

TOM
: Target Operating Model

UI
: User Interface

UK
: United Kingdom

URN
: Uniform Resource Name

US
: United States

UTC
: Coordinated Universal Time

UUID
: Universally Unique Identifier

UX
: User Experience

VA
: Value-Added

VE
: Value Engineering

VUCA
: Volatility, Uncertainty, Complexity, Ambiguity

Index

Made in United States
Orlando, FL
04 November 2026

90200603R00129